I CONFESS
REVELATIONS IN EXILE

Kooshyar Karimi was born in December 1968 in the slums of Tehran, Iran, to a family living in abject poverty. His mother Homa was an orphaned Jew who in order to escape an intolerable family situation, married Khalil, a bus driver and Muslim with two wives and six other children to feed. He was only eleven years old when the Iranian Islamic Revolution swept aside Shah Mohammad Reza Pahlavi's regime. Amidst this post-revolutionary chaos, and the bloodshed of the Iran-Iraq war, Kooshyar pursued his education through to medical school with a determination to avoid war, stay alive, and support his mother. It is from here that he went on to become a published author, award-winning translator, doctor, husband and father by the age of twenty-six.

Kooshyar was kidnapped from the street near his home one evening in the winter of 1998 by the Iranian Intelligence Service. Tortured, burnt, and whipped over sixty-five days, Kooshyar found himself faced with an unimaginable decision...to spy for MOIS (the Iranian Internal Intelligence Service) against his own people or to be tortured slowly to death. His forced co-operation was a significant factor in the arrest of thirteen Iranian Jews in March 1999, a case that caused an international outcry.

Living this intolerable lie and knowing his own execution was imminent, Kooshyar drew on a fateful connection from the past to make his escape from Iran to Turkey. In 2000, he and his family were granted political refugee status by the UNHCR, and a visa to settle permanently in Australia.

He is now an Australian citizen working full-time in General Practice in New South Wales, and writing in his spare time.

I CONFESS
REVELATIONS IN EXILE

KOOSHYAR KARIMI

WILD
DINGO
PRESS

Published by Wild Dingo Press
Melbourne Australia
books@wilddingopress.com.au
www.wilddingopress.com.au

First published by Wild Dingo Press in 2012.

Cover design: Grant Slaney, MAPG
Printed in Australia by Ligare

National Library of Australia
Cataloguing-in-Publication Data

Karimi, Kooshyar, 1968-

I confess: revelations in exile / Kooshyar Karimi.

ISBN: 9780987178503 (pbk.)

Karimi, Kooshyar.
Jews, Iranian–Biography.
Physicians–Iran–Biography.
Physicians–New South Wales–Sydney–Biography.
Refugees–Iran–Biography.
Refugees–Australia–Biography.

305.8924055092

Only wood grown from sustainable regrowth forests is used in the
manufacture of paper used in this book.

To the memory of Habib Elghanian
The first Jew executed by the Islamic regime of Iran, 1979.

And so my atonement begins...

Disclaimer

The story told here is factual. Every care has been taken to verify names, dates and details throughout this book, but as much is reliant on memory, some unintentional errors may have occurred. On occasions, real names have been replaced with substitute names to protect people who remain in danger of recrimination.

The Publishers assume no legal liability or responsibility for inaccuracies; they do, however, welcome any information that will redress them.

Coming to Australia, I lost my language skills. I felt like a painter without hands. I had the heart of the stories, but not the heart of the language. It took eleven years and ten drafts for me to create a perfect body for my manuscript. It was my daughter, Newsha, who brought it to life.

She has been the voice, the language, and the words of my story. I could never thank her enough for being the soul behind the words.

I would also like to express my appreciation to Robert Hillman who dedicated such hard work, research and commitment to the original manuscript in our work together.

1

STAR

It is snowing in Tehran on the night of my birth, a blanketing fall that starts in the morning and persists all day. On a bed in the basement that serves as her home, in a narrow, moulded street of Gomrok, my mother has been battling all day to master the contractions that shouldn't have come for another three weeks. Close to midnight, she has to concede that the child in her womb is about to be born, whether she is ready or not. As young as she is, she has given birth before and knows that no power on earth and no prayer will bring about the respite she craves. No arrangements have been made for the birth. No hospital has been booked, no doctor or midwife is on hand. She struggles, clenching her muscles in an effort to hold me inside for a few minutes longer as she staggers up the steps from the basement to the street. The stale streets of Gomrok hold some of the most notorious, despondent slums of Tehran. In this part of Iran, it would surprise no one if my mother and her child were found dead on the street in the light of morning. Women die in the streets here all the time.

She is barely seventeen years old, my mother. Her first child, a boy, Koorosh, was born when she was fifteen. Koorosh is asleep in the basement room, oblivious to my mother's striving and shrieking. Better that he should remain asleep, since he is now alone in the basement and will remain alone for some time. The pain my mother is suffering is overwhelming, but her distress at leaving Koorosh unattended is just as strong. There will be no sympathy for her at all if Koorosh comes to grief in some way. In Iran at this time, the time of the Shah, the burden carried by a woman is unyielding.

My mother stumbles into the street with no plan other than to hail a passing stranger and plead for assistance. But this close to midnight the streets are empty. She falls to her knees in the snow, stricken by a particularly intense contraction. She is unable to regain her feet and can only remain where she is, stuttering out a brief, repeated cry for help.

As the narrator of this story I can, if I wish, provide the help and support my mother craves, and that I crave for her, in this hour of desperation. I could cause a sympathetic neighbour to come down from one of the above-ground apartments and cry out, 'Ya Allah! Homa, let me get you to hospital!' Or I could give her a hidden reserve of strength that would allow her to find a taxi. But if I were free to distort the truth in that way I would go further, and place her in a warm apartment with a comforting husband and a midwife in attendance. I would fashion my own birth in a way that gives my mother the easiest possible time of it. But my priority in telling this tale is to be truthful and I have to forego the solaces of fiction. My mother is on her knees in agony, my father is occupied elsewhere, perhaps with his other wives, and I am being forced from the paradise of the womb into the grief of the birth canal as the clock is about to strike midnight.

A car crunches to a halt only metres from where my mother is huddled. In the midst of her pain, she realises that this will be the only chance for either of us to survive my birth, for the crown of my head has all but emerged. She attempts to shriek but hasn't the power to shriek and breathe at the same time. The beam of a torch plays on her upturned face. She finds the strength to cry out, 'Please!' And the man with the torch hoists her up with his hands under her armpits and manages to get her onto the back seat of his vehicle.

He stammers in panic, 'The hospital! I will take you to the hospital! Be strong, madam!'

But the distraction of turning his head to address his passenger causes him to lose control of the car and it plunges violently into one of the deep gutters that line the streets in this part of Tehran. The driver shakes his hands at the heavens, cursing his ill-fortune.

'Madam, be strong!' he implores, and leaps from the car, attempting in vain to pull the vehicle back onto the road.

And as he strains with might and an inexplicable determination to move his car back onto the road, my mother grips the pendant on her necklace, gives a final wrenching scream, and I slide into the world covered in the blood and clotted debris of birth.

The driver, shaken by my mother's scream, hurries to the rear passenger door, swings it open and shines the beam of his torch over the gore, over me, over my gasping mother. In the illumination of the torchlight, my mother makes out something she had no time and no strength to notice before. The man, the driver, the Good Samaritan who had chanced by in such an unlikely way, is a policeman. Considering the life that is about to unfold for me and for my mother, this miracle is also a bitter coincidence. For the holy symbol on my mother's necklace—the one which now glimmers in the light of the policeman's torch, with Ruhollah Khomeini little more than a decade away from proclaiming the world's first Islamic Republic in Iran—is a Star of David.

2

ADONAI

At the time of my birth, according to the records of Persia's ethnic complexion which have been kept for perhaps four thousand years, the Jewish population of Iran is at its lowest. The noisy, sprawling city of Tehran is home to some twenty thousand Jews, including my mother, my brother and me. Another twenty thousand survive—even thrive—elsewhere in Iran, largely in the cities of Isfahan, Shiraz and Mashhad. In the distant past—two thousand years ago—Jews comprised as much as a quarter of the population of Persia. Over the centuries, our numbers have waxed and waned according to the generosity or venom of our rulers, none of whom were Jews. It is the same for the Jews of Persia as for the Jews of many other lands. We have made hay while the sun shone, and without any secure destination to flee to, have endured blizzards of persecution when we've had to. The persecution often enough took the form of mass murder, but enforced conversion was also popular: mass murder by a different means, bloodless but agonising. Shylock's shriek of anguish at the end of *The Merchant of Venice* is not the cry of a man separated from his shekels, but of a Jew wrenched from the solace of his faith.

In the earliest years of my life I am not to know that being a Jew in Iran means maintaining the sort of precarious existence that a canary would experience in a house full of cats. I am five years old before it is revealed to me that the Muslim faith of almost everyone I know—a faith that seems to me as natural a part of people's lives as wearing shoes or eating bread—is not ever to be considered a natural part of *my* life. My mother and my brother Koorosh and I are living in the same dank basement in Gomrok that my mother had emerged from to give birth to me on that night of snow and icy winds and amateur obstetrics. It is raining heavily, as it does in Tehran, and water is pouring into the basement through broken windows. It is late at night and we are in bed, Koorosh and I, holding tightly to our mother in the middle.

The fierce explosions of thunder and blinding flashes of lightning seem wicked in their intensity and the storm, in my mind, takes on the character of a great monster with its arms reaching out over Tehran. When the thunder grows louder still, I cry out in my dread that the storm is trying to kill us, and beg my mother to make it stop. She draws me closer to her and strokes my head.

'I cannot make the storm stop,' she whispers. 'But listen to me. I will tell you something. Are you listening?'

'Yes, I am listening.'

'We will not die, my darling. Adonai will protect us, as he has always protected the Children of Israel.'

'Adonai?'

'Yes, darling, Adonai. Have no fear.'

'Who is Adonai?'

'Adonai is our God, my darling, the God of all Jews in the world.'

What my mother has told me leaves me feeling both comforted and baffled. I don't know what Israel is, and I have not heard the word 'Jew' before in my life. But I have heard of God, or of *a* God, of Allah, the God of the Muslims. My mother seems to be suggesting that our God Adonai is even more powerful than Allah and a more reliable protector, and I am glad of that. I picture the marvellous God Adonai confronting the storm monster and subduing him, breaking his arms, slapping his face. I think Adonai might look something like my absent father, but a thousand times taller and with a beard that reaches halfway down his chest. I fall asleep in my mother's arms, murmuring the name of Adonai.

The following morning, after our breakfast of grey bread, I pester my mother to tell me more about Adonai, for I intend to adopt this wonderful champion of the Jews as my lifelong protector. She seems reluctant to say anything more about Adonai at first, and in her bossy way urges me to eat up and sit with my back straight. Koorosh's enthusiasm for this new God of our household doesn't match mine. He was initially amazed to hear that we are Jews, but wakes in the morning with a big smile, relaxed and accepting. He is content to let me do all the questioning.

'Maman, can I ask you something?'

'Ask me nothing!' she says. She is mopping up the storm water that has gathered in pools on the floor, squeezing out the rag into the sink.

'Maman, is Adonai the God of the Jews?'

'Yes! Did I not say so? Why ask me what you know?'

'Maman, please can I ask you something?'

'No!'

'Are we Jews?' I persist.

It is very important to me to get the facts straight, for this new and fascinating information about Jews and Adonai and the Children of Israel has come to me at a moment of a quickening in my curiosity. I feel at that time the urgent, instinctive need to extend my understanding of the world and I want facts, history, stories. Most children of this age experience this hunger, I think.

Or perhaps that quickening is not simply curiosity, but the development of a need to enhance my security, for in addition to truth, I hunger for heroes. In the earliest years of life, one's parents are the heroes, usually adequate enough even with their limitations and flaws. But a little later, fresh gods and heroes with mystical powers exercise a deep allure. My mother could comfort me in her arms, yes, and she could mop up the water after a storm, certainly. But by her own admission, she could not wrestle and subdue a storm monster. I need Adonai for that. My mother pauses in her mopping. She looks at me as if she were weighing up alternatives.

'Alright,' she says.

She wrings out the sodden rag, dries her hands and sits cross-legged with Koorosh and me on our bed. The hesitancy of a few minutes earlier has vanished from her face. She now looks fiercely animated. It only ever requires a sudden gust to make the coals in my mother's eyes glow with an almost maniacal intensity, and the gust of wind this day is my nagging demand for more news about the great Adonai.

'I will tell you of the Children of Israel.'

She interrupts herself time and again to remind us that we are to keep what she is telling us secret. I am delighted to hear that our God Adonai is a secret God, that his powers are only ever employed to benefit Jews. The covert nature of his interventions adds an element of intrigue to his adventures.

The Children of Israel, so my mother's story reveals, were not children at all. The Jews she identifies—Noah, who so pleased God, Abraham the Patriarch, Moses who carried a long stick known as a 'rod', David the King—were grown men. And Israel, so my mother says, is in fact a place, a country, a long way from Iran but not so far as America or China. The most thrilling part of her story concerns the mission of Moses, who led a great many Jews out of slavery in Egypt (I had heard of

Egypt!—I had heard of the pyramids!) and overcame the armies of the Pharaoh by wielding his rod and dividing the waters of the Red Sea and drowning the Pharaoh's soldiers and horses.

Listening to my mother, I begin to feel that Moses might be a more solid sort of hero than Adonai Himself, since Adonai, as she now claims, has another name that cannot be spoken, a name she would write on a piece of paper for me and Koorosh at another time, but that we must never utter. This is awkward. Moses, on the other hand, has a fine, utterable name. My mother says that Moses was 'full of courage' and that his rod 'saved the Children of Israel too many times to count' on the strange and beautiful and arduous and also slightly boring journey (forty years!) from Egypt to Israel. I am enthralled by the ingenuity of Moses, and by his determination, but the sparse diet of the wandering Jews saddens me. Unleavened bread and bitter herbs don't seem much of an improvement on the fare of our famished household. I would have been happier to hear of Moses employing his rod to conjure mountains of watermelon and fish and cheese. She also speaks of Joseph, who became prince of Egypt (the same Egypt of the Moses story—puzzling!) after a great many ups-and-downs, and of Ruth who wept in an open field a long way from Israel, yearning for her native land.

A few questions remain unanswered once my mother has concluded her story. Since we are living in Iran, rather than Israel, does that mean that we are slaves, like the Jews of Egypt? Would Moses or someone very like him, lead us out of Tehran to Israel?

'We are not slaves,' she says. 'Israel is our home, but Iran is also our land. Jews have lived here for thousands of years. Before Allah, came Adonai. Before Muhammad, came Abraham and Moses. Remember that.'

As new as the idea of being a Jew is to me, I still have a pretty good sense of what would happen to me if I ran into the street and shouted out, 'Before Allah came Adonai!' I have no such term in my vocabulary as 'minority', and certainly no phrase as sophisticated as 'victimised, marginalised and despised minority', but my mother's story of the Jews and of their ordeal over the centuries suggests that I should definitely heed her exhortations to keep the whole business secret.

I will wear my Jewishness under my shirt, like a singlet, the closest garment to my flesh. And this is attractive to me, keeping it all secret. The Muslims sing the praise of their God in public day and night. The Muslims have no secrets. To be a secret Jew, praising Moses and Adonai with his unutterable name in private, away from the eyes of the world—yes, this is deeply satisfying. I will walk down the street with the singlet of my faith hugging my flesh and not a soul will know. And then one fine day, my mother and Koorosh and I will follow Moses, or New Moses, or whatever name Moses wishes to give himself in the twentieth century, to Israel where we will be fed watermelon and fish and cheese ten times a day to reward us for keeping our secret so faithfully in Iran.

PERSIA

After Khomeini's Revolution of 1979, the new regime of Islamist puritans makes it difficult to study in any detail the Persia of old, the Persia in which, at certain times, Jews have lived out their lives in relative security. These Islamic puritans regard pre-Islamic Persia as indistinguishable from Babylon in its wickedness: poetry celebrating the beauty of women and the luscious taste of red wine served in silver goblets, songs composed in perfumed gardens where peacocks roam. But even as a boy, I sense that this fundamentalism is a twisting of Islam, not a spiritual interpretation. Politics doesn't yield much in the way of poetry. I also have to remind myself that for long periods of Persia's Muslim domination, Islam has been a more relaxed faith than it is under the puritans. More relaxed and, I imagine, more relaxing.

In my teens, I will come to know, through conscientious and secretive study, of the sunrises and sunsets of the Jews of Persia. By the time of my adolescent studies, the Khomeini regime will have replaced the imperial Pahlavi regime, and much to the horror of many Iranians who had supported the return of the Ayatollah from his Parisian exile and who had harboured a deep disgust with the brutality and corruption of the Pahlavis, the new regime will rapidly develop a reputation of its own for brutality and corruption. One could say, 'What did people think was going to happen? They might have guessed.' But people are allowed to live in hope, surely. I have lived in the glasshouse of hope myself for most of my life, so I know the damage that a well-aimed stone can do. By the time of my teens I will become so practised in the building and rebuilding of this hope, it will lay a foundation for the future, and give birth to my ability to pull through the horrors to be faced later in life. This is the Jewish secret to survival.

Even as I would learn the history of the Persian Jews, the Jews of modern Iran would be abandoning their ancient home in large numbers. My mother would never possess the money needed to back up a decision to flee the puritans for Los Angeles or New York or Jerusalem, where most of Iran's Jews end up over the years. And it has never been my mother's wish to flee, in any case.

At the time of my birth she is married to a Muslim (of which, much more later) and considers Iran her homeland. Israel is precious to her, but only as a land that features in a poetic tale of wandering and miracles and burning bushes. It is more a destination of the Jewish soul than a place where you might set up house and make matzos in your kitchen. There is only one true homeland per life, only one place where the noise of the traffic and the smell of the streets after rain, and the quality of the light of a spring evening, and the breadth of sunsets and the shouting and bickering in the bazaar, and the shriek of children at play gets under your skin and into your entrails and lives there permanently, with pride, or with defiance, or both. My mother is a Persian forever.

Two thousand years ago, women exactly like her baked bread in the Jewish quarter of Isfahan, of Shiraz, of a hundred cities and towns; baked bread and cooked *chelow* and *tsimmes*[1]

---

1. Chelow: national Persian dish of steamed saffron rice; Tsimmes: Jewish dish of sweetened combinations of vegetables, fruit, and sometimes meat, prepared as a casserole or stew.

and garlic fish and pomegranate chicken and maybe kosherfied *dolma* and *aushe sarka*[2]; and went to the *mikveh*[3] each month. At that time, there was no Islam. But there were many other faiths: some, such as Zoroastrianism, highly sophisticated, some primitively pagan. The Jews of that era were the descendants of those who had endured exile in Babylon. Generations had lived and died without having set foot in Judea. They had become Persians and they spoke Persian as their first language. Their version of Judaism itself had taken on the hue of other faiths; they shared customs with neighbouring ethnic groups. When the Achaemenids vanquished the Babylonians and Cyrus the Great gave his permission for the Jews of his empire to return to Judea, many thousands remained. A mother very like my mother was there at the time. She was a Jew who remained, a Jew so Persian that in her temperament and tastes she helped to define the variegated Persia of the Achaemenid Empire.

By the eighth century, empires of cohabiting catechisms, like those of the Achaemenids and of their successors, the Parthians, were no more than historical curiosities. The new faith of Islam swept out of the Arabian Peninsula with irresistible force and gathered more adherents over a thirty year period, 720 to 750 CE, than Judaism that had served as a faith in over two thousand years. Of course, Jews don't proselytise, but even if they did it would be difficult to imagine them attracting fans in particularly large numbers. They haven't got the cuisine.

My study of the Jews of Islamic Persia would reveal to me (not to the world at large, already well-informed on the subject) how susceptible cultures are to the exhortations of the charismatic. An ambitious preacher can cart a faith north, south, east or west, according to the toxins in his system, or

---

2. Dolma: usually rice and beef stuffed in vine leaves; Aushe sarka is a
   noodle soup.
3. Mikveh: Jewish ritual purification bath.

sometimes the generosity. Under certain regimes, the Jews of Persia were permitted to muddle along happily; under others, they were belted from pillar to post. Broadly, the Jews of Persia were accorded the status of *dhimmis*[4]—peoples mentioned in Islamic scripture, and therefore to be accepted, often grudgingly, as having attracted the benign attention of Allah. But today's *dhimmis* could easily become tomorrow's unholy pests. And it was better for Persian Jews to remember that. We survived through a combination of resourcefulness and obstinacy, a complement of chutzpah, a further complement of old-fashioned Can-Do. And we had a fabulous faith to rely on. Extraordinarily subtle, deeply consoling, in places plain crazy, but comfortingly so. No Jew has ever dramatised that characteristic blend of resourcefulness and obstinacy better than my mother.

In the morning that follows the night of the storm, I become a Jew. I think of being a Jew as a gift of my mother, which in a literal sense it is, but I think of this gift as an expression of certain magical powers at my mother's command. And after the night of the storm, after the morning of my mother's gift, I realise that I will never be able to disobey her. With my father so rarely on the scene, my mother is the figure of potency that I so crave in my life. At the same time, I can't help but notice that my mother is just a little bit crazy. At times. Not every day in every way. Just at times. (Even now, in adulthood, I feel that I'm inviting fire from heaven by suggesting that my mother is occasionally crazy.)

Consider: my mother harbours an unalterable belief in her ability to subdue the world, to overcome calamity. It's not just fantasy. On occasions, she can make impossible things happen. I think of her as a genius of a certain sort, powered by the egomania that usually accompanies genius. She is unable to conceive of a world in which things don't eventually go her way.

---

4. Dhimmis: refers to non-Muslim citizens living in a Muslim state.

If she can't bring about the result she wants herself, she knows exactly who to turn to. But this belief in her power to subdue the world...she sometimes takes it a little too far.

It is not long after my fifth birthday, we are in the dim, humid basement of Gomrok. It is the type of summer in which the rippling waves of heat can be seen dancing on the cracked pavement of the streets. My mother fans me with a small piece of cardboard, desperate to bring my temperature down. She is using all of her ingenuity to save my life for I am ill with typhoid. My hair is falling out. I'm passing blood. I myself am not entirely sure that I am alive. My mother has employed her most potent charms and mantras and rituals, but they have failed, so she has moved on to potions. She is convinced that the right dose of the right potion administered in the right manner will save me. She is attempting to feed me a type of broth she has brewed in which the principal ingredient is sheep testicles.

'This will restore you, my love,' she whispers at my bedside. 'This comes from sheep. A sheep is always covered in fleece. The fleece on your head will return when you swallow this.'

After tasting the broth, which is vile, I know for certain that I'm still alive. No corpse could register such disgust. So I swallow. My mother's ministrations can change from whispered entreaty to violent insistence in seconds. I swallow a second spoonful, a third. I swallow the fragments of sheep testicles. I no longer wish to live, but I fear my mother's displeasure more than I fear death. After two days of swallowing, the broth has done me no good. My hair continues to gather on my pillow in strands and clumps. My mother's face hovers above me like a stubborn vision of malice conjured in a nightmare.

'We're going to the doctor,' she says, on the morning of the third day. There's a note of hostility in her voice, as if the persistence of my typhoid has something to do with my stupidity.

'We're going to see Mama Fatima.'

Mama Fatima is what in another land, in another culture, would be called a witch doctor. She is able to call on powerful spirits (well, that's her claim) but she will also rely at times on something as unfussy as aspirin. In the poorer districts of Iranian towns and cities all over the country, there is a Mama Fatima, an *alafi* medical practitioner[5]. The appeal of such healers has its roots in the deep pagan past of Persia. I have said that women just like my mother lived in Persian cities of the Archaemenid era. Women just like Mama Fatima lived at that same time.

My immediate response is dread. But after the bare few moments of reflection the typhoid permits, I have to concede that nothing Mama Fatima does to me could possibly exceed in misery the ordeal of the sheep testicles. So my mother gets me to Mama Fatima. I'm not in any condition to move, but my mother nevertheless gets me moving. Mama Fatima, who cultivates her mystique by studying her patients through half-closed eyes and muttering small sounds of either alarm or wonder at certain intervals, gives me her closest scrutiny, utters a few noises signifying alarm and a few more signifying wonder, sits back on her cushion and prepares to announce her verdict.

'The boy is sick,' she says. 'Bad sick, terrible sick. Take him to the hospital.'

'Take him to the hospital? That's it?' says mother, expecting something more reliant on the intervention of Mama Fatima's spirit allies.

'Yes. Get him to hospital. He's got typhoid; something like that. He could die.'

'To hospital? You haven't got something he could swallow?'

'What swallow? I'm telling you, the boy's bad sick.'

---

5. Alafi medical practitioner: herbal doctor.

Although plainly disappointed, my mother offers a few words of thanks to Mama Fatima and hustles me along to the bus stop.

'We're going to the hospital,' she says. It's not a statement but an accusation. What can I say? What can I do?

'Maman, I'm sorry.'

'So what, you're sorry? Better you were sorry before you got this thing, this typhoid.'

At the hospital, a doctor tells my mother that I will be kept in the infectious diseases ward for some time. The doctor says that I will live—probably. By this time, my mother has recovered from the disappointment of the Mama Fatima visit. She says she will visit me each day. She calls me 'darling', which always thrills me. She also tells me that she wants me to be a doctor when I grow up.

'Look at that man,' she says, pointing at the doctor. 'Nice white coat, lots of medicines, good home in northern Tehran for sure, a car maybe. This is what you will do. You will be a doctor. How much I work to make this happen, I don't care. Are you listening to me?'

Even in my delirium, I don't dare ignore anything my mother tells me.

'You're going to be a doctor,' she repeats, and nods emphatically.

She takes hold of her Star of David necklace after glancing around to make sure she is unobserved.

'If you live,' she adds.

I live. But if the experience of the storm that led to the gift of becoming a Jew enhanced my belief in my mother's magic, the typhoid experience serves to remind me that Koorosh and I are also hostages in my mother's never-ending battle with an unco-operative world. Mama Fatima was shrewd enough to see that I would die without proper medical attention, but if she'd had an off-day and hadn't recognised the symptoms of typhoid, she might have advised my mother to hang me by my toes from the kitchen ceiling and my mother would have done exactly that. Koorosh and I are at the mercy of any sort of spooky scheme that pops into my mother's head, or is suggested to her by people she holds in high esteem, such as Mama Fatima. I certainly don't hold it against my mother. But from the age of five, from the age at which I draw on the garments of a Jew, figuratively speaking, a type of caution lives within me side-by-side with my love and reverence for my mother. This caution, yoked to reverence, will stay with me for years and years to come.

My mother is also training me in the resourcefulness of the Persian Jew. It's not a training accompanied by laments. My mother never dwells on the injustice of our situation as Jews in a land of Muslims for very long. You can't eat laments.

My training in resourcefulness begins with full-time employment. Childhood is not a time of pampering and endearments in the slums of Iran, not for Muslims, not for Jews. My working life starts when I'm five; not an uncommon age for a child to begin earning money if he's from a poor family, and my family is, of course, very poor. A small allowance trickles in from my father, but he has two other families to support and it is only after those two families have been provided for, that he scrapes together a few coins for my mother.

My mother begins looking for a place for me to work before I turn five, but even in Iran it is thought just a little bit barbarous to set a four-year-old to work. My first job is straightening crooked nails for a cobbler in a basement shop. I work all day under the cobbler's watchful eye with my hammer and anvil, singing to myself to overcome the monotony. It is not a job that calls for much intelligence. I have to make sure that I don't flatten the head of the nail while I'm straightening the shaft and also make sure that I don't blunt the point, but that's all the skill involved. The cobbler calls out to me with a rhythm matching the stroke of his hammer:

'Hey, kid! Keep busy! Hey, kid! Keep busy!'

The hours pass at an agonisingly glacial pace. I think of my mother's doctor plan for me and pray to Adonai to speed up my education. What's so difficult about being a doctor? Or more than doctor, a surgeon, which is her most recent embellishment of the plan. I could be a doctor at maybe ten years old. A very young doctor. I think of the meals we could afford if I were a doctor. I think of escaping the tyranny of bread, because my mother's solution to the problem of hunger is always and forever, bread. Bread is cheap. We eat big quantities with very, very small pieces of cheese. Her idea (ah, my mother's ideas!) is that the bread will bloat us and leave us incapable of complaining of an empty stomach. This strategy works, for sure, but you get only so much nourishment from bread. And you can't fool your body for long. Much more cheese is what it wants, and it pleads for it endlessly, 'Cheese, cheese, Adonai, God of the Jews, send more cheese!' My dream is to, one day, eat an enormous clump of cheese with hardly any bread at all.

If Koorosh and I betray our longings with whimpers and little bleats of despair, my mother finds ways, maddeningly, to fashion misery into Lessons in Life: 'When you grow up, never forget that you came from a poor family. Treat all people with honour and respect.' There is not the slightest chance we will forget that we grew up with nothing but Koorosh and I always respond, 'Yes, *Madar jan*, we'll remember, Adonai will witness!' What we really hope is that Adonai will witness us sitting at a table loaded to the ceiling with the foods we most desire, especially cheese in great wedges and rounds.

Another possible solution to hunger is for father to give us more money. But in the same way I can't hold my mother's borderline lethal schemes against her, I can't hold my father's parsimony against him. In fact, if I could choose between seeing more money fall from his pockets onto our kitchen table and seeing him actually sitting at the table, penniless but present, I'd choose just having him nearby, within hugging distance.

For I am a boy who aches. That is my great occupation—aching. My heart aches for my father, it aches for cheese, it aches for my mother's kisses and caresses, it aches for the appearance in our tiny apartment of the God Adonai. Sometimes I tell myself, 'It is because I am a Jew that I ache so much. Jews are born to ache. But a time will come when all the aching will vanish from my heart. The time of cheese will come. The time of fish. The time of fathers who stay all day and all night and every day and every night—that time will come.'

4

HAWOO

The work of a nail straightener leaves a big part of my brain free for thinking. Tapping away with my hammer, I wonder about my mother's life before my birth. I have a few facts to work with, but most of what I know leaves me impatient for more. I know, for example, that my mother married my father because she was pregnant with my brother. How does a woman become pregnant—of that I know nothing, of course. So far as I can tell, a woman might decide to grow a baby on a whim. And everything I've learnt about my mother's temperament tends to confirm the 'whim' theory. So many things in my mother's life—the catastrophes, mostly—seem to develop from whims. As a little boy, I'm sure that she sometimes thinks of children as a catastrophe.

I ask her questions and I'm given answers. The stunning news of our Jewish heritage is just the start of the story my mother is prepared to tell, as it turns out. But I have to choose the right moment to ask my questions. As a child I notice adults are involved in a constant struggle to negotiate opposing impulses when it comes to their children. Often they seem to wish to strangle them and drop them in the river. On another day, they'd be prepared to sacrifice half their complement of arms and legs to spare their child a pain in the tummy. In my mother's case, where these conflicting impulses come from is something I cannot hope to grasp. I can easily tell when she's in the midst of a crisis, staggering about on the frontier of insanity; and it's a simple matter to see when she is blessedly relaxed, but between madness and bliss live a thousand more subtle moods, mini-moods, moods that flicker to life then vanish within minutes. Sometimes I can risk questions when she is frantic, sometimes it's better to wait until she's glorying in some secret triumph. There's no formula. I have to be an artist to pick her mood. I have to rely on inspiration.

My mother was not born in Tehran, but in Isfahan, the glory of Shi'ite Islam. At the time my mother tells me of her birth city I am not aware that Isfahan is renowned for the grace and splendour of its monuments; but later in life, when I have spent time in Isfahan, I will feel a warm sense of how appropriate it was that my mother should have come into the world amidst all this beauty. For she is herself a great beauty, with fair skin and honeycomb eyes. Her hair is coffee and cinnamon, curling around her nape like a sweet mirage, something I only notice subconsciously as a child.

My mother's beauty plays its part in the awe she conjures in me; I am, in a certain sense, in love with my mother. This is not a declaration that a Muslim son will ever make. I think a Jew can love his mother and be in love with his mother because… well…because his mother permits it. Motherhood is different amongst Jews. A Jewish mother is in a position of power that exceeds anything a non-Jew is familiar with, I think. When I sit with my chin resting in my hand as a five-year-old, gazing at my mother with her hair uncovered, she knows that I'm crazy about her. It doesn't displease her, it doesn't make her uneasy.

At the age of seven, I am told that my mother's father died just before my grandmother gave birth to the child who would be named Turan. He became ill, the illness worsened, prayers were offered, and then he was dead. Without a husband to support her, my grandmother could see no way out other than to ask my Uncle Abraham to adopt the child, Turan. From the mixture of sadness and half-stifled resentment in my mother's tone when she speaks of this adoption, I guess that my grandmother was compelled by more than strict necessity to give my mother to Uncle Abraham. Certainly it's very difficult to raise a child without a husband, but many women in Iran manage it. And the stark fact is that Grandma ran away with some man from Tehran not so long after the adoption was arranged. My mother wouldn't have remembered anything of Grandma, but the sadness in her voice when she tells me about the adoption shows that she nevertheless mourned the mothering she had to do without.

Uncle Abraham was not one of those fairytale bear-like uncles liable to drown his niece in the warm honey of his affection, mother made that plain. She said he was as tough as old leather, very tight with his *tomans*, seething with scorn for my runaway Grandma. And he was something of a zealot, fastidious to the point of obsession with the observance of Jewish rituals. Jews negotiate their minority status in one of two ways (and when are Jews not a minority, other than in Israel?). Either they attempt to out-Moses Moses and establish what security they can find on unswerving adherence to ritual, or they make a type of bargain with Adonai, honouring Him in their hearts without making any big deal about it in public. I've always found it easier to get along with the No Big Dealers than with the Obsessives. If you're a Jew, it's part of your anatomy, it's in each cell. There is no possibility that a Jew can alienate himself or herself from Adonai. A Jew honours God by being a Jew.

Uncle Abraham found girls tedious, a misfortune for a man with three daughters. Why he couldn't enjoy daughters, I don't know. How can you not? And a daughter like my mother—a bright and caring child? Hard to fathom. Maybe it was just that he was eager for a son and the sequence of girl babies wore out his small appetite for female children. And, no sooner had my mother joined the family than Abraham's wife, Heshmat, gave birth to yet another daughter; so then he had five. He took out his disappointment on my mother and so did Heshmat, herself no Angel of Charity. My mother became the Cinderella of the household, made to scrub and dust and haul at an age when a girl could reasonably expect to be left in peace to play with dolls. She wore rags, like Cinderella, and endured scolding, neglect and beatings. When Heshmat at last produced a son for Uncle Abraham, a boy they named Mansoor, my mother was left even more marginalised. Her status in the household must have been hardly greater than that of a slave. She went to bed with her face wet with tears and she awoke each morning with a feeling of dread.

Uncle Abraham kept a liquor shop in the bazaar—the sort of business that only a Jew would run in Iran, a Jew or maybe a Christian. A substantial number of Muslims are prepared to enjoy a tipple in secret (how else would Uncle Abraham's gin palace have thrived?), but no Muslim is prepared to make money from the sale of alcohol right out in the open. Among Muslims, a man who runs a liquor shop is held in the same sort of contempt as a man who runs a brothel, and it says something about Uncle Abraham's determination that he didn't care at all, according to my mother. He put her to work in the shop at the age of six, knowing that a girl who served in a gin palace would be burdened with a reputation that reeked to high heaven. The justice of this arrangement was often spelt out to my mother by her uncle: 'You expect me to pay for your school books for nothing?'

My mother tells me that she yearned for love, for a tender word, a gentle touch. What she knew of love, of tenderness, of gentleness, she could only have picked up by witnessing its enactment amongst others, for she herself was never adored, at least not until she turned fifteen, when she fell in love with one of Uncle Abraham's customers, a bus driver from Tehran by the name of Khalil. She says that he was the most handsome man in Iran—tall, strong, jet-black hair, luminous eyes. She herself had grown to a ripeness that attracted the gaze of every customer who came to the shop (only men ever purchased liquor) and often those gazes were full of suggestion, for she was a Jew, and responding to a Jewish girl's allure, a Christian girl's, or to that of any girl who wasn't Muslim, attracted no penalty in the meticulously maintained record of transgressions recorded in Muslim Heaven under the heading of 'Vile Lust'. I have no doubt that my mother enjoyed the attention, more in some cases than others, and how could she have not valued it above its worth when it was the only endorsement she ever received?

So it was Khalil she fell for, bus driver Khalil, Khalil the knock-out, Prince Khalil of the luminous eyes, Khalil who was twenty-four years older than her, Khalil who was a Muslim. She listened to his promises, the Cinderella of Isfahan, and one morning she climbed into Khalil's bus, a pumpkin transformed into a gilded carriage, and escaped from Uncle Abraham's household, from drudgery and disdain, and was installed in a house in Tehran, humble enough, but a palace to my mother.

Khalil might be thought of as a Muslim of a very strange sort, not afraid of a good stiff drink every now and then, and capable of taking up with a very pretty infidel. But he was not so unusual. Muslims are as various in their devotions as Jews or Christians. Most try to strike a balance between the more severe demands of their faith and their natural appetites. Khalil's most insistent natural appetite was for sex, and he squared himself with the demands of his faith by getting my mother to convert to Islam within twenty-four hours of their elopement.

Conversion to Islam is not a protracted business. You simply find a mullah, tell him your story, take the oath, and get used to your new Muslim name, which in my mother's case was Homa. The stunning success of Islam over the centuries is based on the ease of conversion from whatever murky code of beliefs you upheld in the past, as well as the glint on the blade of the sword held before your stricken gaze. It is, in its way, the most generously welcoming of faiths, Islam, much more so than Judaism. But then, because conversion is so quick, it's easy to think of the whole thing as mere accommodation, which is what my mother thought. She remained a Jew in her heart, but, pragmatic being that she was, and is, could see no irremediable damage done to her faith in mumbling a few formulaic phrases in front of a mullah. She was desperate to get into that house, that palace that had been promised to her, desperate to relax into the arms of her prince.

The clock struck midnight two weeks after my mother moved into Khalil's house. The gilded carriage became a pumpkin once more, and a woman my mother had never seen before in her life strolled into the kitchen where a meal was being lovingly prepared and when challenged replied:

'Who am I? Who are you?'

She was Khalil's other wife, away visiting a relative for the past two weeks, a wife whom Khalil, in his haste, had failed to mention to my mother. Plural marriage is widely regarded in the West as common amongst Muslims, but in fact it's not. Muslims of any education tend to regard plural marriage as a hillbilly practice, even though it's perfectly legal. And amongst Jews— even Jews who have mumbled a few sentences establishing conversion to the Islamic faith? Forget it. My mother was heartbroken; the other wife, Parvin, was next to homicidal; and my father, when he arrived home, was at first apologetic, then equivocal, then adamant that my mother was making a big hysterical fuss about nothing at all—the timeless strategy of last resort for men who have been less than candid about their marital status. Homa had reasons other than the violence done to her tender feelings for Khalil to feel distraught. A young woman who runs away from her family for any reason at all in Iran is in danger of finding her life at the end of a noose. The law benefits Muslim paterfamilias principally, but even a Jewish family can invoke the rope if it wishes.

My mother relented. Half a loaf was better than the mouldy crusts she'd been getting by on. She shared the house with Parvin, accepting the role of hawoo, or second wife with as much grace as she could muster. Parvin watched her like a hawk, rebuked her at every opportunity, made her feel very much as if she was still living the Cinderella life she thought she'd left behind. What my mother didn't know was that Khalil had told Parvin that my mother was indeed a servant, hired to help her out. Parvin asked him one day, in my mother's presence, if he was sleeping with this menial, so-called servant Homa person. My father provided some sort of evasive reply—he was a master of the evasive reply—meant to convey that he could not speak of such matters in front of the hired help. My mother wanted to shout out, 'Sleeping with me? Yes, yes, yes! What do you think!' but she kept her cool. Later she heard Parvin and my father arguing. My father denied absolutely that he had ever—ever!—slept with Homa.

It would have been more difficult to deny that he was sleeping with my mother when she became pregnant with the baby who would one day be my elder brother, Koorosh. Before her pregnancy was plain for all to see, Khalil whisked her away and set her up in the squalid basement apartment that she was to occupy for years to come—the very basement in which I became a Jew on that night of storms and revelations. He told Parvin that he had been forced to dispense with Homa's services for complex reasons that he didn't wish to talk about—so Parvin explained in later years, when the darker nooks and corners of Khalil's life were all at once illuminated.

Dreams are the rack of the poor. People like my mother spend their most precious periods of inspiration imagining happiness in loving detail, then all unaware, carry their dreams into the torture chamber to have them wrenched apart. For the sake of a little love and affection, a little comfort, my mother abandoned her family, adopted an alien faith and embraced motherhood when she was herself little more than a child. When she emerged from the torture chamber, the love and affection had become contingent on her obedience, and comfort was reduced to a Tehrani version of the squalor she knew in Isfahan. The poor were offered no choice but heroism. When they couldn't take another step, when their burden was killing them, they picked up their burden once more and took another step, then another, and another. I think of my mother as heroic in her determination to overcome disappointment, but because I know what awaits her, I almost wish I could stop writing and leave her with what little joy still remains in her life. That's not possible, is it? We can never stop writing, none of us. We know what happens. We can't leave anything untold.

Koorosh was a basement baby. My mother spent the first months of motherhood staring up the steps in order to see daylight. Her husband, who denied her existence, came to see her once a fortnight. He paid her a tiny allowance. He said, 'Don't worry. Everything will turn out fine.' My mother made those words her mantra: 'Everything will be fine'. But when she reinforced her mantra with the more formal prayers of a faith, it was Adonai she addressed, not Allah. She saw to Koorosh's circumcision, according to the rites of her faith, and she whispered prayers over the cradle in Hebrew asking that the child should prosper.

She believed in love, in its eventual triumph, as many do. She loved Khalil. In time, he would spend more time with her; in time, he would provide more money; in time, he would see that the Jewish girl he'd married was the only one who really understood him. She kept the basement spotlessly clean so that her husband on his visits would be impressed with her housekeeping. When she had scrubbed the floor, she would wait two hours then scrub it again. Every surface was dusted repeatedly. Khalil kept to his schedule of fortnightly visits, but my mother tormented herself with fantasies of her husband arriving unannounced overwhelmed by desire for her like a lover in a poem by Hafiz[6], and so she kept herself and the basement in a constant state of fragrant readiness. But he never came except when he had to, and Homa taught herself to live on scraps of love just as she was forced to live on scraps of food. She was the hawoo and she would have to get used to an over-committed husband frugal with his kisses.

Something my mother might have given some thought to, but didn't, was that a man who can conceal one wife from another may be capable of concealing a third wife from both. Devastated by bad news already, she probably thought that Heaven or Fate had done its worst and moved on, she did not imagine serial concussions. One morning when my mother was at the *Hammam*, the public baths that all Muslim women of the poorer classes visit twice a week, she found herself showering next to a woman much older than her who gave her name as Layla. Layla usually visited the baths in another part of town, but those baths were being repaired and were closed for the week. After this introduction, my mother and Layla fell into the type of conversation that all women at these communal baths enjoy: the children, the price of rice, the stupidity of men, the perfidy of men, the arrogance of men, the parsimony of men—

---

6. Hafiz: the most celebrated Persian poet who lived in the 14th century.

tell me about it. Traditionally, women don't completely disrobe in these bath houses. They exercise modesty, washing one part of the body at a time. And if they have any jewellery—a bracelet, a bangle, a necklace—they leave it on rather than risk it being stolen. Layla was wearing a gold bracelet that fascinated my mother, because it was a bracelet identical to the one she'd seen on Parvin's wrist months earlier. It wasn't an expensive item but it was pretty and my mother would have loved such a bracelet herself. She asked Layla where it came from and was told that it was a gift from her husband who'd purchased it in Yazd a few months back. When Parvin had flaunted her bracelet to torment my mother, she'd also claimed that it had come from Yazd, a gift from Khalil.

'How strange that is! My husband was in Yazd just a few months ago, and he came back with a bracelet the very image of yours.'

The woman, Layla, continued to smile, but the smile had stiffened a little. 'Do you say so?'

'Almost identical, I swear,' replied my mother.

'A coincidence, then.'

'Oh, certainly!'

'And yet I might ask for your husband's name, if that doesn't seem rude. Please don't say, Khalil!'

'Do you mean to tell me that your husband's name is also Khalil?'

'Khalil Karimi!' said the woman, who had by now lost all of her sociability. 'Ya Allah! You are my husband's hawoo!'

The news at first made my mother feel sick to the point of vomiting, but the sickness was succeeded by rage. She threw her block of soap at Layla and reached for the older woman's hair. Her own hair was seized, she was bitten, she was slapped. Other women gathered around, relishing a full-blooded hawoo fight, one of the regular spectacles of life amongst the poor.

Such fights could break out anywhere—at the market, on the way to mosque—but usually between wives who knew of each other's existence. This fight had the added spice of discovery. The women watching on took sides and offered encouragement.

'The skinny one is in the wrong.'

'It's about nothing. A bracelet.'

'I say it's a shame. The younger hawoo is no more than a child.'

After a further few minutes biting and slapping, my mother and Layla were separated and told to sort out their differences with a mullah. My mother went home to her basement howling her eyes out and had to explain to the neighbour who was babysitting Koorosh that she had been betrayed a second time by her husband. She was consoled in the time-honoured way ('Men, what can you say? Liars all of them. Allah grant you the strength to endure this'), but this latest betrayal had destroyed the last vestiges of her dream.

Although her distress was under control when she next saw my father, something that had remained untarnished in her was now dull, lustreless. She had taken on the burden of a solitary life without having said so to herself in as many words. She had lost her belief in Khalil. Nevertheless, she was married to him and divorce was out of the question for a woman with a baby and little chance of employment. She slept with him on his fortnightly visits and inevitably, she became pregnant again. When her condition was confirmed, she went to one apothecary after another seeking herbs to undo the pregnancy. Nothing worked.

I was the child who filled my mother with anguish before I even drew breath. I was the child who resisted pennyroyal, kingsfoil, belladonna, primrose oil, angelica and black cohosh[7]. I was the

---

7. Herbs that have traditionally been used by women in many parts of the world to induce miscarriage.

child she pleaded with in the chill hours of the early morning to vanish from her womb. I was the child in whose DNA the entire history of Persia—Muslim, Jewish and pagan—was recorded. I was the child who confirmed my mother's prediction of a birth attended by pain and dread and loneliness. I was the child who would have been named Moses if my mother had been free to choose such a name. I was the child who came into the world on the back seat of a police patrol car, with my mother clutching the Star of David and shrieking phrases of Hebrew.

5

SCAR

There is a painting by Arthur Schenck that once hung in a gallery in Tehran which depicted a ewe encircled by ravens, standing guard over the bleeding form of her new-born lamb. The ewe has her front hooves planted over her lamb in readiness for an assault from some of the two dozen ravens around her that have crept closer in their boldness. The artist makes it evident to any viewer of this allegory of motherhood that the single-minded ravens will prevail—the ewe will eventually be forced to abandon her baby. It is we, the viewers, who honour the ewe in her anguish. Nature, red in tooth and claw, has no objection to one species benefitting from the misfortune of another. I have felt—since the time I first studied that painting through my seventeen-year-old eyes—that Schenck sees something particular in the devotion of a mother: hopeless as it may be, it is an impulse modelled by God on His own anguish when we are threatened not by ravens but by wickedness.

My mother stands over me and Koorosh like the ewe over her lamb, but not always. I have agonising memories of vicious ravens tearing at my flesh. Where is my mother in *those* times?

At the age of eighteen months, I am abandoned, left in the care of Parvin, the second of my father's three wives, along with my brother. My mother has escaped to Isfahan, her birth city, in a futile endeavour to leave Iran for a life in Israel. Parvin has no love for me or for Koorosh and she detests my mother. Why should my brother and I have been left with Parvin? Within weeks of my mother's departure, I am in hospital in Tehran, fighting for my life. I have been severely burnt in a house fire. The flames have lapped the left side of my torso and my liver has been damaged by the heat that has cooked the outer flesh. Koorosh, too, is burnt, though less seriously than me. I sink into a coma; the doctors fear I will die. My mother returns from Isfahan when she is told of my condition. She broods at my bedside. Contradicting the prognosis of the doctors, I begin to recover. Bandaged and groggy with pain-killers I am taken back to the basement. We resume our hand-to-mouth existence.

I have no memory at all of the fire, of the hospitalisation, of Parvin's role in my life at that time, of my mother's absence. Creating a coherent story of the episode has taken me decades; it begins with my question to my mother when she is bathing me and Koorosh one evening.

'Why do I have this mark?'

My mother responds that I have the mark because people have marks, and I am not to ask her about it again.

'Koorosh,' I persist, 'has no mark.'

'A blessing that your brother has no scar. Now hold your tongue.'

My mother says, 'scar', and as soon as the word is out of her mouth she hisses, as if annoyed with herself, and annoyed with me, too. A mark is a mark, and people can be born with such a blemish, but a scar is an interpretation of a mark. And I know it.

'I had an injury, then?' I ask her.

'Injury, who knows? Maybe you were attacked by a bear. Don't plague me in this way, child!'

'The scar was made by a bear?'

'Maybe. I can't say. A bear, a tiger, a demon. Don't speak of it.'

'It doesn't look as if a bear made the scar. It looks like a burn.'

'A burn? Are you insane, child! A burn!'

My mother stares at me as if I've revealed a venomous force, something that frightens her, awes her. Then she takes a different tack.

'Alright! Who knows the answer? It could have happened that you burnt yourself. Say no more.'

A scar is nothing like a memory; it is not unstable or wavering. It does not change, fade and lie forgotten in your thoughts. A scar is an irreversible mark, untouched by time. A scar signifies harm, and harm can only come about by accident or by infliction. If by accident, what harm in telling the child—me—that he was burnt when…When, what? When he tipped a pot of boiling water on himself?

My mother remains reluctant to discuss the scar even as the years pass, and I continue to fret that something malicious is going on. In the silent hours of those nights when sleep keeps its distance, I touch the scar with my fingertips and try to fashion an explanation. If the harm that left the scar was deliberate, who is responsible? I don't want to believe that it was Maman herself because my love for her is my treasure. It was my mother who made me a Jew, and at six years of age, at seven, at eight, being a Jew becomes more and more vital to me. If a mistake was made and Maman had to tell me that I was not a Jew after all, I would scream until the life left my body. I think of my mother as having the attributes of Adonai Himself, a woman of strange powers who can rip veils apart and reveal new worlds.

By the age of eight, I'm still giving the sleepless hours of my nights to my obsession, my scar, but now I have more to work with. I've met children here and there in my ramshackle part of Tehran who hobble along with badly mended legs broken mysteriously in their infancy, others with scars not like my scar, but vivid enough; scars from heavy blows to the head. Some children, attacked when they are just old enough to have a memory of it, tell stories of violent vomiting leading to hospitalisation. The children with scars, those who can remember being ill enough to bring up blood with their sputum, they're all hawoo victims—that's what I'm told. When these children say, 'She put a cushion on my face,' or, 'She held me under the water,' they're nonchalant about it. The whole of Iran is nonchalant about it.

A wife who has produced only daughters is jealous of the wife who has produced a son. The husband shared by both wives loves the mother of his son more than the mother of his daughters. She gets more attention. She gets more presents. The mother of the daughters prays for the sudden obliteration of the other wife's son. When the prayers go unanswered, the resentful wife begins to plot accidents. One of the sons—the half-brother of her daughters—falls down the stairs. Or stumbles in front of a bus on Imam Boulevard. Or succumbs to a toxic potion of rat poison and white arsenic which somehow found its way into his *khoresht*. Or is burnt to cinders in a fire that traps him in a basement with a locked door. Everyone knows. Everyone shrugs. It's accepted as an added hazard of childhood amongst the poor of Iran.

My suspicions fall on Parvin. I've met her. I've seen the glitter of madness in her eyes. I've seen passions roused in her that could easily turn homicidal. But when would Parvin have had the opportunity to set me on fire? My mother doesn't leave us alone with her, not ever. Koorosh remembers nothing. But my brother has such a sweet, accepting nature that he could probably watch Parvin raise an axe above his head and merely smile, as if a game were about to commence.

Days come along every now and again that find my mother in a confessional mood. Such days are rare and must be managed with great skill and subtlety. As the world's leading authority on my mother and her moods, I can tell the difference between a true confessional mood and a phoney one. The moods—true and phoney—look precisely the same on the surface. My mother appears dreamy, she acquiesces to requests for a little more to eat at dinner time, she doesn't make a fuss if our chores are left unattended, she touches us softly, she kisses our cheeks, she answers questions, she radiates love. This is the phoney confessional mood. This is the mood in which she will answer questions, as I said, except questions about the scar. In this phoney confessional mood, anger and exasperation lie curled in her heart and will stay dormant so long as the scar is not mentioned. In this mood, she is testing me. She is lulling me. She is almost daring me to poke and prod. Before I master the distinction between the real and the phoney, I suffer slaps.

'Haven't I told you a thousand times, child, a thousand times, let me enjoy some quietness, but you behave like a rat and steal my few crumbs of peace!'

So I wait until I'm certain that my mother's mood is absolutely, truly confessional. When she hugs me, I test the softness of her skin, I make sure that a little nest of worry lines at the corners of her eyes is relaxed, I trace her hands feeling for any residual stiffness in her fingers, I make sure that her kisses linger. And yes—on this day, not long after my eighth birthday, I can tell that Maman is truly, truly ready to spill the beans. She's wanted to do so for three years, and today is the day, or rather, tonight is the night, for we three, my mother, Koorosh and I are sitting together on the bed, my mother making our necks and cheeks wet with kisses—with lingering kisses.

'Maman, was it Parvin who made this scar on me?'

'Hmm?'

'Did Parvin do this?' And I take my mother's fingers and place them gently on my scar.

'Yes, it was Parvin, child. Have I not told you that?'

'No. But I thought it must be Parvin.'

'It was Parvin. Woe to her, that she should harm my baby!'

'Maman, tell me how it happened.'

'How it happened? Have I not told you in the past how it happened?'

'No, never.'

And with a sigh, and more stroking of my head and of Koorosh's head, in a voice that starts as a whisper and rises to a murmur, a voice without any trace of anger but brimming with sadness, she says that Parvin came to our basement one night with her brother Hossein and without warning, as soon as the door was opened, attacked her with her fists and nails.

'Hossein held me, a strong boy. I couldn't raise a hand in my own defence. They hit me everywhere on my body...'

Here my mother stops stroking my head for a moment to point to the parts of her body that were so abused that night.

'Here, and here, and all over my face, striking me as hard as they could so that I screamed in pain, my darlings, I screamed for mercy.'

Bruised and bloodied, cowering on the floor, my mother was forced to listen to Parvin's ultimatum. 'Leave Tehran,' Parvin said. 'Do not return here in your life. Your sons are mine now. If your face appears before me again, I will kill you and your Jew God will not save you.'

'Darlings, my heart broke for the hundredth time in my life. I fled in terror. Parvin's face was that of a demon. I went to Isfahan and begged Uncle Abraham to help me escape to Israel. I told him that Parvin was possessed by demons and had vowed to murder me.'

'To Israel!'

'To Israel. Uncle Abraham's heart was a stone at his birth and remains a stone until this day. I lived like an animal, hunting for tiny pieces of food. He would not feed me. But when I begged him to send me to Israel, he said, "You shall go to Israel." He would not feed me but he wanted to be rid of me, so he said he would help me go to Israel. I begged him to send me home to kiss my babies one last time. He said, "Don't disturb their peace. They are happy with that hawoo." But I came back to Tehran to kiss you both before I departed for Israel. I found you in hospital, dearest child, asleep as if dead, with tubes in your arms and your body bandaged, and you, too, Koorosh, with your hands burnt and wrapped in cloth. Uncle Abraham had not told me this news.'

'So you took us home from the hospital?' I ask.

'I took you home from the hospital. I made you safe. Your father said, "A fire started in my house but by Allah's will the children were saved." It was Parvin who set fire to you both, in her wickedness. Woe to her in this life and the next! And it was because of this terrible happening that I never went to Israel.'

As I sit on her lap, I start to feel an uneasy beating of my heart. There are problems for me in accepting my mother's story. I remain perfectly sure, as I always am, that she has nothing to do with the fire. But she had intended to go to Israel and leave Koorosh and me behind. This distresses me. I can't bear for a second the idea of being parted from her. If she has once thought of fleeing to Israel, she might have such a thought again. If Maman goes to Israel, I decide, I will follow her. I will take Koorosh by the hand and make him follow me and we will cross the deserts and mountains and seas and find the land of Israel as Moses had, and then we will search in every house in the land for Maman.

Then there is the great question of Parvin's motive for me to fathom. I imagine that if my mother had abandoned Koorosh

46

and me to Parvin's care, it would be more in Parvin's interest to keep us safe than to kill us. Parvin has only the one daughter, Nasrin, and she can't be certain that a son will ever be born to her. She might strengthen her husband's love for her by caring well for his young sons. It seems to me that I haven't yet heard the whole story of the burning. Meanwhile, I tell Koorosh to watch Parvin like a hawk if he is ever alone with her, in whatever circumstance. It is not uncommon for hawoos with murder in their heart to make serial attacks on the children of their sister wives. The Tehran police force is not Scotland Yard. Murder investigations are casual unless politics is involved, and even then it is torture that the police rely on, not competent investigations.

It is decades later, when I am myself closely acquainted with the Iranian Intelligence Service, with the way they go about things such as torture, that the blurry outline of Parvin's crime becomes more distinct. I am an adult. I am a father. And I am on the run from a man who has the power to shoot me dead on sight, or if he wishes, to wake a magistrate in the night to sign a document, and with that document in one hand and the scruff of my neck in the other, drag me to a scaffold and hang me. I am making a round of farewells, calling on relatives and friends and puzzling or even alarming them with my valedictory tone. I can't risk telling any of them that I am about to flee Iran, but there's a tension in everything I say and a half-crazed look about my eyes that makes them lean forward in their chairs and say, 'But Kooshyar, you look ill, what is the trouble?'

I am twenty-nine when I visit my father and Parvin in Tehran during this series of farewells. They, too, are struck by the weird light in my eyes, by the fidgeting of my hands, by my pallor, by the mournful note that keeps creeping into my speech.

'But son, you look ill. What is the trouble?'

'No trouble, nothing at all—I'm a little short of sleep.'

They glance at each other, they shrug. Then, as if fearing that I have some terminal illness that I won't reveal, they begin talking in something like my own mournful manner. My father speaks of the past, interrupting the flow of his reminiscences with, 'Ya Allah! Life has been a trial to me!' Parvin, stealing secret glances at me, and convinced, I think, that the life is ebbing from me, begins in halting speech a type of confession. I sit up straight, I listen intently, I don't interrupt.

'Do you know, Kooshyar, when we talk of what is past I hear Allah imploring me, "Parvin, speak up now! Tell your story!" And all my life I have listened to Allah, all my life I have followed Allah's bidding, as you, husband, will witness.'

'It's true,' my father says, but not with much conviction.

Parvin takes up her tale once more.

'A time came—ah, such an unhappy day!—when your mother's Uncle Abraham asked me a favour—he called it 'a favour'—that to this day makes the tears gather in my eyes. He said, "The two children of my harlot niece, neither Jew nor Muslim, half-bloods, let them depart the earth." He gave me a rug, a very valuable rug, worth many, many *tomans*. He said, "This is yours in return for the favour I ask." He did not want two boys of half-blood to claim any inheritance when he died. I can show you the rug.'

Parvin leaves the living-room to fetch the rug. I glance at my father who sits on the sofa leaning forward with his hands clasped on his knees. He keeps his eyes averted. Even in the midst of this terrible revelation, I feel nothing but affection for him. His marriages are a tempest. Events unfold of which he is barely aware. The passions of his wives—their vendettas, their jealousies—whirl around him while he sits in self pity and murmurs.

'Ya Allah! Life has been a trial to me!'

Parvin returns with the rug.

'Here, you see? It was this rug Abraham gave to me. If God granted me my wish, I would go back to that day and refuse the rug. A great stone would be lifted from my heart.'

I don't say to Parvin, 'The rug was your reward for burning me and Koorosh?' and she doesn't confess in such terms. It isn't necessary. The three of us sit in silence, each with his or her sorrows, until I excuse myself from the falsely domestic scene. In sombre silence, I drag my feet down the three front steps, close the rusted grey gate and resume my life as a fugitive. This is the last time I see my father.

Years later, in a country oceans away from my own, and in a place a long way from my father's house, when I finally lie down to sleep, I feel little satisfaction in having learnt the truth about the burning. Abraham, ill for years, is now dead. I can't go to him and say, 'Monster!' I had seen him on his deathbed. He asked for me. He made a rambling apology for unspecified episodes of neglect, an apology that I accepted at the time without much reflection, the words of a man who wanted to face God in a repentant state. If Abraham could speak now, would he deny Parvin's claim of incitement to murder? Ah, but Parvin knew when she made her half-confession that there would be no such contradiction.

Now, thirteen years since I left Iran, I touch the scar with my fingertips, tracing its outline. I think of my mother and, against the tide of my fortunes, a smile spreads over my face. With all her flaws, she is yet the most human of mothers. She has stood up to the ravens that would have pecked the flesh from my body and Koorosh's often enough. And yes, sometimes she has glanced over her shoulder, fixed her weary eyes on the hungering birds and muttered, 'Ravens, to the devil with them, I'm too tired.' I surrender to the strange beast of my mother's dedication. I don't require a martyr for a mother.

6

SYNAGOGUE

I am ten years old, sitting on the hard floor of our basement home. My mother plucks her eyebrows assiduously. I have watched in wonder as she scrutinises her reflection in the mirror, silver tweezers poised like a surgical implement. She is merciless. One solitary misbehaving hair will produce a guttural threat followed by the application of the tweezers. After fifteen minutes or so of interrogating her brow, she lowers the tweezers and looks down at me.

'So?' she says.

'Perfect,' I say.

'You think so?'

'Perfect, Maman.'

Her eyes narrow. Now it's my face she's studying, as if she suspects me of being a conspirator, in league with her tortured eyebrows.

'You think so?'

'I promise you. Perfect.'

Then her lips curl. She snaps her gaze back to the mirror, more certain than ever after my treacherous endorsement that somewhere amongst the tiny pruned patches above each eye, a hair has escaped the searchlight of her glare. And invariably she finds one, confirming her in her opinion of me as a traitor to grooming.

'See!' she says, holding the murdered hair in the tips of the tweezers right in front of my nose. It is barely visible to the naked eye. 'You don't look properly. You want me to go ugly into the street.'

'No, no, Maman. You are beautiful. Very beautiful.'

'So you tell me,' she says, pleased to hear me say so but at the same time certain that I lie as easily as I breathe. 'So you tell me.'

My mother's tweezer attacks express her vanity, of course, but keeping her eyebrows thin and tapered also serves her faith—her secret faith, not the faith she expediently adopted at the behest of her husband, my father. Broad eyebrows, often undivided, are a feature of the female Persian face. In old Persian miniature paintings, the thick, undivided eyebrow is often highlighted as a feature of classic beauty. Young women recline in filmy silk amidst perfumed gardens where nightingales ornament the branches of trees, a single black line arching across their lower foreheads. When my mother plucks her brows, she is distinguishing herself from the hirsute women of Muslim Iran.

She doesn't reveal this motive to me when I watch her at work before the mirror, as a child.

'You are a Jew in your heart,' she tells me and Koorosh, 'but not when you are out on the street.'

She heeds her own counsel at all times. The eyebrow plucking is an idiosyncrasy, not a public confession of her secret faith. There is no rabbinical edict declaring that the Jewish women of Persia must keep their eyebrows pruned. All of our religious observances are covert; we cannot even attend the synagogue as other Persian Jews can. My mother keeps a mezuzah, a small curved piece of metal with a Hebrew prayer imprinted upon it, in a drawer, not on the doorpost. She kisses it before she leaves the basement, out of sight of the mezuzah-despising Muslims. The mezuzah protects us. Our two books, the Blue and the Green, as I call them, after the colour of their respective covers, a Torah and a book of Jewish stories (Ruth in the alien corn, Moses in the bulrushes, Job in a universe of pain) are kept hidden except when my mother reads to us. When she mutters a prayer or an occasional oath in Hebrew, it is never outdoors. Apostasy is a capital crime in Iran; anyone who adopts the faith of the prophet in public but scorns it in private can, in the absence of a lenient court ruling, spend a period of time in uncomfortable quarters, followed by hanging. Under the Shah who rules us, the crime of apostasy is not always prosecuted with the vigour the clergy would prefer, but you can never be sure. In certain jurisdictions, the mullahs get their way.

The return of Ruhollah Khomeini from exile in February 1979, marks the end of all leniency in courtrooms and elsewhere. Blind eyes are no longer turned, friendly warnings become a memory. The puritans of the broad Iranian constituency are the clerics, whose influence had waned under the regime of Mohammad Reza Shah Pahlavi. The Shah had restricted his official involvement with the mullahs to the bare minimum over the years of his reign, treating the clergy as a host of hicks peddling a peasant version of Islam. His land reforms cost the clergy plenty. His secret police force, SAVAK, persecuted the dissenting clergy mercilessly. SAVAK's torture chambers practised refinements in the administration of agony unequalled anywhere in the world. Even security chiefs from states friendly to the Shah's regime, when offered a tour of SAVAK's facilities, went away feeling queasy. The disaffected clergy became the embittered clergy, the embittered became the determined, the determined have become zealots.

As the Islamic Revolution unfolds in the streets of Tehran, the Jews of the city keep to their houses and apartments and cellars. After an ecstatic homecoming at Tehran's International Airport where a crowd of a million has gathered, Khomeini promises that 'No Iranian will be harmed, other than scoundrels.' But within days a bloodletting is unleashed that sees the servants of the Shah's tyranny—those too slow in taking their leave of the state—hunted through the streets of cities and towns. The despots and deputy despots of the old tyranny become the quarry of the new tyranny. Khomeini carries the enthusiasm of the crowds that gathered to welcome him back from Paris into the second and third and fourth months of his rule. But by the fifth month it becomes clear that this grandfatherly figure with his snowy beard has an uncompromising agenda in mind, backed up by a lurking, horrifying menace.

The crowd of a million who welcome him home were brothers and sisters for the day, but their enthusiasm is ignited by different hopes. Some are liberals, some are social democrats, some are conventionally devout Muslims who are happy to see their faith honoured, some are nationalists, some are simply Shah-haters whose great priority is ridding Iran of the Pahlavis by any means possible. Many are happy to have the Ayatollah take Iran down any avenue he chooses. As it turns out, Khomeini's initial embrace of the Iranian people does not include those who have begun to have second thoughts about the rapture of their welcome in February, those who now wish to complain of a new regime of censorship, more severe than that of the disposed Shah.

Rumours are heard that the accommodation in Evin Prison in North Tehran is being extended—it is already a city within a city—now the fortress is growing so rapidly that it will soon become a city of its own. Another rumour, more troubling still, suggests that the technicians of SAVAK—those who have made themselves familiar with the use of pliers, blowtorches, sharp metal implements—have been retained as employees of MOIS— the Ministry of State Security. Before our eyes in some cases, but more often out of sight, the structure of the new tyranny is being erected. When the republic's constitution is revealed, freedom of worship, freedom of the press, the right of citizens to protest is all spelt out in unambiguous language, but these rights are being violated even before a vote has been taken on the adoption of the constitution.

I'm eleven years old when the Islamic Republic is proclaimed. I'm twelve when students invade the US Embassy in North Tehran, and still twelve when Iran and Iraq go to war. The menace in the air is not as new to me as it is to many other Iranians—liberals, socialists and those more thoughtful citizens who see benefit in a division of faith and state are the new Jews of Iran. They are learning, day by day, what it is to live in constant fear of catastrophe. For the actual Jews, the Islamic Republic of Iran is a land of implacable hostility. Under the Shah, we were despised, certainly, but if we kept our mouths shut, we could avoid *koshtars*—our version of pogroms—just about. Now and again, a Jew was lynched or beaten to a pulp or tossed onto a bonfire, but this was more to do with local episodes of hysteria than with anything sanctioned by the Peacock Throne[8].

I develop a type of sixth sense in the years since my mother has revealed my heritage to me. On the streets, in the markets, at school, I pick up the tense vibrations, almost a thrum, of those who wish me ill, who wish every Jew ill. Street art has blossomed in Tehran—whole walls are devoted to caricatures of Uncle Sam reaching out a hand with claw-like fingernails towards a map of the Middle East. Uncle Sam is the Great Satan. Uncle Sam has a homicidal glint in his eyes. One arm embraces his Little Pal, Israel. Uncle Sam's boot is poised over a huddled group of grieving Palestinians. The figure that represents Israel, dressed as a mini Uncle Sam but with fangs for teeth, grins in

---

8. A reference to the Pahlavi monarchy (the Shah).

satisfaction. Other works of art show happy throngs of Iranians with arms reaching towards the beatific figure of Ruhollah Khomeini, the state's Great Father standing against a sky of unblemished azure.

I pause on my way to school or to the cobbler's shop to study these examples of fundamentalist propaganda, the Islamic Republic's equivalent of the Socialist Realist art of China and the USSR. The slogans below the more aggressive works read: Death to the Great Satan! Death to the United States! Death to Israel! I don't stare for too long. It is customary to nod your head in approval when you gaze at these images, even to raise your fist in solidarity with their message, and I won't do that. Boys not much older than me form a fundamentalist militia, the Basij, and you don't want to be noticed staring at the pictures with indifference or outright disgust, because the Basij are everywhere, licensed zealots authorised to crack you over the head with a baton if they have decided they hate you. I move on, schoolbag on my back, my eyes averted, the secret Jew. The air around me hums with menace as I pass below a gigantic portrait of Khomeini fixed to a building on Vali Asr Boulevard. Stronger than my fear is my glee at having a secret to conceal. It thrills me. As I walk along, I murmur too softly for anyone to hear, 'Long live Israel, long live Israel, Adonai is my God...' I am myself a type of zealot—but a very quiet one, and very well behaved.

In 1980, Uncle Abraham's liquor shop in Isfahan is burnt to the ground and Uncle Abraham himself is thrown into prison. He is charged with being a 'pro-Israeli Jew' which is an indirect accusation of being a spy in the employ of Mossad. The anti-Israel sentiment unleashed by the Khomeini regime feeds on more than a sense of the injustices endured by the Palestinian people, it is fuelled by a hunger for revenge. Newspaper headlines that I scan quickly whenever I walk past a newsstand express a rabid loathing for Israel almost comical in its virulence. Israel is 'the cancer that besets Palestine' and Israelis are 'members of a league of murderers feasting on the flesh of our brothers and sisters in the faith.'

When I am older, I will understand that this loathing is a response to the humiliation of political and military defeats inflicted on Muslim militias and Muslim states antagonistic to Israel, going back to the Balfour Declaration of 1917. I will come to know as well as anyone in Iran that humiliation is a type of trauma, and that for many, many of those who experience the trauma of humiliation, fantasies of revenge against those considered responsible for the suffering, rage through the mind like blizzards of hatred, blanking out reason or mercy. I will, in time, stare into the eyes of a man whose hatred of Jews, Israeli or Persian, has taken on a primitive, voodoo cast. He will study me with as much fascination as disgust as if black fumes might start billowing from my ears, a manifestation of the Jew-evil that dwells inside me. I will almost choke with fear under his stare, knowing that no power on earth, no power in heaven can save me. But so much younger at eleven and knowing so much less, I shuffle down the street with my schoolbag past the toxic headlines and rejoice in the protection in which secret faith clads me. Would these people who so despise Moses ever prevail against his power, against the courage of the man who brought down the law from Sinai? Moses—who not even Pharaoh could subdue—who with his wooden staff drowned an army in the tumult of the Red Sea waters? Never.

Uncle Abraham is not a pro-Israeli Jew, or he is, but only in silence. In his thoughts, he honours Israel. So does every Persian Jew. But he would no more brag in public over what is locked in his soul than he would stroll naked into a mosque at evening prayer. He is in gaol for running a liquor shop, not for being a spy. It is not illegal to run a liquor shop, but it is illegal to sell alcohol to Muslims. Maybe Uncle Abraham was indiscreet; maybe he handed over a bottle of brandy to some police stooge. Or maybe—and more likely—he is simply a victim of fundamentalist revenge fantasies. If they can't bomb Jerusalem, they can at least throw a cantankerous old Isfahani Jewish peddler of alcohol into gaol.

Uncle Abraham needs my mother. The Isfahani Revolutionary Guards are not going to listen to pleas for his release from any Jew, but they might listen to a woman who was a Jew but who is now a Muslim; a woman who accepted the faith and married a Sunni bus driver. A message is sent to her in Tehran: 'In the name of God, save Abraham.'

My mother dresses Koorosh and me in our best clothes and we board a bus for Isfahan. On the bus travelling south, she whispers to us, 'Now you will see what a Jewish household looks like. Now you will see what it means to live in faith.' She is pleased to have been implored to intervene. She is not a woman who nurses grievances for life. Get down on your knees and plead for forgiveness and you're going to see a smile, a little smug, at first, maybe, but a smile. I ask if Uncle Abraham is a rabbi, for I know that the mullahs of our faith are called rabbis. My mother says Uncle Abraham is not a rabbi, but he is respected by the Jews of Isfahan and lives in a big house. Gazing from the window of the bus as we pass through Aran and then the holy city of Qom where Khomeini and his deputies the Jew-haters gather, I picture Uncle Abraham as a living version of his namesake the Patriarch, a man of great age with a beard whiter and longer than that of the Ayatollah. The joy mounting inside me makes me squirm in my seat. My mother in her *roosari* (her scarf) frowns and jabs me with her elbow. I try to calm myself by whispering the dozen Hebrew words I have learnt from her.

The words don't make a sentence but just the taste of them on my tongue soothes me.

Uncle Abraham's house lies in the Jewish ghetto of Mahala. Thousands of Jews lived in the ghetto in centuries past, when they controlled sectors of the city's commerce that had by tacit agreement been left in their hands such as the jewellery trade, and hush-hush business loans. For the Jews of Persia, the ghettoes of Isfahan and Hamadan, of Shiraz, Mashhad and Yazd must have had a greater immediate significance than Jerusalem itself. Hemmed in by danger, they were nevertheless in a place where the sweat that dripped from their faces fell onto stones they had lived with for centuries.

Something of the vitality of the lives lived here in Mahala gets into my bloodstream like narcotic fumes as we make our way through the streets and lanes. I forget to breathe in my excitement. I see Jews dressed as Jews. My eyes grow as large as saucers. I'd never doubted that other Jews live in Iran, but to see them! The lines on their faces are not those of the people I see each day on the streets of Tehran, the nuances of their faith and its rigours have fashioned wrinkles distinct from the seams fashioned by worship of the Prophet. But there is a haunted look, too, a version of the expression that Jews in many lands wear in times of heightened persecution. My mother, dressed as a Muslim, rouses a certain degree of alarm. I want to cry out to the people we pass, 'No, no! Maman is like you! We honour Moses!'

Uncle Abraham's house is one of the biggest in the ghetto, and very old. We pass through its doors into a world that exceeds anything I'd conjured in my imagination. My mother switches from Farsi to Hebrew in an instant, chatting with members of Uncle Abraham's family waiting to greet her. On a heavy wooden table with carved legs stands, what I recognise as a menorah and, behind the assembled family, hang tall portraits that I know must represent Abraham the Patriarch and Moses.

In my awe, I take two steps closer to the portrait of Moses and put my hands to my head, holding tight lest my brain should swell and split my skull open. Moses! This is Moses! And in the background, the great River Nile and the rushes on the river bank from which he was rescued by Pharaoh's daughter. Gazing up into the eyes of Moses, a rapture takes hold of me that makes me moan loudly enough for my mother to scold me.

'Kushi! Have you lost your manners? Come to me!'

We sit in comfortable chairs and accept rose water and small biscuits of a type I've never seen before. Uncle Abraham's sons, old enough to have grey hair in their beards, watch us in a wary way that wounds me, for I doubt they accept me or Koorosh as true Jews, but rather as compromised Jews with a father of the tribe of Muhammad. But I'm desperate in my need to be accepted as a Jew.

In adult life, I've thought about this Jew-fever that so overwhelmed me as a child, shaking my head in amusement. I was on track to become a sort of doctrinaire uber-Jew, rather than the casual visitor to the synagogue which more accurately reflects my present level of devotion. It was just me—it was not a family obsession. For sure, my mother held fast to her faith in secret, but that has to be considered in the context of her conversion. It was not just dire necessity that provoked her adoption of Islam, it was also the stunning good looks of her husband. She made me a Jew. She counselled secrecy in public, honesty and stubborn conviction in private. But when it all came down to it, my mother was actually fairly matter-of-fact about her faith. She hadn't caught the fever that drove me into this hectic embrace of Judaism. Nor had Koorosh. My mother could have revealed that we were secret Buddhists or Hindus, and Koorosh would have simply smiled and said, 'Sounds good.'

We are taken through to a second big room to meet Uncle Abraham's mother, Morvarid. My mother has told us that

Morvarid is the angel of the household, endlessly tender over the generations in her concern for the children of the family. She sits at a spinning wheel, a distaff in one hand, her foot on the treadle, the yarn running through her ancient fingers. She seems a figure from a book of folk stories and, indeed, her skin is as papery as the page on which she might have been illustrated. Even through her thick spectacles a gentle light glows in her eyes, as if her great age and experience have wrought a special sympathy in her. As soon as she turns her gaze to Koorosh and me, she utters a phrase that I take to be a Hebrew greeting and stands up from the spinning wheel. She manages the two or three difficult steps to where we wait. Choosing me first, she places her hand on my head, whispers some words and blows at me softly. Then she repeats the ritual with Koorosh. When she's reseated herself and drawn breath, I ask my mother in a whisper what Morvarid had said.

'She gives you her *berakhah*, her blessing. The words she spoke, Kushi, those words make a prayer. Morvarid is the oldest of the family. Her blessing is an honour. Now Adonai will protect you and Koorosh all of your days.'

My mother is occupied with her rescue mission over the next few days. Often Koorosh and I are left in the care of Uncle Abraham's wife and his daughter, Soraya. This suits me fine. The house is a sort of adventure playground of the soul for me—Jew World. I could not be more thrilled if I were being treated to ice-cream and rides on a roller coaster. I only have to gaze at the big beaten-copper plates ornamented with Hebrew letters displayed in the large room with the menorah, a sacred candelabra, to be ecstatically transported. Sitting still, I'm murmuring constantly, 'Shalom...shalom...' When my mother returns from the various sites at which she has to plead for Uncle Abraham, she puts her hand on my brow to check my temperature.

'Calm down,' she whispers as she kisses my cheek. 'You know, I want to tell you something. But should I?'

'Yes, yes, tell me!'

'Maybe you're too excited. Better I should change your Uncle Mansoor's plan.'

'What plan? Please tell me!'

'If I thought you loved me...'

'Maman, I do love you! So much! So, so, so much!'

'So you say. But is it true? Well, I indulge my children, that's a fact. What can I say? Alright, tomorrow is Shabbat. Tomorrow, your Uncle Mansoor takes you to synagogue.'

This is an adventure that had been spoken of on the bus. I'd scarcely dared believe it would come to pass. Now that it has been confirmed, I cover my mother's face in kisses, whispering rapidly, 'Thank you, thank you, shalom, thank you, shalom, shalom...'

The synagogue is within the Mahala ghetto, an ancient building. As Koorosh and I pass through the portals, guided by Uncle Mansoor, I am struck dumb by the magnificence of the interior. Koorosh and I sit each side of our Uncle and respond to his nudges and whispers. The hooded scrolls of the Torah are carried down the aisle as the cantor sings from a corner. That soaring voice eclipses in grandeur any sound I have ever heard. Tears of joy soak my cheeks.

'Oh Moses,' I murmur. 'Oh my Moses, my dear Moses, my Abraham, my Adonai!'

Koorosh, smiling, glances across Uncle Mansoor to me.

'Kushi, what is wrong?'

I don't bother answering him. I go on chanting my private prayer:

'My Moses, my Adonai, my dear Moses...'

7

BUS

Every child of an impoverished urban family in Iran, a boy especially, becomes a jack-of-all-trades. I'm reminded of a famous English folk song that recounts the employment history of a boy in Birmingham who, by the age of thirteen, had tried his hand at every unskilled job on offer, from maker of lice-traps to coffee-grinder to umbrella repairer.

At the tender age of eight, I graduate from my first employment as a nail-straightener to cobbler—a natural progression. My apprenticeship as a cobbler isn't a formal one. I simply watch what the cobbler himself does, recall his techniques and apply them when I'm given the chance. I learn to use an awl, a hole-punch, and shoe lasts of various sizes. I learn to cut rubber strips into the shape of soles without wasting a millimetre of material, and to cut leather in such a way that the greatest possible number of soles and patches can be fashioned from a length.

Every lesson I learn in all of my occupations is a lesson in frugality. Waste, for a poor boy, is the gravest of all sins. If I find a discarded shoe in the street, perhaps with its top peering out of a rubbish bin or left behind in the mud, I dive upon it like an eagle to prey. A shoe of any age, in any condition, is bounty. The sole can be cut from it and used to replace the leaking soles of my own shoes. The leather will do for patches. It always amazes me that anybody would discard a shoe, for a single shoe can have a number of lives. When I patch my own shoes with the carcass of another and experience the sensation of dry feet and dry socks, I feel as if I have duped the world, pulled off an amazing coup—I feel shrewd, masterful.

I always work at more than one job at a time. The money that children bring into an impoverished household makes the difference between severe malnutrition and ordinary malnutrition. You learn to look at the world around you as a place in which tiny niches might be discovered that house opportunities to add a penny or two to your day's take. When I'm not repairing shoes, I'm selling kites in the street—kites being a great playtime favourite of Iranian children. The kite merchant pays me a tiny commission on each sale so that by selling two or three, an extra teaspoon of rice can be added to the evening meal. In summer, I sell ice in chunks to people who rely on ice for refrigeration. I carry a hessian bag of ice chunks with me and accept a few *rials* from customers who transfer my chunks into a bag of their own. There is never any possibility of branching out into a business of which I am sole proprietor, although I embrace the principle, at least. To be an ice merchant, you need a refrigerator—out of the question for me. To be a kite manufacturer, you need the capital to set up a small factory.

I am on a treadmill. If I falter in any of the jobs I take on, I fall. I often start work before the first light of morning and finish when the last light has left the sky. In the space of a day, the faces I see are usually haggard; other children as busy as I am carrying out their tasks in a zombie-like state after labouring all day. I see eyes in which dreams have expired forever—eyes of children my age. But my own dreams have not expired—my mother would not permit that.

'Kushi, a life of ease and plenty awaits you, for you will become a doctor and your skill will make you famous.'

When she sees my spirits lagging, she repeats her exhortations.

'Moses crossed the desert with a following of thousands. Not a word of complaint escaped his lips.'

And, 'Adonai will protect you.'

She says the same things to Koorosh, but I think it is me in whom she places her greatest store of hope. In me, she sees some of the crazed determination that fuels her own dreams. I have inherited some of her madness—and she approves.

One day I walk past a bicycle repair shop and stand there, watching. Akbar, the old man repairing a bike asks me if I would like to become a bike fixer in future. I ask my mother the next day to see if Akbar needs a hand. I know I will make more money than selling ice and kites. Akbar tests me with tools and finds that I am quite handy; he gives me the job. Tehran is a city of bicycles, most of them in permanent need of repair. A man will ask for his front wheel to be straightened, telling me to ignore for the moment that the brake rubbers are worn down to the metal. 'That will be for another day,' he will say, and by the time he can afford to have the brake rubbers replaced, the back wheel will need straightening—and that will be for 'another day'.

I kneel beside an upturned bicycle spinning the wheel to see if the spokes I've added have corrected the wobble. As the wheel spins, I murmur words of Hebrew prayers to keep myself awake. I dream not only of the wealth and fame that awaits me as surgeon of nationwide renown, but of simpler things, of finding a metaphorical ladder that I can climb and see beyond the walls of life. What might lie beyond these walls that tower above me? Green fields, wildflowers, kiosks that hand out free ice-creams, shelves and shelves of books, millions of books, and on each shelf a sign that reads, 'For the benefit and enjoyment of Kushi, the bicycle boy, the cobbler, the ice-seller, the boy on the treadmill.' Ah, how I relish the prospect of walking along those shelves and choosing books at leisure. The ice-cream? Yes, that would be good. But the books? Adonai, send me books, above all, but first send me the sleep that would permit me to concentrate on what I am reading.

A jack-of-all-trades must master the small tools of the workplace. It is not for us to handle lathes and power saws, but needles and scissors, hammers and pliers—the first tools invented by man. I become a good tailor by teaching myself to ply needles of various gauges. My skill with sewing needles and darning needles allows me to make a few *rials* repairing prayer rugs. No conscientious Muslim wants to be accused of praying on a threadbare rug. I inspect the rug, give my quote for its repair, then go to work with the yarns I carry. Huddled over the rug, concentrating closely, I am aware of the great irony of a Jewish boy darning holes in Muslim prayer rugs. It's an irony that delights me, and a way of repaying Adonai for His kindness in sending customers my way, subverting the craft of the Muslim rugmaker with the skill of the secret Jew.

I am constantly on the lookout for discarded garments, just as I keep an eye out for cast-off shoes. Fabric can be shaped in a hundred ways. I repair the holes in my shirts, in Koorosh's shirts and trousers and in my mother's garments. When I find serviceable fabric of any sort, I wear the grin of victory. I feel like boasting of my finds and I sometimes do. 'See this shirt? What numbskull could have thrown it out? See the strength that the fabric retains? Feel it for yourself!' The scavenger's life is not without its moments of exultation.

In the adult life I have come to lead in a land a million kilometres from the dirty streets of Tehran, I see one evening a documentary about the rubbish-pickers of Cairo, children turning over the mounds of debris from the heaving, bustling city; seizing the one fragment of treasure that rewards an hour's vigilant searching and stuffing it in a bundle slung over the shoulder. I know what people in the West would murmur as they watch these children. I know the vocabulary of their distress: 'How sad, how heart-breaking, how tragic!' And yet I can tell you that those children, half-starved, ragged, know joys that those who grow up swimming in cream will never know. God provides consolations in every life.

After I collect all the money from a few months working for Akbar I buy a pair of stockings that I have seen for months in a shop, to keep my mother's feet warm. But the next day she returns the stockings to get the money back, and she tells me that we needed the money more than stockings. I realise how much she is sacrificing for us; I promise to become a doctor and put an end to our poverty and suffering.

The greatest of all consolations in my life is not the sudden discovery of an old shoe, as thrilling as that is. No, it is the journeys that I take with my father on his bus when I act as waiter serving water to the passengers, and as general factotum, responding instantly to my father's instructions: 'Kushi, take the straw broom and sweep the aisle,' 'Kushi, pick up that orange peel on the floor by the fifth row of seats,' 'Kushi, pour me tea,' 'Kushi, wash the windshield at the next stop and check the tyres.'

The joy and pride that swell my heart when I am asked to carry out some task by my father sometimes amounts to ecstasy. For I am the ideal child, the child born to adore his mother and father, the child who will forgive anything, everything, the child for whom paradise is the gentle word of praise withheld for hours, and finally bestowed. Look into my eyes, dark pools of longing, more imploring than those of a spaniel. Look at my expression, woven in its every feature from avid anticipation. If you are my mother, your beauty will be the subject of poetic compliments, so much so that you will come to expect them and will frown if I am a split-second late in providing them. And if you are my father, I will gaze at your handsome profile and the sturdiness of your forearms gripping the steering wheel, and there will be no need for me to say, '*Baba jan*, I'm your greatest fan!' because the adoration dwelling in my gaze will be sufficient evidence of my devotion.

You may at times be short-tempered with me, not because of any lapse in my concentration on your manly good looks but because other things in your life—the never-ending demands of your three wives, maybe—will have vexed you even before you laid eyes on me that day. You will say, 'Kushi, I asked you for tea ten minutes ago. Are you asleep? What goes on in your muddled head?' And I will wince as if a lash had been wielded on my back. The truly amazing thing about me is that I will recover from the agony of the lash and will actually come to agree with you: I was late with the tea—about thirteen seconds late, not ten minutes, but I wouldn't want to quibble—and the next time you ask for tea it will be in your hand almost before the words are out of your mouth. Adonai and Moses—they also benefit from the devotional longing in me.

Do I take time to reflect on the unevenness of my relationships with my father and my mother? Do I ever ask myself if they are as besotted with me as I am with them? Do I ever put this question to myself: 'But Kushi, is this not just a little bit mad, this aching need to devote yourself so completely to your father, to your mother?' No, I don't. I want to be, above all things in life, a son.

My devotion has its rewards, of course. My devotion strives to win rewards. The journey from Mashhad to Tehran and back again is twelve hundred kilometres long and takes fourteen hours. My father drives through the night relying on the tea I provide to keep him awake. Given the opportunity—an opportunity that never comes his way—my father would put his head on a pillow and sleep for hours mid-journey, but I have no desire to sleep. I couldn't bear to miss a second of his presence. The very sight of him so nourishes me that my body would thrive for a week on a kind smile. Sometimes my father reaches out and tousles my hair; sometimes he squeezes my shoulder.

'You're a good boy, Kushi. You make the journey go quicker.'

Words like these are a blessing and whenever I hear them I silently send a prayer to Adonai asking Him to keep my father from harm, to find in his heart a place for this charming and handsome Muslim with three wives to support, this Muslim who is a Muslim through no fault of his own and who would probably make a pretty good Jew if he had the chance.

There is mystery and magic in a journey by bus at night. We are passing through the Lut Desert. A heavy silence envelops everything, suffocating even the loud snorts of the old bus. I struggle to stay awake and, in my twilight state, I see the passing shadows of ancient Persian warriors. Maybe once in an hour I might catch the glimmer of a distant light, a lantern outside a mudbrick house perhaps, or hung from a shepherd's tent pole; a tiny twinkle in the ocean of darkness. Above us the stars extend forever, piercingly bright. The moon stands white and gold but pitted in places with strange shadows. I ride next to my father at the front. Behind us, I can hear the whisper of a mother singing a folk lullaby to her children; the rhythmical chant of old men counting their prayers with their beads; the sudden cry of protest of a baby woken from its slumber when its mother changes position; the muttering and suppressed laughter of a couple of young men sharing an off-colour joke.

'Kushi, peel me an orange,' my father says, and I smile with pleasure.

The roar of the engine has settled into a deep, steady hum as if it has accepted the great distance ahead of it and has adopted a proud determination to arrive on time. The instruments on the dashboard glimmer faintly. The needle of the speedometer hovers just above the eighty numeral. Happiness makes me light-headed. Without some care, I could almost faint. My father stubs out his cigarette and clears his throat.

'Did I ever tell you the story of the king and the white stallion?' he says. 'The white stallion that was famous all over our ancient land of Persia? More famous than any horse of Arabistan?'

'No, I have never heard that story,' I say, even though I have indeed heard it before. 'Tell me the story of the King of Persia and the white stallion.'

'That's funny. I could have sworn I told you the story of the King of Persia and the famous white stallion, once before. Yes, I'm sure I did.'

He's teasing me. He knows as well as I do that I have listened transfixed to his masterful telling of the story many times. He knows I will plead for the story again. And I do.

'Now,' he begins, 'in a time before the birth of our Prophet, the land of Persia was ruled by a king who coveted a famous stallion, as white as snow, that lived below the mountain of Shah Kuh in the desert of Dasht-e Lut...'

The story unfolds over the space of an hour. I relish every detail. Sometimes my father adds a fresh detail to the story—the number of jewels in the white stallion's bridle, the spontaneous acknowledgement of all other horses in Persia that the white stallion is their leader—and I nod my head and murmur, 'Wonderful!' to show my appreciation of the effort *Baba jan* is making.

My favourite of all the stories I listen to while the engine hums and the old men murmur their prayers is the tale of Sohrab and Rustam. It is a story that tears at my heart, this saga of a father and son who are parted when the son is a baby, only to meet many years later on the battlefield, each the champion of a great army. They do not know that they are father and son, only that they are enemies, and yet Rustam, the father, looks on his armour-clad son Sohrab who has come out to face him in single combat, and feels a strange love for the young man kindling in his heart. Rustam has killed many great champions on the battlefield but he does not wish to kill Sohrab. He implores the young man to retire from the battlefield and save his father the grief of burying him. Sohrab says, 'I have no father to mourn me. Show me your mettle!' And the two champions fight. It is Sohrab who is slain, but in his death throes he reveals a secret that identifies him as Rustam's son, and Rustam falls to the ground in his grief. He raises his head and cries to the heavens. He cradles his dying son's head on his lap while the two armies watch on in disbelief. Rustam strikes the ground with his fist, and such force does he impart that a tremor runs across the battlefield and makes the leaves tremble on the trees. 'I have slain my son! I have slain the boy I searched for in every city I subdued!' Such is Rustam's love for Sohrab that he calls for his captains to raise a great funeral mound, and he stalks the perimeter of the mound for days, refusing food and drink, his tears soaking his tunic.

It is not the thrill of the combat scenes that so attracts me to the story of Sohrab and Rustam, although they are vivid enough in my father's telling—'A single swish of his mighty sword and five heads were cleaved from their necks!'—but the poignancy of the father's love for his son, and of Rustam's wracking grief when he understands what fate has wrought in his life. I think, 'This is what *Baba jan* would feel if he accidentally killed me on the battlefield; this is the grief he would know, and he, too, would strike the ground with his fist and cry to heaven.' In my rapture of death and love, I come to believe that it would be well worth the effort of being killed to have my father weep over me in the fashion of Rustam.

Of course, if I were slain I wouldn't know anything of his grief, but maybe, like Sohrab, there would be a few seconds before my eyes closed forever when I would be able to make out the agony on my father's face and see tears run down his cheeks. Because my father doesn't give out many compliments. A few, but not so many. Except when he's telling stories, he's fairly laconic. A word or two here and there, a shrug of his shoulders, a gesture. But it is my conviction that he truly loves me with all his heart, deep down. I need to believe that. He has many children, but I'm the only one who is invited to travel with him on the bus. That might be because I'm such an adept student of his needs and wants, or it may be that he simply loves me, his youngest son, best of all—benign neglect of our welfare, of my mother's and mine and Koorosh's, notwithstanding. That's fine. My father's love for me has to be economical, just as his expenditure in other ways is economical. Three wives, more children than I probably know about. He has a hard row to hoe.

I also enjoy my father's savvy. He knows his way about. Iran under the mullahs is a minefield—so many laws that contradict the natural appetites of people. You can get a beating and be sent to prison just for drinking a beer. My father knows the rules, and he knows exactly when and under what circumstances he can satisfy his thirst without having to put up with the interference of some pimply-faced teenager from the Basaj militia calling shrilly for the police. Like millions of other Iranians, he leads a covert life in which his appetites play out without hindrance. His courtship of my mother when she was a girl of fifteen demonstrates that he's no angel, and that adds to the allure of his masculinity. Just as I respond to the maternal in my mother so I respond to the manliness of my father. Simple, easily understood qualities in my parents attract me. In a way, I'm a fundamentalist myself. No need to go overboard with the parenting for Kushi's sake! No need to get too rarefied and subtle! He's satisfied with the basics!

His savvy extends to practical matters, too, like what to do when an arm is gashed and there is no antiseptic available.

One evening, I'm passing a glass of water to him (he has the only actual glass beaker on the bus—the passengers have to make do with plastic) when it slips from my hand, smashes on the metal of the dashboard housing and cuts my arm. I'm horrified—my father's glass, you've broken *Baba jan*'s glass, you monster! But my father is concerned only with the wound. After all, this is a land in which infection is everywhere. He stops the bus, gives me a rag to dab away the blood, then calmly tells me to go outside and urinate on the wound—urine functioning as an acceptable antiseptic in an emergency. Which I do, thinking of Sohrab and Rustam in a new and improved version. Sohrab is wounded, Rustam says, 'Son, piss on it!'

We climb the lower slopes of the Alborz on the journey from Mashhad to Tehran—the mountain range to the north of the city, snow-capped for half of the year. The road twists and turns, finding its way through the passes. By the time we reach the Alborz on the way to Tehran, we have left Quchan a long way behind us, and Shirvan, Bojnurd, Gorgan, Behshar, Sari, and Babol. All of these towns will remain memorable to me for the stage of a particular story we have reached. It might be that we are in the middle of Sohrab and Rustam when we reach Gorgan, and I will think to myself, 'Hours to go yet, time for three more stories once this one is over.' This is the Persia that stays with me for decades more and will stay with me for life. The terrain we cross is saturated with history and when I'm listening to my father, I see images from his stories extended over the night sky like constellations, as if the ghosts of Persian heroes leave the soil at night and re-enact their triumphs for me on the screen of heaven.

It is at a stop between two of these towns, and at a pause in the story being told by my father that I experience one of those moments of piercing joy that is destined to survive every one of the calamities awaiting me in the years to come. Most people have their own versions of such rhapsodic moments as mine.

We keep them close, like figures on a charm bracelet. This one comes my way in the desert when my father has pulled the bus into the car park of a roadside restaurant. These restaurants in the middle of nowhere are found on highways all over Iran: scheduled stops that allow the passengers to pray, visit the toilets, order a simple meal, stretch their legs. Many of these restaurants—really, combination roadhouses and hotels—also provide beds with simple frames on short legs set up in the open area at the front of the establishment, under the stars, for passengers on particularly long journeys.

It is my job to clean the big windscreen of the bus at such stops, washing away the coating of dust and bugs that builds over the hours of the trip. So here I am, up on the front bumper with a bucket of water, an old squeegee and a dry rag, applying myself with great dedication to this important task. In the restaurant itself, passengers are eating drowsily at tables with plastic covers (often printed with a gingham pattern, curiously) or haggling over the price of four plates of beans and rice, maybe playing cards, maybe backgammon. Mothers are dealing with tired children, issuing slaps to some, caresses to others. Men not occupied with eating or card-playing stand about in groups of three and four smoking and chattering, talking about the war with Iraq, the price of tobacco, the perfidy of politicians, how good it would be to own a television. Mullahs wander about in their long brown robes and turbans looking for opportunities to issue sermons on moral laxity to men who may have ignored their prayers, or abbreviated them; also on the lookout for free food, maybe a gift cigarette or two that can be hastily concealed and smoked later in private.

My father is in there at a table in the restaurant, eating his meal, maybe listening in on someone's story of how boys from his village, fifteen, sixteen years old, have been called up to fight on the Kermanshah front against Saddam's butchers. And here I am, labouring away happily for the reward of a mild compliment from my father like, 'That's good,' or something of the sort, treasure enough. Sure enough, when my father emerges from the restaurant with a cigarette in his mouth and the satisfied expression of a man with a full belly, he looks up at the sparkling windshield and nods.

'That's good,' he says. But on this fabulous evening in the desert, he goes further. He says, 'I miss you when you're not here, Kushi. Yes, I do.'

He puts his hand on my shoulder and squeezes for a second or two. Then he calls out loudly to a few tardy passengers, 'We're going!' and climbs into the bus.

I climb in, too. No, I float into the bus on a cloud of bliss with a smile on my face that would quite possibly do me some medical mischief if it were any wider.

8

HAJI

More than a year has passed since Sayed Ruhollah Musavi Khomeini flew into Tehran International Airport on a Boeing jet and changed the world forever. He has sent the Peacock Throne to a museum. He has extended the section of Evin Prison that houses the torture chambers of the Ministry of State Security. He has sanctioned the death by hanging of a great many people he could not abide. He has established a regime that in the audacity of its intrusiveness rivals that of North Korea—not that I am properly aware of how far the Supreme Leader has taken things. Life is more fraught than ever. That is what I know. My Bar Mitzvah is coming, and may never be celebrated—I know that, too. And my father has moved my mother, my brother and me to the holy city of Mashhad for some mysterious reason. To Mashhad, and to a hole in the wall even more squalid than the hole in the ground we occupied in Tehran. I look sulky about the whole business.

'Get used to it,' my mother says.

And I do get used to it. I still have my mother, occasionally my father, and always my fledgling faith. These are the foundations of sanity in my childhood. The irony is that I guard them with a zeal that borders on madness. My mother must remain

75

beautiful, brave and admirable (seemingly). My father must remain handsome, masterful, heroic. And my faith must shine down on me like the sun and the moon. Anything that strikes at these foundations sends tremors up my spine that open fissures in my mind.

Haji Heydar becomes the enemy of my sanity when I am twelve. His entry into my life, into my mother's life, into Koorosh's, threatens me in every important way. My father's heroism is blemished, my mother's bravery is compromised, my faith is demeaned. I'm a wreck. Haji Heydar, crook, adulterer, and anti-Semite, arouses hatred in me for the first time in my life; a hatred too powerful for my small frame to accommodate. At times, contemplating his arrival at our tiny apartment in Mashhad, a fever seizes me and I find myself whispering prayers of toxic ill will.

Before the coming of Haji Heydar, my prayers to Adonai were those of an earnest, respectful supplicant: give my mother more rest, more peace, make more food appear on our table, send books and many more books into my life. Now I am beseeching Adonai to visit disaster upon Haji Heydar: let his great big Mercedes Benz plunge into an abyss, let the electric shaver he employs go berserk in his hand and swallow his face into its electronic interior. Such a curious thing that the intensity of my love for my mother and my father should become the engine of hatred for Haji Heydar. When people talk of 'the tenderness of love' they should remember that love will fight for its survival with the ferocity of a wolf trapped by howling dogs.

Haji Heydar is a businessman, the owner of the Gilantour bus company for which my father works. But he is a businessman of a type who thrives in Iran, completely free of scruples while at the same time expressing the piety of a mullah. One ill-fated day he comes to our tiny apartment to enjoy tea and biscuits and is treated like royalty by my mother and by my father. He is tall in stature, good-looking, abundant with grey hair carefully barbered and, unusually for a man of such piety (it had been impressed on us that Haji Heydar is a man of fastidious religious observance), clean shaven. Muslim men of any real spiritual ambition are encouraged to keep a beard, but Haji Heydar apparently feels that a beard diminishes his good looks. He shaves with an electric shaver—a weird loophole in the grooming code, for the relevant commandment speaks of good Muslims 'refraining from shaving the hair of the face with a *razor*'.

On this day of his first visit to our ramshackle dwelling (there will be many more visits, and the fare provided will exceed tea and biscuits) Koorosh and I watch on in bafflement and unease while this large man, a complete stranger to us, is fawned over and courted and pampered. Koorosh and I shoot secret glances at each other, both of us asking, in effect, what's going on? I study, from my cross-legged position on the floor, the rings on his manicured fingers: on the right hand, two large stones in silver settings, possibly jasper; on the left, a ring of solid silver, but without a stone. I have known, since a young age, that Muslims are forbidden to wear gold on their bodies, but I also know that any Muslim of genuine piety would extend the proscription to flashy jewellery of any sort. And this man is supposed to be super-holy? It doesn't add up unless you were to take into account the vigour of Haji Heydar's vanity, which I'm not quite equipped to judge on that first visit.

Something I *am* able to judge is Haji Heydar's insincerity. One look at him and I instantly distrust every part of him. It's the same for Koorosh. Children are often good at this sort of thing—grasping the essential feature in a person's character. By the time we reach adulthood, all of us have learnt how to deceive ourselves about others. It's an ability that we can't prevent ourselves from acquiring. We can turn it on and off, almost as if we say to ourselves, 'I'm going to permit myself to believe this person when he says that he will never do me harm, although he's certainly lying.' At the age of twelve, I'm too young to rationalise and excuse and adjust the lighting to put another person's less attractive features in shadow. I know he's a crook, Haji Heydar, and I know that he's a threat to me, to my mother, to my father, to Koorosh, to Adonai Himself. I watch him on this day of his initial visit while he smiles and waves away apologies from my mother for the meagreness of the delicacies on offer, and rolls the beads of his expensive *shamaqsood* rosary between his fingers. I watch him glancing at my mother when my father is looking the other way, the way his gaze sweeps the miserable interior of our apartment with a distaste he quickly disguises. And I ask myself, what does this crook want from us? What have we got that he values?

He arrives in a big shiny Mercedes Benz, and he leaves in it. We wave him goodbye from the front door. Up and down our dank little street, neighbours are peering from their own front doors. They know who it is in the Mercedes. And they're dying to know more, asking themselves why the Karimi family has been so honoured. For the first time since our arrival in Mashhad, people envy us. But all I want is for Haji Heydar to dissolve into a mist and float away into space.

The next day, my mother asks me what I thought of our visitor.

'I don't like him,' I say.

'What? Are you mad? Of course you like Haji Heydar!'

'No I don't. I don't like him and Koorosh doesn't like him either. I hope he never comes back.'

'Listen to me,' my mother says. She stands before me shaking her finger. 'Haji Heydar owns two bus companies. Not one, but two. Do you know what else he owns?'

'No.'

'Then listen with your ears. He owns many, many fields, more than you can walk across in two hours. And a hotel, a very big hotel. What else do you think?'

'I don't know.'

'Shops! Many shops! He is a wealthy man, Haji Heydar, a very, very wealthy man. And he came to our house. Your father invited him for tea and biscuits, and he came. Do you think he goes to every house when he's invited? No! But he came to our house. Now, show some respect!'

'Yes, but *why* did he come to our house?'

'Why?' She doesn't have her answer quite ready. 'Well, he had his reasons. He respects your father.'

That night, I turn over in my mind the aspects of the unease that Haji Heydar arouses in me. I'm attempting to go a bit beyond the visceral and actually put my finger on the thing about him that so threatens me. The trouble is, I don't yet have the vocabulary I need for such an analysis. The word I require eludes me. Instead I have to settle for something as unsatisfying as 'He's not a good man.' I toss and turn in bed while shadows dart about in my mind like bats in a night sky. All unaware, I am rehearsing a night twenty years into the darkness of a future that has not yet formed. I will have the vocabulary I require when that time comes. I will look down at my surgeon's hands, so steady in the theatre, but trembling as I wait to be interrogated by a man who takes a very close interest in my vocabulary. He dwells on the words I use, on the sentences I fashion. He wants to hear everything I have to say. Everything.

Let me speak a little of what awaits me. Let me tell you of the Hotel Laleh in central Tehran, with which I am to become very well acquainted, and of the craft of the interrogator in the Islamic Republic of Iran.

In the late 1990s, the Hotel Laleh, in common with all of the larger hotels of Iran's major cities, keeps a room at the permanent disposal of the Ministry of Intelligence and Security. The room is maintained in the same manner as any other suite in the hotel. It is not usually employed for protracted interrogation or for forms of interrogation that involve torture. The room is always referred to as Number 113. They are essentially meeting rooms, all of the 113s. State Security officers transact business with informers, both salaried and coerced (always referred to as 'clients'), listen to reports, utter threats on occasion, perhaps administer the sort of discipline that is more likely to produce bruises than bleeding. Severe interrogations are usually carried out in houses set aside for the purpose, isolated houses properly equipped.

The five-star Hotel Laleh is one of the hotels favoured by MOIS agents but, in light of its status, it is reserved more for debriefing than interrogation. The Laleh caters to a sophisticated clientele from Middle-Eastern nations comfortable enough with the Iranian regime—to Saudi moguls, Syrian oil brokers, princelings from the Emirates, and post-Soviet plutocrats from the -stan states, Kazakhstan in particular. There is nothing remotely menacing in the look of the hotel's spacious lobby; no overweight men in dark glasses, for instance, pretending to read a newspaper under the standard portrait of Ruhollah Khomeini. The lobby is designed for commerce and comfort with signs guiding guests to the in-house branch of the Tejarat Bank, to the jewellery store, leather shop, one-hour photo kiosk, boutiques, barber, swimming pool and sauna, travel agency, the bookshop, and to the hotel's four restaurants, including the Tiare, specialising, oddly, in Polynesian cuisine.

When MOIS officers arrive for an interview, they arrive late. Their client on any particular day will be expected to wait patiently in the lobby for up to an hour. I am the client on this particular day and I'm very used to waiting, very used to looking up at the clock on the wall before glancing down at my trembling hands. I am just shy of thirty years old.

Compelling a client to wait reinforces the control that MOIS agents exercise in any transaction, but the practice is often an expression of simple bloody-mindedness. Like intelligence officers everywhere, MOIS agents operate within a narrow range of behaviours that are easy to learn and easy to enact. Bloody-mindedness is a reliable tactic and difficult to turn off. Arriving late keeps the client on tenterhooks, anxious. Another explanation for making the client wait is related to the professional suspicion that agents nurture. The suspicion is so pervasive that doing anything differently arouses what might be termed 'suspicion of self', the agent's fear that some rogue sympathy for a client might emerge and be witnessed by a colleague, or worse, by the client.

For the client is always the adversary, even when, like me, he is co-operative. MOIS agents do not rely on any finely-honed ability to read deceit in the face of a client, they do not study tics or subtle movements of the eyes in the manner of accomplished card players. They assume from the first that the client is lying and never stop believing that the client is a liar. Even when the client does exactly what he is told to do (and I always do what I'm told to do), or regularly provides reliable information, he is still a liar who, acting out of self-interest, has suspended this vice for a lesser or greater period. There is never any trust between agent and client no matter how long the relationship lasts. And if at any time it becomes necessary to murder a client, the deed will be carried out without regret, and usually, without much malice.

Today's interrogation could follow a format I'm familiar with. I will probably be asked, 'Did you do what we asked you to do?' and I will answer, 'I did what you asked me to do.' Then my interrogator will sit back in his chair and say, 'Tell me everything.' Or it could take a different turn, concluding at another location—Evin Prison, perhaps—in a room in which a scaffold stands erected. In the years since I became a 'client' of the Ministry of Intelligence and Security, I have experienced every type of abuse short of being murdered but I know with certainty that murder is the ultimate destination of these sessions.

I am a spy. Once my benefit to the state comes to an end, there will be no point in keeping me alive. If I am to hang, it won't be a vindictive execution, just the permanent retiring of a resource that would be a nuisance to have around. The hangman will take me in hand in a business-like way, test that the tethers on my ankles and wrists are firm, hold me by the shoulders and position me over the trapdoor and fit the noose securely around my neck. He will know that I am a Jew and so will not bother telling me to commence my prayers once the noose is tied. He may or may not bother with fitting a cover over my head before activating the lever that releases the trapdoor. He might wish to witness the expression a Jew wears at the moment of death. He may not have hanged a Jew before and, if he is like his colleagues in MOIS, he will have built up a colourful catalogue of beliefs and prejudices about Jews. He might have heard that a Jew turns bright red at the moment of extinction and bursts into flames, or that a Jew sprouts horns when he dies and reveals the satanic form that he has kept concealed throughout the years of his life.

The man I am waiting for in the lobby of the Laleh I know as Haji Samadi, probably not his true name. He is in his early forties, of medium height, solidly built. He has a beard and moustache, as do most Iranian men—Haji Heydar excepted—but his facial hair is not as thick and lush as my father's and he is almost bald on top. He has the prominent cheekbones and Asiatic eyes of the Hazara, a people who trace their ancestry back to the soldiers of Genghis Khan of Mongolia. Many thousands of Hazara escaped to Iran from Afghanistan after savage persecution at the hands of the Barakzai Khans, and it would not be the first time that a member of a persecuted minority found a new career in a new country as the oppressor of another persecuted minority. His customary expression is of fierce intimidation. I think he wants to convey the impression that he has an appetite for cruelty that he is barely able to keep in check.

In my early meetings with Haji Samadi, I assumed that I was the heart and soul of his professional life, that my case occupied most of his time. But that was just the egocentricity of the victim. What I now think is that I am only one of many clients he meets within the course of a week. Sometimes when we reach Room 113, in this hotel or in another, I notice in his eyes the look of a man who is rapidly attempting to recall all the details of a particular case. He may have arrived at the hotel from a meeting with someone very much like me, or from an execution, or from a couple of hours of paperwork in his office. I'm not the biggest catch of his career. I'm nothing. I'm sure that's what a client takes so long to learn—that he is nothing. Even when I knew that Haji Samadi would not feel a second's remorse if he were required to shoot me, I still hadn't accepted my absolute nothingness.

Perhaps some of the European Jews who were despatched to death camps by the Nazis experienced, for a short time, this same psychological impediment: that you don't matter *at all*. Your terror, your pain, your wretchedness—they don't matter to the people compelling you to form a line, to sink to your knees, to clasp your hands on the back of your head. It's not a simple thing to learn. Even when most hope is gone, a persistent vestige remains. You think, 'But he's a human being like me. He feels pain, he feels grief, he can weep, surely.' And that's true. Samadi is a human being like me, in a thousand ways, but his higher duty is to his calling. What if I had a calling? What if I considered it my sacred duty to destroy the enemies of Israel, for example? Perhaps I would sit opposite a Samadi judging whether today or tomorrow would be the best time to put a bullet through his head. Those who have a calling are the most dangerous people on earth.

In the time of waiting, I may think of my wife and children, but not always. I may think of my mother and my father, but again, not always. But Haji Heydar makes an appearance, each time. Why? He doesn't physically enter into my life any longer so why should my imagination conjure him at times like this? Is it that he initiated me into the world I have inhabited ever since, the world of imminent catastrophe? And that he introduced me, unintentionally, to a longing that has hovered beyond my reach, but been visible, since my boyhood? The longing for peace, a personal peace, a freedom from dread?

This is the life that I have created for myself: that finds me sitting in the lobby of a hotel waiting in fear and trembling for a man who marks off the months, the days and now perhaps the minutes until he can watch me hang. Haji Samadi is the nightmare that began to form twenty-two years earlier when I lay in bed with Koorosh struggling to locate a word that was not in my vocabulary, but which I knew existed: ruthless.

Through the glass doors of the hotel's entrance strides Haji Samadi. He glances at me and instantly I sit more upright in my lounge chair. He glances left and right, scanning the lobby, then back at me. It is a warm day, but he is wearing a light-grey suit, as he always does. Beneath his jacket he carries a two-way radio and a gun. He motions me to follow him to the elevator. I keep a respectful stride behind. As we wait for it, his gaze settles on my face. He is checking to see that the fear he put there remains. That is the limit of his interest.

THE GOLDEN
THREAD

My father owns one third of the bus that he drives between Mashhad and Tehran. The other two-thirds are owned by Haji Heydar's Gilantour agency, and that's the problem. Haji Heydar owns half to two-thirds of all the buses that leave Mashhad for destinations north, south, east and west; and he owns one hundred percent of the traffic. In the manner of a Mafia padrone, Haji Heydar rewards drivers in favour with him by sending their buses along busy routes such as the Mashhad-Tehran route, and he shows his displeasure to drivers who have disappointed him (in any of a hundred ways) by giving them poorly patronised routes— Mashhad to Nowhere, three passengers. A driver earns income based on the volume of passengers he carries. The simple lesson a driver learns is to please Haji Heydar in every way possible.

Heroes die protracted deaths. They are wounded by your doubt one day, resurrected the next, given a second, a third and a fourth chance to redeem themselves, and any diminishment of their status in one's personal pantheon is resisted. I watch the obsequious manner of my father during Haji Heydar's visit to our hovel. It wounds both me and Koorosh to witness our bold and handsome father reduced to such a feeble state. I'm left now with a suspicion that pierces me whenever I dwell on it.

'He likes Maman,' I whisper to Koorosh one morning over breakfast, then look back down at my bread before my mother notices anything going on. I want Koorosh to contradict me. He is older so maybe he knows things about the world that remain veiled to me.

But Koorosh says, 'No!' which is good, then 'Really?' which is not so good.

'I think so,' I persist. '*Baba jan* should punish him.'

But punish him for what? For sneaking glances at my mother's face and form during his visit? Yes, exactly that. When I say, 'He likes Maman,' I am using a euphemism without even being aware of it. I don't yet have the experience of life to suggest that Haji Heydar lusts after my mother, but that's what I mean.

A few days after Haji Heydar's visit, my father's bus has been repainted in the colours of the Gilantour agency, and along both sides the route he follows is proudly advertised: Mashhad–Tehran. When I see the new lettering, I know I'm gazing at my father's reward for smiling at Haji Heydar and for passing him cake and biscuits and for not noticing those glances. A transaction has been completed. I smile my face off standing beside my smiling-his-face-off brother when we're invited to applaud my father's good fortune, but my head and heart are fighting to rescue my father from shame. I say to myself, '*Baba jan* didn't punch Haji Heydar on the nose for looking at Maman. So what?' And '*Baba jan* knew what he was doing. Maman's very beautiful.' I'm attempting to add a complement of craftiness to my father's talents, to give him some of the attributes of an Odysseus. But deep inside, my true self is sickened.

Two weeks after the transformation of my father's bus, my mother begins to complain of a pain in her wrist that is likely to require medical treatment.

'Do you know what I'll do?' she says, as if the idea has come to her quite out of the blue. 'I'll go to the physiotherapist and ask his opinion.'

Koorosh and I look at each other in astonishment. Since when do the Karimis go to such a person as a physiotherapist, with a sore wrist? Since when do the Karimis go to any medical man for anything at all? It was only when I was at death's door with typhoid that my mother agreed to get me to hospital. In our family, anything up to amputation of limbs is a task for the neighbourhood witch doctor. Is it possible that a pain in the wrist is a far more serious ailment than we think?

'Is it a bad pain, Maman?' says Koorosh.

'Oh, most certainly. I can barely move my hand.'

Koorosh and I become neurotic when something threatens my mother's physical health. Her mental health we've got covered; we know she's crazy, we've made allowances for it. A potentially fatal sore wrist, though—we tremble, we hug each other, we sob, we pray.

It's an evening appointment my mother has with the physiotherapist—oddly. Koorosh and I are left alone in the apartment fretting until well after nightfall. We have school each morning, finishing at midday, then it's our practice to race back to the apartment and slave away at our homework like the conscientious little students we are. From three in the afternoon, we make the few *rials* we can bring in from our various jobs. Now and again we have a chance to play with other boys in the neighbourhood, kick a ball about, chase each other. My mother is always at home from five in the afternoon. But not today. Between fits of sobbing, my brother and I think up emergency plans should bad come to worse: start running and not stop until we reach Israel, kill ourselves, or maybe we could live on my father's bus, journeying forever between Mashhad and Tehran.

It is after eight before my mother returns. Koorosh and I leap all over her like a pair of hysterical puppies. She doesn't look as if she is about to die. On the contrary, she's flushed and smiling and full of affection.

'Maman, Maman—what did the doctor say?'

'Oh, the doctor! Well, he said that I have rheumatism, unfortunately, my darlings. Rheumatism in my wrist. Rheumatism in both wrists. There you have it.'

'Maman, Maman—don't die!'

'Die? Don't be foolish. Die of rheumatism? No, no, no! But it will need treatment for a long time. Yes, for a long time, unfortunately. You will be by yourselves in the evenings for… well, for a time. Unfortunately.'

It sounds much more serious than my mother is admitting. Rheumatism in *both wrists*.

The treatment continues. Every second evening my mother hurries off to see the physiotherapist, but at least she's arranged to be home for a short time before the appointment. We plead with her to get better, as if it were a matter of will. She sighs and shrugs.

'My darlings, it's in the hands of our God, whose name is Adonai. The worst thing is not the pain, though God knows it's a sore trial to bear. No, my darlings, the thing that hurts far more is leaving you alone. But it's only for two hours. Two and a half, maybe.'

To ease the burden on our mother's wrists Koorosh and I do the laundry. We pray as we wash sheets and shirts and underthings, almost as if we were involved in a ritual cleansing designed to win favour in heaven. The praying helps keep our fear under control for an hour or so, but then we suddenly find ourselves in each other's arms, howling for our mother like the children in the folktale I read years later, Hansel and Gretel. Though it was not their mother, or stepmother, they yearned for, as I recall, but their feckless father. No, it was the stepmother who regarded them as a nuisance and wanted them out of the way.

Often we're too scared to remain at home by ourselves in that lawless part of Mashhad and we sit in the street a little way off, holding hands and sobbing. If we were more sure of the benefit of the physiotherapy, maybe we'd be a little less hysterical. But every time our mother returns from her appointment, she sighs and says, 'Still the pain, my darlings! I must go again.'

We have, however, a particular friend amongst the children in our street, a boy of Koorosh's age by the name of Reza. We play at his house now and again, always enjoyably. Reza is a version of the friend that all boys have sometime in their childhood, the wise one, the one who's clued into the way things look to adults. And the one who sees trouble coming way before you do.

At Reza's house a couple of months into our mother's Amazing Near-Fatal Rheumatism Experience, he pulls Koorosh and me aside to tell us he has a secret to disclose. If I'd been a little more mature, the expression on his face might have warned me that the secret was likely to make a mess of my life and my brother's life, but all I'm able to read in his eyes is the sort of sadness you see in the eyes of adults at their weariest and most disappointed.

Reza urges us along in his quiet way to a corner of his backyard remote from where the other boys are playing.

'Do you know what gossip means?' he asks us. 'You know that word, gossip?'

I say, 'Of course.' Then, less confidently, 'What do you think it means?'

'It means when people are talking about you.'

'That's what I thought.'

'Well, they are.'

'They are what?'

'Talking about you.'

'About me?'

'About you and Koorosh. About your family.'

A wave of sickness sweeps up from my stomach to my chest. Koorosh glances at me, experiencing the same thing, I think. He's leaving the questioning to me, as he often does.

'There's nothing wrong with my family,' I tell Reza. 'It's not right for people to talk about us. It's not right for people to gossip,' I add, remembering the word.

Reza nods his head, agreeing with me up to a point.

Then he says, 'When you go to school each morning, a car comes to your house. A blue Mercedes.'

'A blue Mercedes?' I know exactly who the car belongs to, but I don't say the name.

'Haji Heydar's car,' says Reza. 'Kushi, your mother and Haji have been together. Doing things. Every day when you go to school. And in the evening.'

Just for a second or two, I think I've found the flaw in Reza's information. My mother couldn't possibly be seeing Haji Heydar in the evening because she's at the doctor's having her wrists fixed up. The words that I am about to use to contradict Reza's claim reach my lips, but the exultant feeling dies before I can utter them.

'Kushi, your Maman is having an affair.'

I don't say, 'What's an 'affair'?' but my ignorance is written on my face.

'He loves your Maman. Haji Heydar loves her. He kisses her. And other things.'

My embarrassment takes away the power of speech. I look at the ground. My hand reaches for Koorosh's and once linked, we walk away. We don't glance at each other, we don't say a word.

All the way home, I'm imagining the ways in which my mother might explain the visits to our apartment of Haji Heydar in his blue Mercedes. But what I realise is that I'm not imagining valid explanations, but lies. I accept that Reza is telling the truth and that she will soon be offering us some frenzied fiction to silence us. My love for my mother lives side-by-side with the agonising knowledge that she is a born liar. How do I reconcile the gentle and the coarse features of her personality? The beloved and the hateful? I don't. I believe that all that distresses me about my mother will somehow fade away, in the way that an illness can pass. I believe this right now, on my way home with my brother's hand in mine. I will believe it ten minutes from now when she throws her fabrications at us. Twenty years in the future, when I have heard a further thousand lies, I am sure I will still believe it, even on a certain distant day, still in Mashhad, when my mother slips a noose around my neck and whispers, 'No, no my darling, this is not a noose, what a foolish thing to say!' I'll be telling myself, 'Well it *is* in fact a noose, and she does intend to kill me—oh, but deep down she loves me, I am sure.'

My mother's strategy of denial is actually far, far more violent than I'd envisioned. It is Koorosh, my infinitely gentle brother, smiling Koorosh who runs ahead of me when we reach the apartment and without any preamble, like an outraged husband demands to know if she is 'having an affair' (he uses those words) with Haji Heydar.

'What lies! How dare you! You will both be thrashed! As heaven is my judge, I will dash your brains out on the floor!'

We are seized and shaken, my mother's rheumatic wrists suddenly no impediment to the force she can impart to a whack over the ear. And here's her story, a version of the one I've been imagining.

'It has come to this! Dear God in heaven! The children I raised and bled for—yes bled for!—over and over! You have torn my heart out! There, look!—*there* is my heart on the floor all in pieces! You listen to these disgusting Mashhadis when the whole world knows what liars and fanatics dwell in this evil city! These wicked people with their wicked tongues! They are jealous of me, little fools! They are jealous of any woman who steps out of her house! They want women like me to live like prisoners inside four walls! Liars, every one of them! But how much worse to have sons who listen to such vile deceit!'

There's a lull in the onslaught. She stands above us, her chest heaving. Koorosh and I cower together crouched on the floor. In desperation, I risk one final throw of the dice.

'Tehran, Maman! Take us back to Tehran! In Tehran there will be no gossip!'

'Hah, you think so? You think in my life I will ever be free of wicked tongues wagging? Do you think such good fortune is intended for *me* in this world? Hah! And once in Tehran, how will it make you feel when Parvin puts the blade of a knife to your throats? Will that make you happier? When your throats are cut?'

My mother's reprisals are not yet complete. The tropical cyclone of her anger is succeeded by a polar chill. Within a couple of days, my brother and I are reduced to quivering wrecks. We know that justice is on our side, but being in the right is a thin, thin blanket to keep out the cold. I make a deliberate effort to avoid thinking about what my mother is doing when I'm not with her. It takes discipline. I'm already sharing my father with two other families, and now my mother has contracted herself out to a disgusting old crook about a hundred times her age. I want to kill him. I *will* kill him. Or if not me, then my father. Oh, but then it occurs to me that he *knows*. He *knows*. Believing this thrusts me into a darkness so dense that I pray, not for deliverance, but for annihilation. I can't find my way in this adult world of smiles that are not smiles, of lies spoken with such fierce conviction. Or I could find my way, yes, but only if I accept that my mother and my father deserve no special distinction in my heart. And I can't do that.

Over the weeks my mother's rheumatic wrists fail to respond to the skill and heroic dedication of the physiotherapist. I begin to find that I can live with lies as people do all over the world, every day. Someone you cannot abandon, someone you're not free to hate, insists on your acceptance of an ugly fiction, and with a heavy heart and rising gorge, you accept it. It is easier for your soul to detest itself than to detest the one thrusting fictions at you. And for periods of time sometimes of quite some length—a whole day!—you even allow yourself to believe the lies. Look at my mother. Look at the way she rubs her wrists when she returns after dark from the doctor and murmurs, 'Ah me, when will I be free of this torture!' Look at the calm way she meets the sullen gaze of her children. Listen to her creating the layered tale of deceit: 'Well, he is such a nice man, the physiotherapist, and so busy! He leaves out magazines for us to read while we wait. A good idea. I sometimes get so caught up in a good article that I forget all about the pain in my wrists. Yes, I forget all about it, if you can believe such a thing!' And now the one you are not at liberty to loathe gathers such confidence from your appalled silence that she is ready to reveal an even more shameless side to herself.

'Oh darlings, what do you think? We are to go out and eat in a proper restaurant next week! We are to eat till we burst! A man who feels pity for us will pay the bill! What do you think of that? Oh, say you are glad! Say you are happy that God has sent this angel to our doorstep!'

'We're glad, Maman.'

'Of course you are, darlings! Who would not be? An angel, a blessing! I wonder how long you would have waited for your father to grant you such a treat? Oh, he cares for nothing but his bus and his foolish wives in Tehran! Is that not the truth?'

We know the identity of this angel. And yet her trilling and cooing and giggling succeed in creating doubt. She is a mistress of this sort of manipulation. When we ask what name the 'angel' goes by when he comes to earth and dwells amongst us mortals, she admonishes us for our impatience.

'Wait and see!'

Little by little, day by day, she erodes our determination to spare ourselves the disappointment of Haji Heydar. And after six days Koorosh and I are smiling at each other and whispering, 'Who will it be?'

Whenever my mother has had to choose between her own firmly secured self-interest and the interest of her sons, she has never failed to vote for herself. And yet, here we are whispering and smiling, waiting for our benefactor in the way in which Christian children wait in giddy expectation for the arrival of Santa Claus.

It will be Haji Heydar. It *is* Haji Heydar. Here we are on the evening of the promised feast dressed in our best clothes (such as they are!) waiting on the footpath in Garagdara Road when the blue Mercedes pulls up. My mother is smiling with her whole face. Haji Heydar steps out of the Mercedes and opens his arms to us in benediction.

'Kushi! Koorosh!'

My heart squeezes itself, clenched, like the fists at my sides as I stand shaking in silent anger. The rear passenger door of the Mercedes is opened for us. I stand anchored to the pavement, refusing to enter the car. But Koorosh gets in. I watch appalled. What is this? He's suddenly grinning with delight, an 'Oohh oooh! Look at me! I'm sitting in a big fancy car' sort of grin. That's something you have to understand about Koorosh— he can only be outraged and miserable for so long. It's an exhaustible resource in him, moral conviction. I want to scream at him, 'Are you this shallow? Are you this easily bought off?'

'Get in!' my mother hisses into my ear. She is still smiling even as she hisses.

'No.'

'Get in, damn you!' Still smiling.

'No.'

'Get in or I'll kill you, as Allah is my judge!'

'No!'

Koorosh shoots me an imploring glance. He doesn't want to join me in my death-or-glory stand against our mother's tyranny. His glance says, 'Don't make me feel bad, please?' My mother seizes hold of me and crams me into the rear seat alongside Koorosh and slams the door. The great big smile is back on her face—just a slight misunderstanding, ha ha ha! In sullen silence, I sit with my arms folded, refusing to look at my apathetic brother, at my treacherous mother, at my mother's contemptible lover.

So, the food at the restaurant is good. I admit it. I eat my fill—I admit that, too. But not once do I allow my eyes to meet the lizard eyes of Haji Heydar. I think, 'You want to feed me, Haji? Go ahead, feed me. You want me to smile? Alright, I will, when you're dead.'

After the third course of the meal, Haji clears his throat in preparation for a speech. The clearing of the throat is a signal to my mother and Koorosh, and to me, to stop eating and pay attention. I keep on eating.

'Children,' says Haji Heydar, 'listen to the words I have to say. Your family is a good family, a Muslim family, embraced by Allah Himself. Once your mother was a Jew. A disaster, but not her fault. Children, your mother saw the light. Your mother embraced the true faith and gave up this folly of being a Jew. Such nonsense. I have heard the voice of Allah in the night whispering to me. "Raise the children of that family, who cast off the disgrace of their Jew folly, out of their poverty!" That is what the voice of Allah said to me in the night. I am your uncle—yes, that's the truth. I am your uncle. I am your protector. And that is

the truth, too. I am your uncle and your protector. Your father...
who has the right to condemn another human being? But let
me say this, your father is a cold, hard man who has turned his
face from you. That is the truth. His face is turned away, turned
toward Tehran and his children in that city. When is he here to
protect you? When did you see him last? Three weeks ago? Yes,
three weeks ago. The man is a scoundrel. The man treats your
mother like a rug on the threshold on which he wipes the mud
from his shoes. Children, close your hearts to that man. Close
your hearts, forever. You have found a protector in your uncle.'

My mother sits with her chin raised and the prettiest smile
she can find lifting her lips while this steaming heap of elephant
dung is shovelled onto the dining table. She looks as if she's
smelling newly-bloomed roses. Oh the smiles, oh the blushes! I
hate her for those smiles. I hate Koorosh for his bland acceptance
of Haji's speech. But this is what I do love, what I rejoice to hear:
that my father *doesn't* know of his wife's faithlessness. The relief!
Our father *doesn't* know.

I resolve right then and there to tell him. I'm enjoying already
the sock to Haji Heydar's jaw that my father will deliver.

'Enjoying your dinner?' says my mother, with her Jew-
betraying smile.

'It's fine,' I reply, and give the same answer to all of her enquiries
until we're mercifully delivered back to our hovel in Garagdara.

She places on the kitchen table a fifty *toman* note that Haji
Heydar, the Great of Heart, ostentatiously pressed into her hand
as we left the restaurant.

'Oh darlings, why is Haji so good to us—that is what I ask
myself. Why is he so good to me and to you boys? He has a big
heart, oh yes, a very big heart!'

'He's a liar,' I say.

My mother's pretty smile disappears in an instant. She seizes
me by my ear.

'Is he a liar? Is that what you think? Well listen to me now, because this is the truth. You will be polite to that good man. Do you hear me? Do I have to twist your ear until you hear me? You will be polite to him. And you will say nothing of this to your father. Nothing!'

'I'm going to tell him!' I wail through the pain of her professional ear-twisting.

'Oh yes? Is that so?'

She gives my ear a particularly agonising tweak.

'Are you sure of that, you barbarian? Because I will kill you with my own hands if you breathe a word! Now what do you say?'

I can't respond. The pain is awful. I notice Koorosh backing away from us, keeping out of harm's way.

'And another thing,' she says, 'you will not say a word to Haji Heydar about the books I read to you, not a word about our prayers, not a word about Adonai. To him we are Muslims, and that is the way it will stay. And tell him that you pray every day to Allah and the Prophet.'

I muster enough bravery to shout at my mother that I will never tell Haji Heydar that I pray Muslim prayers. And she musters enough disgust to push me away and hiss the words, 'Idiot boy!'

We glare at each other from opposite sides of this arena of disdain. Koorosh is the audience. I'm waiting for my mother's next move, because there will be one. If threats don't prevail, she'll try something different. And she does. She sighs and shakes her head, lifts her shoulders and lets them fall.

'Can I love a child like this?' she asks the air. 'Surely my love will wither away when I meet, every single time I speak reason to him, such obstinacy, such selfishness. A terrible stone sitting on my heart—this fear that I will cease to love him, cease to care.'

It's done. I can't hold out against such a threat. My mother looks away, still sighing. I recant. It's done.

In later life, I come across stories that illustrate my childhood predicament better than any available to me at the time. Or perhaps it would be more accurate to say that I do not require illustrations when I am caught up in the hurly-burly of my mother's strategies. All that matters is endurance. G.K. Chesterton in his *Father Brown* stories speaks of a golden thread that joins the lapsed or erring Catholic to the priest of his neglected faith. Let the sinner swim far out to sea where he wallows in worldliness. The priest can reel the sinner in at any time he wishes for the golden thread ends in a hook, and the hook is the sinner's allegiance to his Catholic faith; an allegiance the sinner may try to forget, may despise, may try to overcome, but cannot.

My Jewish mother has me snared on a golden thread of her own. She has given me cause to believe she loves me, and I can never forget it no matter how far my anger, my disgust, even my better judgement takes me from where she stands, sighing, lamenting, calculating. In Father Brown's claim of being able to reel in the remote sinner there is an insufferable smugness, enough to make you vomit, for what he is talking about is a tyranny over the soul. My mother's tyranny is as indomitable as any in the universe. My disappointments do not accrue until they reach a critical level of eternal alienation. No, they fade and die.

10

SHAME

Life is a constantly refreshed banquet table for Haji Heydar. I think of him holding his capacious plate in one hand as he surveys the dishes prepared for him and his companions in good fortune and gluttony, perhaps humming a tune softly as he serves himself a portion of this delicacy or that. For the Haji Heydars of the world, the only concern is how to master fortune in order to further enhance their delight in living.

I am rushing back home from the local bakery, clasping the steaming fresh bread against my panting chest. It is a rarity to even hold such warm tender bread, but I am entrusted with this mission every time Haji visits us. I can smell the aroma of my mother's cooking from all the way down the crooked street of our house. I open the narrow door, and find Haji Heydar sitting on the only chair in the house waiting to be served his bread and kebabs. I murmur a quiet *salaam* as I join Koorosh on the floor. My mother places the pan of old dry cheese and dates in front of us. I try to ignore the way my mouth waters from the drifting scent of Haji's kebabs. As I try to chew the stale, stiff bread that has been laid out for me, I cannot help glancing at Haji rolling his delicious, tender kebab into his soft, steaming bread. I want to be angry but instead I feel pity. I wonder why Adonai would create people so incapable of kindness.

A natural hypocrite himself and a robust zealot, he finds himself, after the Islamic Revolution, living in a land *ruled* by hypocritical zealots. The burden of prescribed religious observance that bears down on the shoulders of the average Iranian merely adds duck feathers to the pillow on which Haji Heydar rests his head. Business opportunities go to the regime's most pious friends, and what more pious friend has hidebound puritanism ever had in Iran than Haji Heydar?

And even that important though awkward appetite of Haji's for variety in carnal expression—awkward because it might be seen by some as contradicting his endorsement, at other times, of sexual continence—is catered for by my mother's eagerness to satisfy him a number of times per week. And that's week after week, month after month, year after year. What I know of 'affairs' is kissing. I picture (because I can't help but picture) the chubby mottled lips of Haji Heydar coming into fleeting contact (I can only manage, fleeting) with the gorgeous contours of my mother's lips. In the West, a boy of my age could be expected to have secretly gazed at, or at least glimpsed, glossy pictures of naked men and women having sex. But for me, kissing is the whole thing.

So imagine the shock it is to me when I witness, halfway through Grade Six, in three living dimensions what the boys and girls of the enlightened West have studied in lurid magazines. I am a super-conscientious student at school, on most days. But every now and again I get sick and tired of it—the rote learning, the lack of adventure in the curriculum, the ease with which I can negotiate every subject, the whacks on the knuckles or bare legs with a metal or wooden ruler as punishment for phasing-out, however briefly—and I take off.

I have a rusty old bicycle purchased cheaply from a junk merchant and this gives me the opportunity to go with my friends, truants like me, from school to the airport. We have to cross a desolate paddock or two before we can sit and watch the big planes landing, passenger jets emblazoned with the livery of their airlines. And this is thrilling. The great fuselages angle down and down and down, floating towards the runway, and then the wheels on their struts hit the tarmac with a shriek, blue smoke rising in a cloud. Now, with the great roar of the jet engines reversing and the sudden slowing of the plane, the impossible has been achieved! I feel, each time, a surge of joy and admiration; one of those moments in a child's life when he feels the exhilaration of being alive in the world.

Why would I be at school when this sight awaits me at the airport? What dreams does the classroom promote to rival this? And at school, it's not only the tedium of the way in which we're taught that so irritates me, it's also the propaganda: the Revolution, the Revolution, the Revolution, the Beloved Supreme Ruler, the Glorious Triumph of the Truth of Islam over the lies and hypocrisy of the infidel, the Great Mercy of Allah, the duty we owe to His Prophet Muhammad. I would come to know in time that fanatics of all religious persuasions generate slogans for their various faiths without the least hint of shame, and that all fanatics are enemies of the richness and variety of life. But at my school, the slogans are generated only by Khomeini's besotted followers and I have to sit with my own faith cloaked, and smile and smile and smile in feigned delight.

I cycle home with Koorosh to find a blue Mercedes parked outside our apartment block. Sickness sweeps up from my stomach and I close my eyes and whisper a curse. The boys playing in the street—Jamal, Kian—grin at me and cast taunts my way.

'Haji Heydar is here, Kushi!'

'Kissy kissy kissy!'

'Kushi, where is your Maman, Kushi?'

Only Reza refrains. He looks embarrassed. He has lost his

mother to cancer. His father barely acknowledges his existence. He understands that I am enduring the loss of my own mother, losing her by degrees, just as he lost his mother bit by bit.

'Don't think about it,' he murmurs to me.

But I can't take Reza's well-meant advice. I throw my bicycle to the ground and climb up the door to peer through the fanlight above it. I find footholds where I can on the architrave, on the doorknob. I peer through the glass of the fanlight.

By the time a son reaches the age I am as I stand balanced on the doorknob, he has seen his mother in many types of situations, in practically every type of mood. He has seen her transformed by passions of various sorts and he's seen expressions of tenderness, and of kindness. He has seen things that reflect great credit on his mother, other things that puzzle or distress him, other things that appal him—his mother picks her nose, scratches her behind, occasionally breaks wind. His mother is a crucial subject of study for a boy; the person whose heart, whose manners, whose mood, whose demeanour he knows best. The one situation that I had never seen my mother in was that of passionate sexual transport, and that's what I see now.

My response comes in three stages. First, I tell myself that I am not witnessing what is happening before my eyes, that my mother is *not* lying on the bed in a weird position with the fat naked figure of a man on top of her covered in hair, spluttering and gurgling grotesquely. Then I concede that what I refused to believe is actually true. Finally—and all this happens in a matter of a few seconds—I wish my mother dead, the fat naked man dead, and myself dead.

I am no longer looking through the fanlight at the sickening sight. I am simply hanging there, gazing at nothing in a paralysis of disgust and detestation. Reza, Kian, Koorosh and Jamal stare up at me. 'What's wrong, Kushi? Come down!'

Only Reza seems able to guess at what I've seen. He pays me the compliment of not looking at me in my stricken state.

'Hey! Numbskull!' Jamal calls. 'What's wrong with you?'

Finally I clamber down, but I refuse to respond to any questions. I seize my rusty bicycle, mount it, and speed away. I have no destination in mind. I pedal furiously, dodging traffic, twisting and swerving, putting as much distance as I can between me and my home. When I find an empty street I brake to a halt, let my bike fall to the ground and huddle against a wall. A great torrent of tears overwhelms me. My body shudders with the rigour of my grief. Every time I lift my head I see only the squalor of the wretched cul-de-sac I've escaped to, the rubbish left in bags on the pavement, the grimy cobblestones. It's like an alleyway in the precincts of hell.

One of the children in my class at school, a boy by the name of Abbas, had told me that my mother often goes to a hotel with Haji Heydar. He'd said that he knew someone who worked in the hotel and that this person had told him of these meetings between my mother and Haji. And I'd thought, 'How ridiculous!' Now, in this filthy alley of a filthy suburb I recall the shrewd expression on Abbas' face as he told me what my mother and Haji Heydar were up to. I recall the excitement underlying the shrewdness, the desire to see me wince in pain. I don't think Abbas particularly dislikes me—no, he was just doing what children do, acting out the casual cruelty of a boy with some especially wounding information to relate.

Together with the agonising knowledge that my mother is probably considered cheap and immoral by our neighbours, who would have guessed at her arrangement with Haji, I am also struggling desperately with this further confirmation of Haji Heydar's hypocrisy. The pious Haji Heydar is an adulterer. But if his adultery were to come to the attention of the authorities, it would not be Haji who would be punished, it would be my mother. Haji would bribe his way out of punishment, but my mother would be condemned to death, which is to say death by stoning, buried almost up to her shoulders in the ground while a number of officially appointed executioners fling rocks almost the size of a fist at her head from a distance of one-and-a-half metres. When I'd stared in through the fanlight to see my mother writhing under the figure of Haji Heydar, I'd wished her dead. But I don't wish her dead now.

It's almost nightfall, but I don't return home. The prospect of gazing at my mother's face while she fabricates some story about where she'd been this afternoon is too much to bear. No, I ride my bike through the gathering gloom to the house where Reza lives with his brother. He will offer me the only solace that can dull the pain I'm in. He will say, 'Kushi, maybe your mother is not the best human being on earth, but at least she's alive, at least she can hold you and kiss you. My mother can't hold me and kiss me because she's dead. And my father couldn't care less about me. Count your blessings, Kushi. Forgive your mother.'

I have already written the script that will lead me to forgiveness. I have already put into Reza's mouth the words that will permit me to accept my mother's lies. Riding my bike to Reza's house, I am seeking out the only person on earth who can restore me to life, to the world. An orphan who lives each day with a despair that exceeds mine.

11

A TWIST OF
THE KNIFE

My mother always has a strategy. Everything she says, everything she does plays its part in whatever scheme she's crafting at a given time. Even sincerity. This is a feature of her personality that I am beginning to grasp. If she is being honest and open, it is because being honest and open better serves her plans than being deceitful and secretive. It has nothing to do with virtue. It is always the plan, always the bigger picture that compels her.

I return from Reza's house comforted by his advice. And his advice is exactly what I'd anticipated: 'Your mother has her failings, too bad about that, forgive her.' But my mother only accepts my forgiveness on her terms. The most insistent of her terms is that I learn to hate my father and she takes every opportunity to corrupt my vision of him.

'You think your father loves you, Kooshyar? Do you think he cares about you? He doesn't care about you. He doesn't even remember your name.'

'He knows my name.'

My mother is quiet for a few minutes, busying herself with housework but glancing at me and at my brother out of the corner of her eye. She knows that I am the one she has to break. Koorosh doesn't suffer in the way I do. He is calmer by temperament.

'You think your father loves you, do you?' she says. 'Isn't it strange that he never buys you presents! Fathers who love their children buy them presents. How many presents has your father bought you? One hundred? Ten? Even one present?'

'He doesn't have enough money!' I shout. 'How can he buy presents when he has no money?'

'Oh, so that's the reason,' she retorts. 'He doesn't have the money. But it's strange that he can find money to buy toys for Katayoon. Oh yes, there is always money for Katayoon, always toys for Katayoon.'

Katayoon is the youngest of my father's children—the youngest whom I know about. Her mother is his first wife, his Tehran wife. The mere mention of her name is agony to me. I don't hate her, only envy her.

I look down at the book I am reading and try to hear nothing. But I am no match for my mother. She has the tip of her knife in my flesh and is waiting for exactly the right moment to twist it. I am much more aware of her shape on the periphery of my vision than I am of the words on the page before me. Koorosh is attempting to catch my eye, to exhort me to close my mind, ignore the torment. The harsh shouts of the boys outside playing in the slum occupy one tiny corner of my consciousness. I know each boy out there, and I know that not one of them would be as sensitive to their parents' taunts as I am to my mother's. To them, life has already revealed its plan and they don't expect kindness, they don't expect tenderness, and they definitely don't expect toys. My yearning for love is laughable to them.

'Oh, yes, he likes Katayoon the best,' my mother continues. 'He loves Katayoon so much you wouldn't believe it. When he goes to Tehran in his bus, he hurries to his house so that he can sit Katayoon on his lap and kiss her cheeks. Do you know what she says to him? She says, "*Baba*, did you bring me a present?" And do you know what your father says? He says, "For my beloved daughter, for little Katya, would I forget to bring a present? Would your father, who loves you, forget to bring a present? Of course, I have a present my dearest darling daughter. Of course, I have brought you a dolly. Do you want to see the dolly I've brought for you? Here it is!" That's what he says, Kushi, as God is my judge, that's what he says.'

I know what my mother is trying to do. I know, too, that she is capable of every sort of lie in pursuit of her object. And yet I can't make myself ignore what she says about my father. This is my mother's genius. The knife she twists in my flesh has been dipped in poison. Even if I can find the strength to bear the blade, I can't escape the poison.

I lurch from the table at which I'm sitting with my book and rush downstairs to the basement. I crouch in front of my Star of David scratched on the wall and clasp my two hands. I close my eyes and whisper prayers to Adonai, to Abraham. 'Make *Baba* love me more than Katayoon.'

I revive in my memory every example of my father showing me affection such as the time he told me how to pee on the cut I gave myself when I dropped a glass in his bus, the poor man's disinfectant. But no matter how long I search my memory, I know I will not recall a toy, I will not recall sitting on my father's lap and enjoying his caresses in the way my mother claims Katayoon does.

Gradually, remorselessly, my mother's poison is withering my love for my father. But nothing she says will make me accept Haji Heydar as a substitute. On the contrary. In my fantasies of revenge I take on the stature of a giant and with fists like hammers I bludgeon Haji to death. In other fantasies, I have grown into adulthood and accumulated mountains of money. From my bulging pockets I draw wads of *tomans* and hand the notes to my mother. 'Buy yourself some new clothes,' I tell her, 'and new shoes. Buy fifty pairs of new shoes. Shop all day and in the evening, treat yourself in the best restaurant you can find.' My mother weeps with gratitude. She puts my hand to her lips and kisses it.

The second front of my mother's battle with me is as violent as the first. She attacks our faith. She denies that we are special. She throws her arms wide open and embraces Islam.

One summer night I am feeling suffocated as we take our seats at this fancy restaurant Haji has brought us to, as he does when he wants to impress my mother. Haji smiles in his special 'what-a-great-and-benevolent-super-rich-fellow-I-am' way, and my mother matches it with her, 'what-a-tender-and-indulgent-mother-I-am' tilt of her lips. If it weren't so wrenching to watch them and if I were not so scared, I'd say, 'Excuse me, *Madar jan*, excuse me, Uncle Haji, I have to step outside for a minute to throw up.'

'Eat up, boys! Eat up!' says Haji. 'Use the knife and fork.'

'Yes, Uncle Haji.'

'Listen to me, boys, listen to me. Tonight I am very happy. Tonight I am glad in my heart to be sitting here with you and your mother. Tonight your mother is beautiful. Because why? I will tell you. Because your mother is no longer a Jew. Your mother is a Muslim. This is what she has told me. No longer a Jew. Our faith welcomes her. Our faith welcomes you too, Koorosh, and you, Kushi. No Jew can ever be truly beautiful. Only our faith can make a person beautiful on the inside and beautiful on the outside. Your mother has come to our faith and it is my duty to welcome her. She is my guest. It is my duty to care for her, and for you Koorosh, and for you, Kushi. It is my responsibility. I must guard you against all dangers. All dangers. Do you see?'

My mother is smiling and nodding, as if this horseshit of Haji's is the wisest thing she has ever heard. She is utterly shameless. My gorge has risen so far up my throat that I am likely to choke to death. Koorosh glances at me in his way, telling me silently to keep cool, keep calm. I imagine the shame that is felt by Abraham, the Patriarch, as he listens to this treachery of my mother's.

'Your father,' Haji resumes, 'is a cold-hearted man. His heart is like a stone. He is not a human being. Do you understand? He does not love you. He does not love your mother. It is not only Jews who have cold hearts. There are bad Muslims, and that is the truth. Your father has a heart like a cold stone. When he comes in his bus to Mashhad and stays with your mother, it is only to have a place to sleep. It isn't love, boys. No, no, not love. The only love in your mother's life comes from me. This is the truth. Is that not so, Homa?'

My mother dimples and smiles like a giddy little girl at her own birthday party.

'Oh yes, Haji. Allah knows it is the truth!'

'And boys, would I let you keep living in Garagdara?' says Haji Heydar. 'In that evil place? No, no, no! Boys, Allah has sent me into your lives. You are not alone in the world anymore. Not anymore. I am your uncle now. That is how you must think of me—your uncle, who loves you. We are all the one family.'

Haji drives us home in his blue Mercedes, his work for the night accomplished. When people see him with our mother, we're expected to say, 'Oh yes, that's Uncle Haji. We're all in the one family. No Jews here, absolutely not; we're all good Muslims!'

Like an actress on the stage abandoning her carefully crafted role once the curtain has fallen, my mother turns a sceptical gaze on me.

'Now listen to me, trouble-maker!', she says. 'God has sent Haji Heydar to us and we are grateful, do you understand? Your father is a scoundrel. He'd let us starve if he could. But Haji puts food in our mouths. As far as he is concerned, we are good Muslims. Don't you say a thing about Moses, don't you say a thing about our books, nothing about Israel, and not a thing about Jews at all—not a thing! If Haji asks, you tell him you pray five times a day to Allah.'

Keeping our true faith secret from the millions of Muslims around us is something I understand, something I can go along with. Adonai knows the reason, and forgives us. But keeping a secret like that is something you do in sorrow, wishing it could be otherwise. And each time you pray, you remind Adonai that it is He you worship. What my mother is doing is nothing like that. There is no secret sorrow working in her when she tells Haji that she is a Muslim now; there are no tears in private and she does not ask our God for forgiveness and understanding. She courts the gains of saying she is a Muslim. She is like a spy who has forgotten her mission. Pretending to be one of our enemies, she has *become* one of our enemies.

In my own years of spying for Islam, or at least for the Islamists of the Iranian regime, I think of my mother's deceit many times. Many. I ask myself if the way I carry off my deceit is any different from the way my mother managed her deception? Is it something I learned from my mother—how to be a spy? I remind myself that unlike my mother I have no choice. She could have kept her integrity by accepting grinding poverty. But the human mind is capable of such great subtlety. I can't be sure that my, and my mother's, spying stand in such distinction, one from the other. During the times when my dread holds me like a vice—those times when I look into the eyes of my handlers and see nothing that could save my life if they decide I am no longer useful to them—at those times, even in the midst of my fear, I ask myself if my mother also told herself that she had no choice. Maybe she thought that she too was compelled to spy or die.

I furtively start a file on my father in my mind, listing all the questions I would like to ask him and those I wouldn't like to ask him because I'd hate the answers. A secret dossier.

Why does Baba *have more than one wife?*

Actually I know why he has more than one wife: because he can. I am perfectly well aware that an adult Muslim male is permitted more than one wife. I think my real question is this:

Why does Baba *want more than one wife?*

One wife is difficult enough—haven't I seen the evidence? Why should my father multiply his problems? It's not only wives who cause trouble. With each wife comes children, and each child is an expense. I know for a fact that my father provides more money for his Tehran wife than for his Mashhad wife, and certainly he complains about never having any money. So what's the story? I have a dim idea that it's all related to what my mother and Haji Heydar were doing when I saw them in bed through the fanlight. It appears that grown men and maybe women are addicted to it. It's vile. Pray God such an obsession doesn't come into my life.

Why doesn't Baba *ever remember my name?*

I see *Baba* in my head; he closes his eyes and screws up his face. He opens his eyes and shakes his head. He's baffled. He's just called me 'Arash' and he can tell from my wounded expression that he's mistaken. He's struggling to recall who I am. He says, 'Um—what's your name again?' I say, feeling sick, 'Kushi.' I say it softly. This might mean, or probably does mean, that he has more children than I know about. Maybe many, many more. He drives his bus a couple of times a year all the way to Mecca for the Haj, his vehicle bursting with the faithful.

He travels through three countries. He's been doing it for years. I'm thinking, 'He has children everywhere. He has Kushis and Rezas and Husseins and Abbasses and Bahmans and Hajirs and Arashks and Jafars and Karims and Erfans and Farids and Hamids and Ahmads and Habibs; and just as many girls.' The desire to be thought special is not to do with ego. It is to do with being cared for. Who wants to be loved by someone who packs you together with a hundred others? Who can believe in love of that sort? But I'm Kushi, and surely my father can make the effort to remember me, the son with the Jewish mother, the son who adores him.

Why doesn't Baba *ever know which year I'm in at school?*

Under this heading my mind's eye conjures: *because he doesn't care.* Then my imaginary hand hastily crosses it out and writes instead: *Baba jan's memory is not so good.* I'm not yet ready to concede that he doesn't care. But I'm getting closer. My mother's plan is working.

Why do I love Baba, *but he only loves his bus?*

This question thinly disguises the beginnings of a bitterness that my mother is crafting in me. But it's there in the sarcasm.

Why do I want to scream all the time?

This question should really be a statement: I want to scream all the time. Maybe I'm insane and don't know it.

If Baba *is a Muslim and* Maman *is a Jew, then what am I?*

This question is just a way of starting an argument with myself. I know that I'm a Jew. I never have any doubts. So what's the issue?

Why can Baba *hear his bus engine but can never hear me?*

It is true that my father is extraordinarily sensitive to what the engine of his bus is telling him. A certain sound means that the pistons are slightly out in their timing. Another sound means that there is the barest commencement of distress in the carburettor, just a whisper but one that he is attuned to recognise. Yet another sound, when he turns on the ignition, suggests that the starter-motor might need new carbon brushes, another that the wheel bearings are wearing, another that the distributor is misfiring. If he were to apply this degree of sensitivity to the modulations and fluctuations in the tone of my conversation he would pick up evidence of wear in every part of my brain, my heart, my soul; evidence of distress, of approaching calamity. And more than that, he would hear the true register of my love for him, or he would have, once. Now he would hear the slight hesitancy that should suggest that my love is labouring, like an engine with badly worn rings. Even my silences, if he were to notice, are cataplexic attacks, the dissociation of mind and body.

Other questions that occur to me are more broadly philosophical. *Why are so many people lonely? Why is our neighbour's little girl with Down Syndrome kept in the basement all the time?* I am thinking of the poor child and of poor me at the one time. The child is a shameful secret so far as her parents are concerned, and my own shameful secrets—that my father barely knows who I am, that my mother is an adulteress—are also kept locked in a basement of sorts.

'Adulteress' is not a word that enters my vocabulary until years past the time of the secret dossier, but now that I've written it here I'm reminded of another question I asked myself all the time from the age of twelve—that is to say, past the age at which I came to know of the regular reward that my mother provided Haji Heydar: *How many others?*

Let me conjure a scene in the street at that time. Koorosh and I are sitting on the curb after school waiting for my mother to return from one of her infamous physiotherapy sessions. We are miserable, of course. Koorosh tries to comfort me, holding my hand, and I try to comfort him by murmuring, 'It'll be fine, don't worry, it'll be fine.'

I don't believe for a second that it will be 'fine' but the words are spoken as an incantation, as if something magical might intervene in our lives and take away the wretchedness just for a moment. Or perhaps I should say that the words are spoken in the way that people prepare themselves to shriek when they tear a bandage from a wound, using the shout to distract the senses from the pain for an instant.

Our slum is home to a number of derelicts and vagrants in advanced stages of decline, some likely to drop dead in the gutter at any time, others likely to survive in a fashion for some years yet. One of the worst is a drunk by the name of Abdolrazaq, a dirty old scoundrel with rheumy eyes and mottled lips, his long hair a feculent thicket, his drooping moustache crusted in filth. Koorosh and I are so used to him that we barely register when he passes. He's just part of the squalor, like the debris that blows about the lanes and alleys. But this day he stops in front of us, swaying as he attempts to focus his gaze.

'I love your *Madar*,' he says. 'Really love her.'

Koorosh and I are too shocked to say anything. What does he mean, he loves our Maman? He has no right to even mention her, let alone say he loves her.

Abdolrazaq hovers over us, barely holding himself up. The stench of his breath causes a retching nausea.

'D'yer hear what I said? I love your Maman. You tell her. Got it? Tell her I love her.'

I turn my face away as a shudder of disgust runs through my frame.

'She won't talk to me. Won't talk to me, no. You know why? Hey? You know why she won't talk to me, your Maman? Because I got no money.'

Abdolrazaq gestures toward the pockets of his trousers.

'No money! Nothing! That's why she won't talk to me. If I had money like Haji Heydar, yeah, she'd talk to me then.'

Abdolrazaq bends at the waist and thrusts his face closer to us. His stink is now overwhelming.

'You tell her, I love her. See you do, boys. Abdolrazaq—me! You tell her, I love her.'

Koorosh suddenly lets out a wail of horror, perhaps more frightened of this looming form with its nightmare disfigurements than he is outraged by the suggestion of Abdolrazaq loving our mother. I am normally no braver than my brother, just as inclined to panic. But not today, I raise my fist and push it into Abdolrazaq's face—it is a push, not a punch. But it's forceful. In his unsteady state, I almost knock him off his feet. He regains his balance, swings his arm back and smacks me across the face.

'Little brat!' he splutters. 'Little shithead!'

Other people in the street, picking up Koorosh's siren-like wailing come running, partly out of curiosity. Abdolrazaq hurries away. Our neighbour, Mr Beheshti, hurries up to us.

'Ya Allah! What is this, what is this?'

He speaks soothing words to Koorosh, who's still wailing, while at the same time examining the blood on my face.

'What is this? What has happened here?'

I can taste the sickly sweet blood in my mouth, and obey Mr Beheshti when he tells me to spit it out on the ground.

'You come with me, boys. You come home with me and let Mrs Beheshti have a look at you.'

Mrs Beheshti is a kindly woman, one of those stoic and resourceful wives who holds a family together. She makes us drink a glass of water each, all the while making sympathetic sounds and promising Koorosh (who is still shaking violently) that he will survive.

'Abdolrazaq is a disgrace,' she says, 'striking a small boy! Believe me, Allah will punish him one day, surely. Eat some dinner, children.'

My brother and I attempt a few mouthfuls but neither of us has any appetite. On top of the assault by Abdolrazaq, we are suffering from the intense shame of being rather like derelicts ourselves, our mother nowhere to be seen, the Beheshti children stealing glances at us then averting their eyes out of pity.

When my mother does arrive, well after dark, she embraces us in front of the Beheshtis, making a great show of her concern. The Beheshtis themselves say little, just a brief account of Abdolrazaq's assault. Our neighbours know that my mother is not providing the security for Koorosh and me that she should. They know that something unsavoury is going on with Haji Heydar but they don't want to embarrass her further.

Back in our own house, we implore our mother to come home from now on before dark.

'Yes, boys, yes children, but God knows how long I have left. God knows, boys.'

'*Madar jan*, don't die! Please, please, *Madar jan*, don't die!'

We cling to her, clutch at her, now in more distress than when we faced Abdolrazaq.

'Ah, children! Who can say, who can say? But promise me this, children. Promise me that if I die, you will be good boys. Promise me this.'

My face and my brother's are sodden with tears.

'Maman, Maman! Don't die, *Madar jan*!'

'Well, I may recover. I hope so. Who can say?'

But in bed that night, Koorosh and I clinging to mother in the darkness, the thought comes back to me and burns like liquid fire. *How many others? How many others?*

The patterns of experience in our lives reveal features that in a secular universe would have to be considered mere coincidences, but in a universe governed by God, must be thought expressions of a complex sense of humour. There is another question in my secret dossier and it is this.

How many children does Baba *actually have?*

This question is related to a further question. *Why doesn't* Baba *remember my name?* But when I write this question down, later in life this time—in my teens—I have more knowledge of what goes on between a man and a woman when they are naked in a bedroom. And I know something about birth control, mostly about condoms. And there's another thing I know by this time: my father has never bothered with condoms. He doesn't 'believe' in them. He has told me this. He says he is allergic to rubber, which is the excuse that every negligent seed-carrier with an urgent erection resorts to.

So far as my father is concerned the likely and expected result of sexual intercourse is insemination. Muslims don't have any basis in scripture for a reluctance to use condoms. There's nothing against it in the Koran, naturally enough, and nothing against it the interpretations of the Prophet's philosophy. No, all that my father can rely on to explain his aversion is his tragic medical condition, his latex allergy. I'm pretty sure it's not just a raincoat-in-the-shower thing with him—a diminution of pleasure. I think it's just as much to do with a sort of macho dynamic, the need to leave the seed in the *kos*.

But I am speaking of the patterns of experience, the dark humour of the Deity. Because in years to come it is insemination that leads to my handlers from the MOIS looking at my neck and thinking of a noose every time I face them. I become a surgeon and as a surgeon I am approached by young women, and very young women and girls, and occasionally older women, to provide an abortion. Most of these patients have been raped. But what I do is a capital offence. I can be tried in the morning for just one termination, and hanged in the afternoon. My handlers from the MOIS come to know about the terminations and this becomes the basis for my compliance as a spy.

But think of this: my father is criss-crossing the Middle East leaving a trail of babies and creating terrible distress, often chaos. Later I, Kooshyar Karimi, one of my father's negligently conceived babies grown to adulthood, become Iran's leading abortionist, criss-crossing the country with my surgical kit, my bottle of pills, undoing some of the terrible distress, and sometimes chaos, left behind by the seed-carriers.

12

TOGHI

It takes a long time for my mother's campaign of subversion against my father to work its way into my bloodstream; and even when I accept the essential fact of my father's negligence, I still love him. He can never be the hero to me he once was but maybe it's the fate of all heroes to lose their lustre over the years. At twelve years of age, I'm still glad to see him when I do. I still relish the sound of his roof rack brushing against the branch of the tree at the entrance to our alley when he arrives home with his bus late at night. He comes clumping into the tiny house, and a tang of diesel enters with him. The reek of the diesel in my nostrils is as welcome as the smell of fresh bread. To this day, the smell of diesel acts on my senses in the way that a madeleine cake soaked in tea acted on Marcel Proust. A type of joy fills me, and a smile spreads slowly across my face. I am slow to relinquish the people I love, or have once loved. I hold on with a tenacity that may not be all that well-advised.

There's no privacy in the life of a slum dweller, and next to no secrets. If you're the sort of ruffian who beats his wife, everybody knows. If you keep pictures of naked women under a floorboard and only take the pictures out when no one's around, everybody knows. The complete lack of privacy breeds a type of slum-dweller psychology. You think, 'Whatever I don't want people to know, they will know in time.' And so you become nonchalant about other people's vices and foibles. In a way, you become more tolerant. Even if you have a secret that you've assiduously preserved, you still look like a person who has a secret. I'm a Jew, and that's a secret—or so I believed at the time. But looking back, maybe other people knew it. Probably the important thing is not that your secret is absolutely secure, but that you believe it is. A closely-guarded secret is, after all, the only precious possession in your life. The slum dweller's other possessions are junk. And your junk is no better than your neighbour's, so nobody envies you.

But even those who own nothing crave a different sort of privacy at certain times. Not the sort of privacy that permits you to spend time alone with pictures of naked women, but the sort of privacy that your soul demands. You live in a shoebox, so where do you go when you can't bear the sight of anyone on earth just for the time being? I find a place for myself, which as humble and tiny as it is, saves my sanity.

It is the ramshackle roof of our ramshackle toilet at the back of our ramshackle house. I swing myself up onto the roof acrobatically by using the door as a grip, and once up there I gaze down at the squalor of the backyard. The endlessly extended city of Mashhad spreads out north, south, east and west—a city seething with poverty, but in all of this city not one person wants to take my toilet roof away from me. It's mine forever: and it's up here that I dream. The first of all my dreams is to have a bus like my father's and drive it to Tehran and back, or to Mecca—a special delight because my cargo of Muslims would have no idea that their fate on the twisting roads over the mountains was in the hands of a Jew.

Up here above the stink of the toilet, I could not be more

content if I were a king in a gilded palace. And it's up here that I delight in the great consolation of my young life: my pigeons. I own four of them. I became attracted to pigeons when I watched a friend tending his birds, and saw their response to grooming and feeding and affection. This is why we keep pets, of course, so that they can soak up the surplus love in our hearts. And I am a boy with a great deal of love to direct somewhere or the other.

Keeping pigeons has a long history in Persia, over two millennia, going back at least to Darius the Great whose grooming and training of the birds is mentioned in the surviving literature. In Mashhad you can find shops that sell only pigeons, from your economy pigeon up to your fabulous princess. But the strange fact is that keeping pigeons is now against the law in Iran. When the puritans came to power they outlawed this custom that had survived for three thousand years. And why was it outlawed? A man who keeps pigeons will in all likelihood build their dovecotes on a roof. And he will spend a lot of time up there on the roof with his birds. What else might he do while he is up on the roof? He might well use his elevated situation to peer in through the windows of other houses and apartments. He might see girls and women dressing and undressing. Just on the off-chance that this pigeon fancier will abuse his lofty perch in this grotesque and criminal manner, best to prohibit the dangerous practice of keeping pigeons altogether. If any defining evidence of the sheer insanity of fundamentalist thinking were required, the prohibition on keeping pigeons would provide it.

Illegal though it is, many Iranians still keep pigeons. But the pigeons have to be purchased if you're starting from scratch, as I am. It's summer and it's hot in Mashhad. I make a few *rials* a day by selling ice blocks in the sweltering streets for Haji Alaska ('Mr Alaska', as he's known) the Ice King of Mashhad. When I've saved enough for four pigeons, I'm off to Koocheh Seeyaboon, a street on the wrong side of the tracks where all sorts of illegal stuff, including pigeons, is sold under the counter to wicked people.

My pigeons need a dovecote—a house to come home to—and I put together the best structure I can manage on the toilet roof. As soon as I become the owner of these four pigeons I regard them as my family. Each has a name, each is given an equal part of my heart, each is spoken to as if it were capable of understanding every word I speak. Parpa has a fine dusting of feathers on her claws and feet; Baghdadi is white and elegant like the snowcaps of Mount Damavand. The birds soon know that I am Jewish, that my father and mother are a very problematical pair of parents, that my brother's name is Koorosh and that I hope one day to be husband to five wives, all of them stunningly beautiful. The birds thus fulfil two functions in my life: they provide an outlet for my competitive instincts and they act as my confessional. Sitting cross-legged on the toilet roof, I take each bird in turn and hold it firmly but not forcefully in my left hand while I stroke it gently with my right hand.

I enter the fraternity of pigeon keepers, pigeon lovers. At school and back in the slum, I chat for long stretches of time with other boys who keep pigeons, making big claims for the intelligence and beauty of my birds and setting dates for competitions. The competitions are mostly striving to have my birds climb higher in the air than anyone else's, to fly more gracefully, to complete aerobatic rolls and swooping dives. And I do quite well; my birds are not duds, but I'm a pauper and my birds are the birds of a pauper.

The most beautiful and coveted of pigeons are those with a lovely crest on their head, but my birds have no crest. I can afford only the economy brand. To compensate for the lack of a crest, I adopt a plan that is quite frankly nuts and in certain ways, very typical of me. I have to have what I can imagine, which is always going to be a problem because I can imagine more than I can have. When Reza says, 'Your mother has her failings. Get over it', he's reminding me of this restless feature of my character that won't allow me to accept sensible limitations. My pigeons have no crests, so what is my solution? To make a crest of feathers and glue it to my pigeon's head! This is what I do with my mother and father again and again. My mother has no crest, my father has no crest, so I make a crest and glue it on. But the crest is a distortion and it makes my mother look ridiculous, makes my father look like a freak, makes my pigeon look like some sort of monstrous mutant. Ambition is all well and good, except when it makes fools of us.

Another type of highly desirable pigeon is one with pure white plumage all over its body, except for a black band circling its neck. It's called a *toghi*. I put aside every *rial* I possibly can until I finally have the huge sum I need to purchase one of these beautiful creatures—twelve thousand *rials*, or twelve American dollars. I hurry down to the shop in Koocheh Seeyaboon after school and stand with my money in my fist. I permit the shopkeeper to ask me what I want. He does, adding, 'The usual?'

'The usual?' I say. 'What do you mean by "the usual"?'

'What you bought last time. Yes?'

'Oh, I think I might buy a different bird this time. Yes, I think I might buy a *toghi*.'

'A *toghi*? Boy, a *toghi* is one thousand five hundred *tomans*. You know that! You're not telling me you've got that sort of money?'

I put my money down on the counter, looking as casual as I can.

'I think you will find that this is enough for the *toghi*.'

I already have a name ready for this most gorgeous of pigeons: Fereshteh, which means 'angel'. I take her home and introduce her to the other pigeons. My four other pigeons are not nearly as enthusiastic as I am. As far as they're concerned, Fereshteh is just another pigeon. I hold her in my hand and stroke her, marvelling as I always do at the trust of these creatures. They don't try to evade you when you wish to hold them; they seem to sense that you mean them no harm. I can feel Fereshteh's heart beating in my hand. A balmy tide of pleasure creeps through my body.

At school the next day, I saunter over to the group of pigeon owners and join in the chatter—technical pigeon talk and big boasts. At the right time, I nonchalantly mention that I now have a *toghi*.

'You have a *toghi*?' says one boy who owns three times as many pigeons as me. 'That's bullshit. You don't have a *toghi*. How could a slum boy afford a *toghi*?'

He doesn't have a *toghi* amongst his flock, and is furiously jealous, which is just fine by me.

'Oh, I just saved up. Her name is Fereshteh. I'll show you after school.'

My *toghi* is not only the most beautiful bird in our neighbourhood, she is also the most talented. She flies higher than any other pigeon and at the peak of her ascent she levels out then dives with not one but two astonishing rolls before returning to me. It is as if she's celebrating her own beauty, but even more than her good looks, she is celebrating her freedom. Because that's the wonderful thing about pigeons: they can belong to you and yet still be free. The sky is a paradise for Fereshteh, and she is the mistress of this vast, blue domain. How it catches my heart when I gaze upward, with my hand shielding my eyes, and see Fereshteh still climbing, until it seems that she will disappear completely—and then just when a panic begins to grip me, she rolls and plunges and rolls again! Oh, this is why I love her!

Keeping pigeons up in the sky is a skill, and one that is acknowledged by other pigeon fanciers. It is the natural inclination of pigeons to return to their dovecotes and to their keepers after a certain period of time. To keep them high and circling, it's necessary to make them recognise the signal of a black object—almost any black object—thrown skywards. They come to associate the thrown black object with your wish for them to remain airborne. And the black object I choose is a pair of my mother's black socks, made into a ball. You can't throw the black signal just once. You must do it again and again, timing their stay aloft. But there is competition for those socks. Not unreasonably, my mother wants them for her feet, and it becomes necessary for me to tell her lies when she storms into the backyard demanding her hosiery.

'Kushi, where are my socks? Don't tell me any lies!'

'No idea what you're talking about, *Madar jan*. Ask Koorosh.'

'Koorosh has no use for my socks! It's you who has them, you scoundrel! Give them to me now, or I'll do something bad to you!'

I'm up on the toilet roof. There's no way my mother can lay a hand on me. Gazing down at her upturned face, I take the opportunity to pay her back for some of the grief she has caused me over the years.

'Something bad? What would that be?'

'I'll kill you, that's what! Now give me my socks!'

'No socks up here, *Madar jan*. As I said, talk to Koorosh.'

'These pigeons of yours cause nothing but trouble for me!' my mother shrieks. 'The police will come for you!'

'Do you think?' I laugh.

I am in more danger of police intervention in my life than I realise. Our neighbours have complained to my mother that I have been spying on their daughters from the roof of the toilet. The idea is absurd. What, look at our neighbour's ridiculous daughters when I could watch Fereshteh climbing into the heavens? I know that our neighbours wouldn't actually go so far as to report me to the police. 'But what about my mother?' I say to myself, 'No, no! She would never denounce her own son to the police—no way!' And yet there is a doubt—a doubt of the very same sort that torments me years later when MOIS agents stand over me hissing, 'We know all about you, Jew. We know about the abortions.' How do they know? From my mother? No, no—my mother would never report her own son to the MOIS. No, that is impossible.

Another danger to my pigeons clouds my life at this time. It is September 1980, and war has broken out between Iran and our neighbour, Iraq. The war is all to do with the ambitions of Saddam Hussein. He sees the opportunity to subdue Iran to his will at a time when Iran is in turmoil after the Islamic Revolution. Saddam is a Sunni and all of the most important people in his regime are fellow Sunnis. Iran is overwhelmingly Shi'a. Saddam doesn't want Shi'a Iran lending support to Iraq's own Shi'a majority. And with relations between the US and Iran at an all-time low following Khomeini's siege of the US embassy in Tehran, Saddam can count on American military support in any war with Iran. Not that I understand any of this at the time. All that I know is that something strange and frightening is going on and that the dangers to the survival of my family have increased, as have the dangers to the survival of my pigeons, from Iraqi jets thundering through the skies over Mashhad.

The war persists beyond the winter of 1980, and I begin to comprehend more of it. In the lurid propaganda of the regime, Saddam is characterised as a monster marching over the bodies of dead Iranian 'martyrs' with American missiles tucked under his arm. Although I'm a Jew and therefore exempt (in my soul, at least) from partisan commitment to the regime's cause, I nevertheless have enough Persian in me to feel that the good guys in this conflict are the Muslims of Iran and that the bad guys are the Muslims of Iraq, principally Saddam, himself. Some of the propaganda posters plastered on walls around the city suggest that Israel is also Saddam's great pal but I find it impossible to credit that this salivating monster with his fat black moustache has any friends in Israel.

At school we are told of the unspeakable atrocities carried out by Saddam's soldiers. We believe every story we hear of women and children being butchered, of bombs raining down on civilian targets in cities further to the west than Mashhad, in Tabriz, Kermanshah, Borujerd, even Tehran. Living in Mashhad at this time is like inhabiting the nightmare of some cartoon genius. It's all monsters and good guys, and our Chief Good Guy is Khomeini, the Father of the Revolution and Supreme Leader of the Islamic Republic. Khomeini is depicted in posters in very much the way that the Patriarch Abraham is depicted in the books I have at home and in the portrait on the wall at my mother's uncle's house in Isfahan: long white beard, a paternal gravity in his expression, limitless wisdom in his gaze. Khomeini doesn't make me feel safe from harm in the way that Abraham can at certain times. But I am glad in a complicated way that we have a big wise good guy on our side.

We don't experience any aerial bombing in Mashhad; we are too far east from the Iraqi border. But Iraqi MIG-21s regularly scream through the skies overhead, probably just to put the fear of God into all of us in the city below. Air-raid sirens wail, people scatter from any open area; some, like me, dive into a gutter and hug our heads with our hands. The jets terrify me, utterly. While a million or so Mashhadis are furiously imploring the intervention of Muhammad, at least one small Mashhadi is furiously imploring the intervention of Adonai, of Abraham, of Moses. When I glance through my fingers I see red anti-aircraft tracers climbing into the sky. Although the Iraqi jets are not equipped to drop bombs they can still fire rockets—and what I imagine is a blazing rocket flying straight towards the gutter in which I'm cowering, and blowing my body into a dozen pieces. How will the ambulance drivers ever find all the bits of my body? Maybe they will only find my head and put it in a box and return it to my mother and father and brother. 'If we find any more bits, we'll let you know,' they'll say, and my mother will throw up her hands and wail, 'What trouble this boy causes me! He can't even die in one piece!'

Huge rallies are held in the square outside the Holy Shrine of the Imam Reza—Astan-e Qods-e Razavi—and in Malek Abad Park in the west of the city, Rezvan Park in the north, and in Basij Mustazafin Square to the south of the Holy Shrine. People stand shoulder-to-shoulder at these rallies, native Mashhadis and refugees from cities to the west fleeing the bombing. Koorosh and I are often enough compelled to attend, even if it is only to avoid the sort of suspicion we'd arouse by staying away. I never get caught up in the emotional outpouring of the crowds. You'd have to be an extremely naïve Muslim to be moved in the way that these people are. Mashhad is the holiest city in Iran, one of the holiest in the Muslim world and the rallies always begin with paeans of praise for the Imam Reza, the eighth Imam of Shi'a Islam, who was murdered here in Mashhad—or nearby, there is some dispute—twelve hundred years ago. 'Poisoned grapes,' so it is said. The faithful outside the Holy Shrine would be emotionally wrought to the point of hysteria even if there were no war going on. Just the experience of standing close to the burial site of Imam Reza would be enough to produce howls of ecstasy. But now the dread of what Saddam might do if his armies invade Iran magnifies their fears and at the same time, their need for deliverance. 'Imam! Imam!' the faithful chant, raising their hands to heaven, tears streaming down their cheeks in torrents. 'Imam Reza! Beloved of the Prophet! Beloved of

Allah!' The mullah calls on the faithful to brace themselves for years of war against the despot, Saddam.

'Allah will guide us to victory!' he cries. 'Do you doubt the strength and faith of the Iranian people? Do you doubt the love of the Supreme Leader for those who follow his path? Never can you doubt it!'

What the mullah doesn't say is something I only learn years later. The reason for the dominance in the air of the Iraqi air force is that many of the Iranian air force's best pilots have been shot or hanged or imprisoned over the past year by order of the Supreme Leader himself on the grounds of their 'ideological impurity', meaning that they did not wholeheartedly embrace the Islamic Revolution.

It is one of the tasks of the mullahs and leaders of the armed forces addressing these war rallies to encourage young men to join the army. Not that there is any need to wait for these young men to enlist. Conscription is in force for all boys who are eighteen years old or more. (In the years to come, the army will conscript fourteen-year-olds.) The real purpose of the rallies is to reinforce support for the Revolution and ensure that the conscripts report to military bases full of fervour rather than full of resentment. And the young men are in fact as fired-up as the regime could possibly wish. They are to become 'martyrs', which is to say, they are to become corpses. The Koran, including Sura Three, Al-Imran, speaks highly of martyrdom in the cause of the faith, and Khomeini has himself promised members of the Iranian armed forces that they will be received in Paradise should they die in battle. It is a sort of deal with Heaven: a brief period of discomfort on the battlefield ending in death, to be followed by an eternity of happiness.

'Martyrdom' is rapidly becoming a growth industry in Iran that is, in fact, benefitting the mullahs who officiate at burials, the coffin-makers, those who sell winding cloths or shrouds, and, of course, the grave-diggers. As the war unfolds, the bodies of those who have died in battle are returned to villages and towns and cities all over Iran. Huge gatherings of the bereaved and their sympathisers receive the corpses of these young men and carry them shoulder-high through the streets. Women lift their heads and wail their threnodies, like choruses of lamenting ravens. When Koorosh and I watch on at these funeral processions winding through the mean streets of our slum we hold hands, half terrified, half fascinated. We recognise the fundamental contradiction in the spectacle: these dead boys are heading for an eternity of joy, according to the Supreme Leader, but the mourners are weeping and wailing as if the dead are headed for an eternity of pain.

We witness funeral processions every day, for the battlefield casualties are unending. If we were on the frontline west of Ahvaz, west of Kermanshah we would see exactly why they are so high. We would witness young men being ordered to advance through minefields, each soldier with a blanket wrapped tightly around himself in order to keep his body parts compact when a mine explodes underfoot. And we would watch other young men writhing in shell-holes and ditches as poisoned gas drifts across the battlefield. We would stare in horror as Iranian troops launch suicidal frontal attacks on entrenched Iraqi positions.

For this is a war that is being fought in the same primitive manner as the conflicts on the Western Front in Europe during World War I: a bloodbath every day and, back in our slum, five, ten, twenty fresh funerals. If the war lasts long enough, first my brother and then I myself will become conscripts.

The war brings hardship to everyone, even to those who are already familiar with hardship. Rationing creates endless lines of people at shops where milk, bread and butter are sold. Cheese is scarcely to be found apart from the tiny quantity permitted under the rationing system. Petrol is also rationed—strange for a country that pumps millions of barrels of oil a day.

In our household, my mother wails that we will all starve to death. But the wailing is really just a part of my mother's own propaganda campaign. She is reminding Koorosh and me that we have a friend in high places. She wants her sons to know that it is Haji and Haji alone who stands between the Karimis and death by starvation. It is fascinating how closely her propaganda mimics that of the regime. The mullahs promote Khomeini as the Great Father of the Nation, the Supreme Leader, the True Benefactor of the Iranian People. My mother's propaganda places Haji Heydar on a pedestal to be worshipped as the Great Father of the Karimis, the Supreme Leader, the True Benefactor of the Karimi family. I have to say that my mother has a real gift for rhetoric. If the regime put her in charge of their rallies, they wouldn't be disappointed.

My special dread is that the Iraqi MIG-21s will spook my pigeons. What would I do if I lost my *toghi*, my Fereshteh? Pigeons have been one of the most successful species of life on earth. They're found almost everywhere; they're brave and not easily traumatised. But the scream of a MIG-21 overhead is a truly terrifying sound. When I hold my birds in one hand and caress them, I speak soothing words and promise them that no harm will come to them. To Fereshteh I say, 'I will shield you from all harm. Saddam will not hurt one feather on your body, Little Angel, not one feather.' But my promises, like all promises, are expressions of hope rather than fact. I can be fairly confident that Fereshteh will not climb high enough in the sky above Mashhad to be sucked into a MIG engine. But what I don't know is that the real danger to the great consolation I take in training my birds is not in the heavens but on the ground.

In English-speaking countries, Asgar would be called 'a rag-and-bone man'. He's a dishevelled-looking fellow who rides a rickety old bicycle up and down the streets of our slum on a certain day every second week buying and selling junk of all sorts. If you've got a broken coffee pot, Asgar will buy it for a *toman* or two, repair it and sell it for twenty *tomans*. And the same with anything you're happy to get rid of. I always give him a wave, recognising in his struggle for survival something of my own struggle. Arriving home from school on this searing summer's day, I would normally expect to see Asgar with his heaps of junk secured on the front and back of his bicycle, for this is the bi-monthly day of his visit. Or if I don't see him immediately, I would at least hear his call, 'Bring it out! Bring it out! Asgar is here with his pockets full of *tomans*!' It's no problem that he's not yet on the scene, he could be ten streets away.

I think nothing of it because I am bubbling with joy at the sight of my father's bus parked at the front of our house. After a couple of weeks' absence he has returned from his travels and will spend a night with us, maybe two nights. I leave my schoolbag just inside our front door and grab the broom to sweep the bus. My father will be sleeping after his journey, but when he wakes he'll inspect the bus and find it spick and span, all the rubbish gathered from under the seats, the floor hosed down, the outside of the bus washed with the long-handled mop. And he'll say, 'Kushi, good work, very good work,' and he'll feel in his pocket and give me enough to buy a bottle of Coca Cola from the shop.

The anticipation of my father's approval makes me oblivious to everything else for half an hour or more and it is only when I have mounted the roof of the bus with the mop that I notice something that stops me dead. My pigeons are not roosting on the toilet roof. For a moment I am baffled, then I throw the mop aside, climb rapidly down from the roof of the bus and race to the toilet. I swing myself up on the door, calling the names of my birds as I always do when I first greet them after school. If I keep to this ritual it will work a spell and my pigeons will be where they should be when I look.

'It's Kushi! Here I am. It's Kushi, home from school...'

But there are no birds to respond to my greeting. The cote is empty. A great many feathers, plenty of birdseed scattered about, but no birds. My heart stops beating. That sickening hollowness that succeeds moments of profound disappointment leaves me paralysed for a minute or more. I look about, left and right, above and below, as if—impossibly!—Fereshteh and my other birds will suddenly appear out of nowhere.

'No!' I whisper to myself, unable for the moment to accept that the birds are gone. 'No, no, no!'

I pick up a feather and study it, as if it will yield a clue to this mystery. It is one of Fereshteh's feathers. Tears spring into my eyes. I swing myself down from the toilet roof in a fever of anxiety and rush inside. My mother is draining rice at the sink in preparation for baking it in the oven. She doesn't so much as glance at me when I burst in. I stand panting, almost hyperventilating, my cheeks wet, waiting for her to tell me what she must know. Finally she turns her gaze on me.

'The pigeons are gone,' she says softly.

'But where? Where have they gone? And why?'

'Your father took them.'

'Took them to where, *Madar jan*! What do you mean?'

'Yes, he took them, all of them, all of the pigeons.'

By now I am on the verge of insanity. 'Where did *Baba jan* take them! Where? Tell me!' I shriek, stamping my foot.

My mother releases a sigh as she dries her hands on a cloth. She puts those dry hands on my shoulders in a way she would never do unless she were certain that I was hurting badly inside.

'Kushi,' she says, 'He sold them to Asgar. I am sorry to tell you this. Yes, truly. He sold them to Asgar. A bad deed. I said to him, "Husband, you will destroy the boy!" But he didn't listen.'

'He sold them?' I whisper. Then much louder, 'No! They're my birds! He can't sell my birds!'

'Alas, sweetheart! I said, "Please no, the boy loves them!" He didn't listen, my love. He didn't listen.'

She returns to the rice, but as she does so she says, 'Playing with pigeons is dangerous. You know that.' And this makes me feel that's she's overplaying her innocence in this...this crime. She must have agreed with my father. She could have stopped him if she'd truly wanted to.

I go down to the basement and huddle in a corner, my face in my hands. I don't go to my Star of David and beg Adonai to make my pigeons return. I believe in Adonai's goodwill, I believe in his power, but I don't believe that he can make my father change his mind. Why would my father change his mind? He knew it would tear my heart out if he sold my pigeons to Asgar. My tears would not mean anything to him.

A KNOCK ON
THE DOOR

It is a mystical experience to stare into the eyes of a man who intends to kill you. From an age as young as six, according to some psychologists, a child knows that the ultimate destination of life is death. It ought to be experienced as a profound shock, but it isn't. A death that is decades away is a death you barely think about. And who knows? You might be the first human being in the history of the world to live forever. Every child believes in his or her immortality, except for certain times when danger enters the bloodstream like a fever.

But as you grow older, you imagine more vividly the many, many ways in which you might meet your end. You have a friend who fell under a bus—might this also be your fate? You have a friend who cut his throat when the love of his life spurned him, and you think, 'I will one day have a great love, and when I do, I will certainly cut my throat if I am spurned.' You think of cancer—naturally, you think of a brain tumour, you think of murder, you think of being propelled at a great velocity through the windscreen of your car, of emphysema, of heart failure, of botulism, of a mystery virus that makes you bleed from the ears. And so each of us faces death a thousand times, and each of us asks, 'Will I keep my courage? Will I be able to show consideration for those I love gathered around my sick bed and say, "It's nothing. Don't weep. I'm not afraid"?'

When it's an individual, identifiable human being who intends to kill you, you are—finally!—looking at the face of fate. You notice a number of details. The stubble on this man's cheeks, the eyebrows that meet above his nose. The hair on his temples that is beginning to go grey, his slightly laboured breathing, suggesting that he's nursing the disease which will one day kill him, too. But most of all, you notice the eyes. This man has spoken with you a hundred times, he knows almost everything about you, he knows almost everything about your family. He doesn't hate you—that's not what you see in his eyes—nor does he care if he has to kill you. Not in the slightest. It's his job to kill people. It means nothing to him. He is not a poet, he is not a philosopher. He's an assassin.

I look into the eyes of the man who intends to kill me and I have just the one thought, 'No!' A battle of wills has commenced. His will is that I should die with a bullet in the back of the head, or with a noose throttling the flow of blood and oxygen to my brain. My will is that I should continue to experience a pulse, respiration, thoughts, passions. The man who intends to kill me says, 'You're full of shit.' And I say, untruthfully, 'No. I'm telling the truth.' I calculate that I have maybe a week to live. This man, Haji Samadi, my handler, my boss, in fact, must go away and talk to his colleagues. He will say, 'This Jew I've got, Karimi, what do you think? Shoot him? Or maybe put him on trial as a Zionist spy? We could do that.' And someone more senior will say, 'It's your call.' And Haji Samadi will say, 'He's full of shit. We're getting nothing out of him. He's a Jew, he doesn't know what the truth is.'

There are patterns in any life that we cannot discern because we are too close. Our noses are pushed up against our lives. If we could step back—and we can't—we might notice a certain figure repeated; we might see the part this figure plays in a much, much broader pattern. In the week that Haji Samadi is contemplating my fate, a figure reappears in this pattern. With maybe a week to live, I have no way to ascertain the intentions of this figure, and I deeply doubt that I have any allies on earth. But one man *is* an ally; and in this moment, I recall the gravity of friendship. Reza comes to my mind, and the belief he impressed on me: that the Middle East honours, firstly, the code of brotherhood.

To explain this figure in the pattern, I must go back to a time before the pattern, back to the year before the puritans triumphed in Iran, that is to say, before Khomeini landed at Tehran Airport in February 1979 to be greeted by a host of millions. Those who oppose despots get every possible opportunity to study the mechanics of tyranny. The man you hate, the man who oppresses you—how does he do it? What are the secrets of his success? You see the vital role played by informers; you see the tasks given to the secret police, those given to the torturers. You acknowledge, ruefully, that the tyrant makes effective use of propaganda. And as you study the tyrant you wish to destroy, you make a promise to yourself and to your followers, and the promise is this: 'When we finally succeed, when we take control of the country, we will never employ the methods used by this man we so detest. We will never torture, we will never ask one person to inform on another, we will never resort to propaganda.'

The mullahs and middle-class intellectuals and devout communists who oppose the tyranny of Mohammad Reza Shah Pahlavi over the twenty years of his reign in Iran know all about the mechanics of tyranny. They have been tortured, they have been exiled, they have seen members of their own families, haggard from their experience in the torture chambers of SAVAK, confessing that their own brothers and sisters and uncles and aunts, even their fathers and mothers, are committed enemies of the state. And their hatred of the Pahlavi regime grows deeper and more intense. But not in my family. The Karimis have nothing against the Shah. My father in particular considers him the Father of the Nation, a noble human being. My mother never takes an interest in politics. My brother and I, being Jews, are mostly on the side of whoever is on the side of the Jews, or at least whoever ignores the Jews. We are not equipped by education or ethnicity to care about the Shah in any vital way, Koorosh and me. The Shah is the Shah—what else is there to say? And so we are baffled when people, with more interest in the Shah than Koorosh and me, take to the streets in 1978 and demand that this king and his family be put on trial for crimes against the nation, or some such thing.

I say to Koorosh, 'What are they talking about?'

'Maybe they're insane,' he replies.

Koorosh probably got this idea from our mother. She regards revolutionary movements of any sort, anywhere, anytime as bad news. Hers is that immemorial suspicion of many mothers when it comes to people with Big Ideas. What she believes in is her family, comfort, rice in the pot, a little lamb, bread, cheese. If a revolutionary movement started up with the highly specific aim of giving her personally, Homa Karimi of Mashhad, twice as much rice and lamb and bread and cheese as she presently enjoys—just her, not her and a million strangers—then she might support it. But a movement that wants to restore liberty to certain people now in the Shah's prisons, out of the hands of professional tormentors, out of the hands of the hangman— what good would that do her? So as the protests of those who want what they call 'freedom' grow more clamorous, and the reprisals of the Shah's military and secret police grow more vicious, my mother becomes more and more certain that she wants no part of whatever the revolutionaries are after, and

Koorosh and I become more and more baffled.

The Shah imposes a curfew: everyone indoors by eight in the evening. If you're on the streets after eight, you get shot. By implication, anyone on the streets after eight is an enemy of the Shah and deserves to be shot.

We are at home one evening during the curfew. We are obedient people. Our door is locked. My father is in Mashhad on one of his visits, his bus parked out the front of the house. The Shah's thugs in the police and the military have been hard at work all day. People protesting down at the square have been slaughtered. There is an atmosphere of alarm in our household, and in thousands of others in Mashhad. Most people are also confused. The confusion comes from powerlessness. In Iran at this time, power is invested entirely in an elite, and it is only the elite who know what is happening at any given time. The great irony is that the members of the elite maintain that they are doing everything in the name of the people, while the revolutionaries— also an elite—maintain the same thing. But the people in whose name so much is being done sit terrified behind locked doors praying for an outcome that doesn't endanger them. That is all they ask. In a way, what is swirling around outside our locked door is a tempest of Big Ideas, a great clash of ideologies, and you can be sure that whatever Big Idea wins in the end will barely benefit those locked away in fear. It is as if we are being told, 'Listen all of you! Shut up, do nothing, and we'll tell you when you can come outside again! That's all you need to know!'

On this evening, well after curfew, we hear a loud knocking on our front door. My father has been in an especially anxious state not only because he supports the Shah but also because his bus is exposed to whatever mischief the rebels in the streets might wish to subject it to. Cars and buses have been set on fire all over Mashhad, shop windows smashed. His bus is his livelihood. If it is set on fire, he will be without an income and in addition, Haji Heydar will probably hold him accountable for its loss. The knocking startles all of us. My mother looks up from her knitting, my father glances quickly towards the door and turns down the BBC news on the radio, Koorosh and I look away from the television presenting the local news and instinctively reach for each other's hand.

'Don't open the door!' hisses my mother.

'Ya Allah! Who would be knocking at nine o'clock?' replies my father.

'Khalil, listen to me. Don't open the door!'

My father stands up with a worried and puzzled expression. The knocking becomes louder.

'Husband, have some sense! Who would knock in such a way at this hour? We have no business with such a person! Are you listening?'

My father approaches the door, more to investigate the cause of the insistent knocking than to offer hospitality to whoever is outside. As he does so, a voice calls wildly.

'In the name of Allah, open the door! I beg you, open the door!'

Now my mother is absolutely certain she wants nothing to do with the owner of the voice. She stands quickly, leaving her knitting on her chair. She goes directly to my father and seizes his hand, holding it in her own two hands.

'Now hear me, husband. Hear me. We have no business with this rogue, whoever he is. Look at your sons! Do you see their fear?'

The voice—and it is the voice of a young man, so far as can be judged—calls loudly, the panic of its owner mounting.

'They will kill me! For Allah's sake, let me in!'

My mother grips my father's hand even more fiercely. She can see by his expression that he is wavering. My father is not callous. He is always ready to respond when someone asks for help. And it is this side of his nature that my mother fears at this moment.

'Hear me, husband! Would you invite a criminal into our home? Such madness!'

For my part, I can't decide what is right and what is wrong. My mother's fear excites dread in me, and yet I am curious. Koorosh, I think, feels the same.

'He must open the door,' I whisper to him.

Koorosh says, 'No!' then, 'You are right.'

My father has made up his mind. He shakes his hand free of my mother's grip and eases the door open, not very far. I am able to glimpse the form of a man in the dim light that shines onto the street but I can't see his features.

'What do you want?' says my father, keeping his voice low.

'Let me stay here for a few minutes,' the man whispers urgently. 'That is all I ask.'

Koorosh and I move a little closer to the door. I can now see that this man who is pleading for sanctuary is as young as he sounds, perhaps not yet twenty, but bearded. And his face is grazed. Blood has seeped onto the collar and breast of his white shirt. My mother has glimpsed the blood, too, and the sight of it sets her wailing, not in Farsi but in Hebrew—an urgent prayer for deliverance addressed to our God, to Adonai.

My father is blocking the young man's entry into the house. Perhaps the blood has frightened him, too. He seems to be having second thoughts.

'I have a family,' he says, still keeping his voice low. 'See? A wife, two sons. If I let you in we are all in danger.'

My mother, with her hands cradling her face, wails as if she is already in mourning, 'All of us will be taken by SAVAK!'

The young man puts a hand on the door to prevent my father slamming it shut.

'Sir,' he says, 'You are an Iranian; you have the same blood as me—the same blood! The soldiers will kill me before your eyes, believe me. They have killed many tonight and they will kill me. I am begging you, sir, for a few minutes, let me hide.'

'Listen to me,' says my father. 'I am not on your side, do you see? I have nothing against the Shah. Nothing. People like you are making trouble that gets you killed, and now you want someone to save you who doesn't even believe in your nonsense. You heard my wife. If you are found in my house, SAVAK will kill every one of us—me, my wife, my sons. Go to another house. I can't help you.'

By this time I can see the face of the young man quite distinctly. I believe everything he says. The games of genius that are played by whatever forces control the cosmos—no, a lifetime of reflection has not yielded me any insight into those games, those cosmic schemes—that I concede. But I am now gazing at the face of the individual who will one day save me from certain death of the most horrible kind, and whose name will be revealed as Ali Mazaheri. And something passes between us— between Ali Mazaheri and me—some brief glimmer on a circuit of energy that girdles the universe leaving a mark or a message that will come to life again in two decades. I rush forward and swing the door open.

'*Baba*, don't make him go! Please, they will shoot him!'

Koorosh runs forward to support me.

'Hide him, *Baba*! You must!'

My father looks at me, aghast. The tendency of his thought is towards denying the young man his wish. Now my intervention has aroused his better angels, and they have gone to war against his fears. Even as he struggles, we hear the sound of gunfire from close by. The young man looks over his shoulder, clearly terrified.

'Alright,' says my father, 'But not in the house. In the bus.'

To me, he says, 'Get the keys.'

I take the young man, who will soon become known to me as Ali Mazaheri, to the bus. I unlock the boot that forms a cavity along one side of the bus—this is where passengers would stow their suitcases and bundles. The young man climbs into the boot and lies down on his stomach. Although there is no need for me to join him, I do, closing the door of the boot firmly behind me. I think I want him to feel just that tiny bit more secure, for with me beside him, he could be sure that my father and mother—especially my mother—will not betray him if the soldiers come to our house. We lie side-by-side in the pitch dark, each smelling the stench of fear escaping from the other's body.

The soldiers come, as my father feared they would. In the sightless world we now inhabit, we can distinguish each sound as surely as if we were watching on in broad daylight. We hear the shouts coming from the soldiers as they demand that doors are opened, that questions are answered. It feels as if the young man and I are encased within a single womb, as if we're twins, bound to share the one fate.

Now the soldiers are at my house. I can make out my father's voice denying that any rebel is to be found inside. I pray beside my Muslim twin to my Jewish God that my mother does not break down and betray us. And it is not only my mother who could reveal our hiding place. Our neighbours may have heard the knocking. They may have said to the soldiers, 'Go to the Karimi house, you will surely find the rebel there!' But now the soldiers are thudding out of our house, shouting to each other in their frustration. 'Nobody here. Nothing!' It occurs to me that the soldiers are almost as terrified as the man they are searching for. They are under pressure to come back to their commander with a dead body—or with a living one, to torment.

We remain in the darkness of the compartment, waiting for complete safety. The intimacy of fear is surely as close as you can get to the intimacy of love. Nothing is said. I can hear the young man's stifled breathing, I can smell the sweet reek of his fresh blood. Finally I hear him take a deeper breath and exhale as he accepts that the immediate danger to his life has passed. I, too, take a deep breath, and I, too, release it slowly.

'What is your name?' he whispers.

'Kooshyar.'

'Kooshyar?'

'Yes.'

'Kooshyar, you are very brave. Very brave.'

'Thank you.' It is the only response I can manage.

'You saved my life. The soldiers would have shot me before your eyes. It is because of you that I am alive.'

'Thank you,' I murmur once again, most unpoetically.

'What grade are you in at your school, Kooshyar?'

'Grade Five,' I whisper.

'Grade Five. Good. You are the future of our country.'

I do not say, 'Well, I am in fact a Jew, so maybe I am not quite part of Iran's future.'

I say instead, once more, very politely, 'Thank you,' but this time I add, 'And what is your name?'

There is a pause before the young man answers, a hesitation. He is an enemy of the state. He would probably prefer to keep his name to himself. But he wishes to show his trust, and so he says, softly, 'My name is Ali. Ali Mazaheri.'

Made a little bolder by this trust, I ask Ali why he is fighting the government. 'Such danger for you,' I say. 'Why do you say, "Down with the Shah"?'

The tone of Ali's reply changes from the hush of our first exchanges. He is now speaking like an educator, imparting a lesson.

'The Shah is a traitor to Iran,' he says. 'We want freedom. We want independence. Why does the Shah do everything that

America tells him to do?' Now Ali's voice softens again. 'You
are too young to understand these things, Kooshyar. But believe
me. A great change is coming to Iran. A change such as you
would not believe. We will have an Islamic government, a true
government of Allah. We will have no rich men and no poor
men. The people will share. Kooshyar, a great leader is coming.
He is coming very soon. Imam Khomeini. The Imam is beloved
of Allah. He is coming.'

I barely comprehend two words of what Ali is saying, but
I am intoxicated by the romance of his vision. Khomeini, I
know nothing about. Some great man like Abraham, like Moses
maybe, or like the Prophet of the Muslims. I am all in favour
of great men arriving in a golden cloud to right the wrongs of
a nation, of a world. Ali's ardour makes me tingle all through
my body. I believe in Ali. In a shorter time than I could possibly
credit at that moment, the Ayatollah will step from the door of
a Boeing jet at Tehran Airport and around him, stretching for
kilometres, his adoring followers will experience ecstatic waves
of pure joy. Six months later, perhaps half of those who enjoyed
such delight will be asking themselves if they were mistaken,
after all. By that time, many Iranians alive at the time of my
communion in the darkness with Ali Mazaheri will have been
shot, hanged, tortured to death by many of the very people who
have gone about shooting, hanging and torturing for the Shah;
except that the killers, the torturers, will then be in the employ
of the Islamic Republic of Iran. But I don't know that. Of course
I don't. I only know the ardour, the hero-worship I experience,
lying beside Ali Mazaheri.

Silence returns. The man who will one day hold my life in the
palm of his hand has said all he wishes to say. He is the figure
in the pattern.

I push the door of the boot open. I murmur to Ali, 'I am
going.'

Ali is looking to me as though I am his brother of blood, and in his eyes, I read, 'I owe you my life'.

The passing of years through one's twenties renders the world less mysterious, less enchanting, and much more menacing. In fact, the danger you experience increases with each passing year. You learn of more people who don't like you, who wish you ill, perhaps because, like me, you are a Jew, or perhaps because you are a Muslim, or a Christian. For whatever reason, the people who might forgive you everything when you are a child forgive you less when you are a man. It is not only the ill will of people you become aware of. You come to know of all the diseases waiting to attack you, of all the accidents that could befall you. And if the world confronts you with no dangers, you still know that in the end, the world will kill you and consign you to history, one of many, many, many who once lived but who live no longer.

It is now June 1999. The danger I face twenty-one years after my communion with Ali Mazaheri is not abstract, not existential, not philosophical. The danger I face is insistent and immediate. I have made a pact with State Security, or more precisely with *Tashkilat*, which is how those who work for State Security speak of their particular agency: *Tashkilat*—the system. I will spy for *Tashkilat*, and in return, *Tashkilat* will allow my life to continue for a further year, or month, or week, or day. I have become a resource, no longer a human being. My value could diminish to such an extent that I am no longer worth considering.

When my handler, Haji Samadi, calls me on my mobile phone and tells me to come to a familiar hotel for a meeting, I respond immediately. At the familiar hotel in a familiar room, Haji asks me if I have any fresh information for him—a familiar question. The only unfamiliar feature of this day is the presence of another man, introduced as Mohammad. This man has a brutal look about him, the embodiment of cruelty, the reincarnation of Himmler. I feel instantly that my relationship with Haji Samadi has altered in some crucial way. This new person has been invited along partly to take a look at me and give his opinion on what I am worth. His presence suggests that my usefulness to *Tashkilat* is under review. I may not be about to be shot here in the hotel room, but the time is surely coming. After all, what have I provided for Haji Samadi over the past two years? Trivial stuff: stuff they already knew. The activities of converted Jews in Iran, and who of these converted Jews is having a birthday, who is travelling from Tehran or Mashhad to Tabriz on business, who is keeping a mistress. It's nothing.

The really big thing happening in Iran at the moment is serial assassination. Members of the so-called Reform Movement are turning up dead, a bullet wound in the back of the head, one after another. I have met many members of the Reform Movement, and whenever I do I feel an immediate sympathy with their agenda, almost as if I'd written it myself. But the sympathy doesn't prevent me from telling everything I learn (very little) to Haji Samadi. If I don't, I die. Such is the miserably conflicted state-of-mind I'm in when I'm sharing tea or coffee or a glass of homemade wine with these reformers. I want to shout, 'For God's sake don't say anything incriminating about yourself!' even while I'm making meticulous mental notes of everything that's said. Wherever I go, I feel the cold edge of an axe on the back of my neck.

The unfamiliar Mohammad and all that he makes me fear brings on paranoia. I leave the meeting believing that every stranger on the street is watching me. Because something else is unfolding in Iran at this time: a round-up of Jews and converted Jews who have been accused of spying for Israel—a preposterous accusation. Mossad would never recruit Jews as spies in Iran. Every Jew and every former Jew in Iran is on a database and almost all of them are watched by informers. Why would the most sophisticated espionage agency on earth turn to people who are regarded with intense suspicion as spies? And there would be no need. The spies Israel has in Iran—and it no doubt has many—would have impeccable Muslim credentials. People who spy for a living, earning good money, are more reliable than people who spy out of powerful political conviction. As long as the paid spy gets what he or she wants—folded notes— he or she is yours forever.

But the Iranian security agencies entertain fantasies about Jews. They believe that we are far more devious than we actually are, that we are agents of the Devil, and that the Devil has given us extraordinary powers. As I have said elsewhere in this story, Palestine has suffered such terrible humiliations at the hands of Israel that they would rather capture a genuine Jewish spy with a Zionist agenda than a hundred Muslims who merely take money from Mossad. It would be almost impossible to overstate the hatred that Iranian Security feels for Israel. Like the Nazis before them, they attach themselves to monstrous stories of Jews drinking the blood of babies and holding séances at which Satan is summoned from hell. This very day, the vile Mohammad tells me that stories of Jews being murdered in World War II are Zionist fabrications. 'America and the Jews dreamed up these stories. Rubbish, every word. No Jews died.' If Mohammad and Haji Samadi were shown incontrovertible proof of the Holocaust, they would still deny that any such thing happened, ever, anywhere. Their loathing of Israel, of Jews, means more to them than almost anything else—probably more than their own faith. One could almost say that their faith is their loathing.

Meanwhile, my paranoia continues to develop. I think of all the times that Haji Samadi has met me without witnesses. I get into a running sweat as I recall the way in which he always looks around, north, south, east and west whenever he meets me, making sure he is not himself being watched. The information he asks me to gather! What about that? It could easily be made to appear that I am spying for Israel. I have provided him with five hundred pages or more of information of various sorts, some of it quite crucial, of course, but how easy it would be to use those five hundred pages as evidence against me. I know exactly how they would go about that. The prosecutor would say, 'This Karimi, the defendant, he is a Jew. He has a whole network of Jews working for him in the Islamic Republic. We will show the jury pages and pages of secret information gathered by the wicked spy, Karimi, about his fellow spies.' And all the tapes I've made—they too could be used against me in a court of law. Maybe they have kept me alive in order to stage this amazing show trial, sometime soon. When *Tashkilat* first blackmailed me into spying, it was surely part of a much bigger scheme to put me on trial as a Zionist spy.

The idea has lodged in my guts. I am put into contact with a beautiful, young woman by the name of Roxana—she shares her name with Alexander the Great's girlfriend. Roxana is a walking honey trap. Her role in the intelligence service is to purr and simper and smile and flatter and at a certain critical moment, reveal her breasts and stick her tongue down your throat. That's her initial set of tasks. Her second role, the more crucial, is to coax stories from you, details of the sabotage you are planning, of the plans you have hatched for the destruction of the Islamic Republic of Iran. You are not likely to tell her, of course, that you are working day and night for the destruction of the Islamic Republic. You may only tell her that you intend to meet your Uncle Moshe in Isfahan on the occasion of his birthday. But Roxana will remember everything you tell her, and pass it on to Haji Samadi, and Haji Samadi will fashion what you whispered to Roxana into a scheme to destroy the Islamic Republic.

Roxana simpers for me, and whispers to me, and smiles at me, flatters me, undresses herself for me, asks me to reveal my deepest secrets to her. I don't reveal any of my secrets to her but the mere fact that she is let loose on me confirms (so I tell myself) Haji Samadi's scheme to implicate me as an agent of Israel, a Jew spy. Why he should go about it in such a complicated and melodramatic way is a mystery, but in my paranoid state I believe everything I tell myself. Roxana, succulent Roxana, is after my head.

I wake one night bathed in sweat. What I have been dreaming of I can't recall but from the instant of waking I know with absolute certainty that I am being set up for a show trial. Paranoia does this to you. You don't think to yourself, 'I'm half insane!' You think, 'Oh I see it all so clearly now!'

I'm in Tehran at the time this terrifying conviction of being set up grips me. I'm lying in a hotel bed, the sweat-soaked linen wrapped around my body like the winding sheet of a corpse. In my state of glittering dread, my eyes focus on the cornice of the room, on the light fitting, on my shirt and coat and trousers dropped over a chair. Dear God, it's come to this! Two years of ducking and weaving, two years of nauseating, chilling fear, two years of moral squalor, two years of rationalisations, and all of it has led me down a cul-de-sac where I now stand with my back to a brick wall and a searchlight trained on my haggard face. My hunger for safety, my vision of one day being patted on the head, told that I had done a good job and then permitted to lead a normal life—what a futile and fatuous hope! I hold my hand up, and in the dim light that enters under the door from the passage outside, I gaze at my palm. Is it written there, on my hand, the wretched, scurrying life that I'm now living? Has this life been my fate from the beginning?

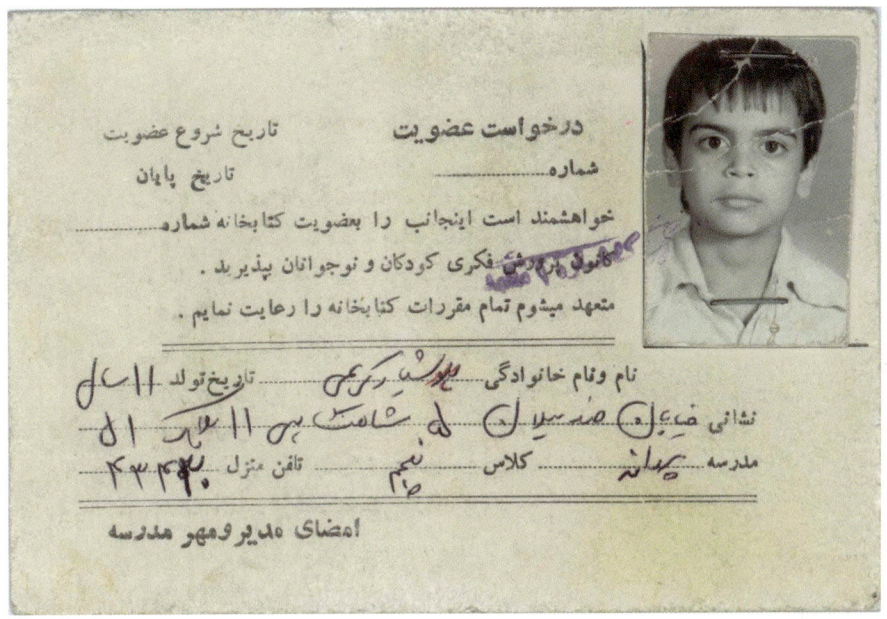

My library card when I was 11 years old. This is so precious to me as it signifies my passion for books from my earliest years and is the only picture of me as a child, since no one in our neighbourhood could afford cameras or photographs. I have carried it everywhere I've travelled, till now.

Me with my friend Majid Vahedi whom I met at the after-school Maths tuition classes, 1984.

Azita and me at our wedding, 1991.

My mother at my wedding.

My brother Koorosh, my father, and me at my wedding.

Haji Heydar with my mother at my wedding.

Receiving an award for Best Translator in Iran, 1994, from the Speaker of the Iranian Parliament. The Dean of Tehran University and the Minister of Education are to the left in this photo.

My daughters and me in Sydney on Newsha's 18th birthday in 2011. From left to right: Newsha, Niloofar and me.

In all the world, there is only one person close to my heart who knows of my ordeal. My wife, Azita, pregnant with our second child. Our first child, Newsha, only five years old, is the light of my life and will soon be a sister. I yearn to see Newsha grow and shine, as I long to see the face of my child yet unborn.

I get out of bed and shuffle to the balcony. In my boxer shorts and t-shirt I light up a cigarette and draw in the smoke. I'm like a man facing a firing squad enjoying one final cigarette. The sounds of the city have diminished by three in the morning but there are still things to hear. The racket of the traffic that never stops, an ambulance siren, and closer by, the muted voices of strangers on the street below, perhaps heading home from shift work.

Back in the room, I dial Azita's cousin's number from the hotel phone, as she is staying there for the night.

'Azita? It's me.'

'Kushi? Where are you?'

'In Tehran. I'm in bed. Well, I was in bed, now I'm not.'

'Kushi, it's after three in the morning! What's wrong? Is something wrong?'

Is something wrong? What a question! Is something wrong? No, not 'something'—everything!

'Azita, they're going to kill me.'

A gasp comes down the line.

'What are you saying? Dear God, husband! Why would they want to kill you?'

'I don't mean they want to kill me now. They want to put me on trial as an Israeli spy. Then they will kill me. Or put me in gaol.'

I'm aware that I sound hysterical. I try to calm myself.

'Listen, all the times when I meet Haji Samadi, we're always alone. Why? Because he doesn't want any witnesses. He wants to tell the court that I'm an Israeli spy that he discovered.

151

He doesn't want all of our meetings known about. Do you see? I've been set up from the start.'

'But Kushi, why would they want to create an Israeli spy? You're not making sense!'

'No, no—listen! All the information I've given them, all the tapes I've made. That will be evidence against me. Listen, Azita, they're going to have a show trial: "Look, look! We captured this evil Zionist spy, this Jew who's trying to destroy the Islamic Republic!" Believe me, Azita! I know in my bones they want to kill me.'

Azita says nothing for a few seconds. When she speaks again I can tell from her tone that she thinks that the best policy is to speak quietly and reasonably in order to calm me down. She thinks I'm having a panic attack, that I'm off my head and need to be coaxed back to commonsense.

'Kushi, if they wanted to kill you or put you in gaol, they could do that any time they like. They don't need all the information you gave them. They can invent any evidence they need. What you are saying makes no sense in the world. No sense! But I do know this: you have to keep doing what they want you to do for now. Just for now.'

Listening to Azita, this thought comes to me out of nowhere: is she working for them, too? Is my wife part of this whole, elaborate scheme? The fact that this suspicion has come into my head is enough to make me question my sanity. Who would I be suspecting next? I know I'm right about this whole Israeli spy thing, but I don't want to alarm Azita.

I speak quietly. 'Azita, enough is enough. I can't do this another day. I can't.'

And this frightens Azita much more than any wild tantrum. She has taught herself to cope with my hideous situation over these past few years, and now I want to change everything. I can hear her fear in her voice when she speaks again.

'Kushi, no! Don't you see that they will crush you like an insect if you stop giving them what they want? Don't you see that?'

'Not another day. I'm sick and tired of it. I'm sorry, Azita.'

'Please, please listen! Listen to me! Don't do anything silly! Are you listening?'

'Yes, I'm listening.'

'Don't do anything silly, anything mad. Let my baby be born and then we'll talk about it. Are you listening?'

'Yes.'

'After the baby is born, maybe Allah will help us.'

'Maybe,' I say, but I don't believe any such thing. Azita is a person prone to finding comfort in superstitions. She believes in divine interventions. She thinks goodness triumphs in the end. I wish I could agree with her but in the state I'm in, the triumph of goodness seems a very remote possibility.

I say good night to my wife and go back to bed.

My thoughts are a spiralling hurricane of dread containing the faces of all those I've encountered over the past few years as a *Tashkilat* agent, as a spy, appearing and disappearing—Haji Samadi's face in particular, and Roxana's. I see Roxana calling to me from the bathroom of that hotel a month or so ago; I see her standing naked in the doorway, offering her breasts. And I see the face of my mother, confessing that it was she, above all others, who had fashioned for me this grotesque life I am leading, this life of lies and betrayals and heart-stopping fear.

I will speak in more detail of this time of frenzy, of running scared, of my mother's treachery, of Haji Samadi's schemes and of Roxana's flattery, but for now let me employ a kind of springboard, and from this springboard launch myself into the office of a passport official in Mashhad, some months later.

I have travelled through half the night by bus from Tehran. I have had no sleep for thirty-six hours. My nerves are so raw that it feels as if they are bleeding under the strain. My thoughts swarm in my head like ants searching for shelter in a sudden downpour. I am wearing sunglasses, and a good thing, too, because the dread and panic in my eyes would excite suspicion in every person who might glance at me. I am waiting on a sofa in the ante-chamber of the passport official's office. His secretary has twice told me to go away and make an appointment. But I have no time to make an appointment. A week's delay would kill me. Or if it didn't kill me, I would be a no-more-than-pathetic shell of a human being paraded before the cameras and spoken of in some grim voice-over as a hateful spy for the hateful state of Israel. My hands are unsteady—my surgeon's hands, capable of manipulating a scalpel with perfect control, now trembling like those of a drunkard. I'm a wreck.

The man I wish to see—the passport officer—is the man who shared that hour with me in the darkness of the bus compartment. I came to know some time ago that he survived the Shah's purge, that he lived to see the Ayatollah step from his jet at Tehran airport. I have come to know that he has prospered under the regime, rising to the important office he now holds. What I don't know is what you never know about people with powerful political convictions. Will they honour you for the service you did for them in the past, or will their ideologies convince them that you should be put into the hands of the authorities? I am going to ask Ali Mazaheri for a passport.

I am not going to tell him exactly why I need a passport so urgently. I am going to ask him to trust me. In a way, what I say to Ali Mazaheri and what he says to me will stand as a test of whether life is worth living. If a man who is in your moral debt can acknowledge that debt and extend a helping hand—more than helping, a life-saving hand—then yes, life is worth living, something important about the hearts and souls of one's fellow human beings is established. But if he says no, or if he says yes, then hands me over to the police, then I may as well be dead because I would cease to believe that our existence on the planet amounts to anything more than self-interested lies and casual treachery.

Once more Ali Mazaheri's secretary, with a disapproving frown, tells me that her boss is a busy man and will probably not find the time today to respond to my imploring.

'You should come back another time. I told him you were here. He doesn't want to see you.'

'But did you tell him my name? Did you say, 'Kooshyar Karimi'? It will make a difference if he knows my name.'

The secretary is not without a certain amount of goodwill. She is not entirely dismissive.

'I'll tell him. Wait here,' she says.

She returns again from the office of the man who whispered to me in the dark: 'I will never forget you.'

'Alright,' she says, 'He's coming.'

I wait in seething anxiety. God knows, I may have no power of speech when Ali Mazaheri finally steps out of his office and turns his gaze on me.

And he does step out of his office. He looks about quickly, not sure who it is he is supposed to recognise. Then his gaze settles on me and something of the young man I hid from the Shah's police comes to life in his eyes. His hair is now grey, or half-grey; he's in his forties, after all. His beard is turning grey. He is a man of fuller figure than he was twenty-one years ago. What do I now mean to him? Perhaps no more than a nuisance?

'Dr Karimi?' he says. 'Is that you? It is surely you!'

I stand and offer my hand. 'It is me,' I say.

Ali Mazaheri shakes my hand with genuine warmth. There is no hint of annoyance in his gaze. He is glad to see me.

What I once meant to him has not been eroded away by time. Such a volume of gratitude and relief works its way up from my heart into my throat that I can barely keep myself from falling to my knees and weeping.

'Kooshyar, how good it is to see you,' says Ali Mazaheri—Haji Mazaheri, as he is now known. 'Come with me.'

He takes me into his office to hear my story. And he honours the unspoken code of brotherhood.

So there is something for me to be glad of in life. I am rescued from the worst sort of despair, if not from fear. I have stepped back and seen the pattern, the figure. The world is not given over entirely to the squalor of lies.

'I have something to ask of you,' I say when I am seated before Haji Mazaheri. 'A favour. I only pray that you can help me.'

'Tell me everything,' he says.

14

HELL

Part of my training for the role of spy that I play out in adult life is the subterfuge I master as a boy while concealing my religion from the zealous officers of the Islamic Republic. That concealment goes on night and day. At school, I learn to sit perfectly still and listen to tirades of abuse directed at Jews and at Israel by the religious zealots the fundamentalist government sends to my school to instruct me. For once Khomeini hits his stride as Supreme Despot, he sees fit to prohibit the teaching of boys by women, and so the largely intelligent and well-educated female teachers who give me cause to enjoy my schooling up to the age of eleven are replaced by male ideologues. The ideologues know next to nothing about the world, they are as ignorant as if they'd emerged from caves in the mountains. What they know about—so they believe—is the wickedness of Jews and the vile machinations of the State of Israel and America. Sometimes I listen in dread, sometimes I listen in anger, but whether it is dread or anger that seethes inside me, on the outside I appear calmly attentive. The Kushi Karimi poker face is being nurtured right here in my classroom.

When I say that the fundamentalist instructors are cavemen, I am not merely exercising my spleen. These people regard it as a virtue to know so little, just as they regard it as suspicious if you or I or the person next to us knows a great deal. Tyranny thrives on ignorance. The mentality the fundamentalists wish to promote is one that remains obedient even in the face of the grossest contradiction of the laws of logic. If they say that black is white, they don't want anyone raising his hand to object: 'But how can black possibly be white?' As I sit listening with my poker face, I experience a disgust for the contravention of the laws of logic. I am Galileo staring at the enraged features of some agent of the Pope as he—the Pope's agent, or maybe the Pope himself—tells me shrilly that the sun is *not* the centre of the solar system, never *has* been the centre of the solar system, and never *will* be the centre of the solar system.

And I am spying as I sit here. I am a spy in the employ of science, sense, intellect, reason. I am making mental notes as the fundamentalists rant. I am thinking, 'Tomorrow you will deny that you ever said that black is white. But I know you did'. I am also taking note of the various responses to this cant of the instructors amongst my classmates—classmates who are all male, now; the girls having been dispatched, if they're lucky, to schools restricted to female enrolment, and if they're unlucky, to their homes, where they will live without education. And there is some hope for reason and sense in these varying responses. I can tell that there are others like me—other spies in the service of reason—who harbour serious doubts about what they are being told; others who sit with a poker face pretending to drink all this bilge in mentally, without disgust. But naturally, the majority is prepared to swallow everything they hear uncritically. What none of us students knows, and what keeps us in a permanent and heightened state of anxiety is this: which one of our classmates, sitting next to us maybe, or which teachers—perhaps of Biology or Chemistry?—is an informer. For this is what our life has come to.

Out in the broader world, out in the streets of Mashhad, the thing I notice most after the first three years of fundamentalism is the monochrome quality of the city, of its people. Colour has died, since colour itself is regarded with suspicion—even with hatred—by Khomeini's people. Women and girls above the age of eight now wear the hijab. And the girls and women had better make sure they remember that the hijab is compulsory. Muslim fanatics are licensed to take the law into their own hands when they see a woman who has left a little too much of her hair exposed, and throw acid in her face—a favourite punishment. The men, who are technically free to wear colour, also abstain. I hear no music coming from shops in the bazaars, for music itself is banned. At times in the pre-fundamentalist past, you would hear music both local and international issuing from shops, even from cafés (Michael Jackson was a great favourite with young people in Iran) but not anymore. Advertising posters have also disappeared. The only colour one sees is in the grotesque propaganda posters and wall paintings that promote loathing of Uncle Sam and of Israel.

Iran has become a barbaric place to live—there's no other way of putting it. I have no experience of any other country but I know, somehow, that what's happening in Iran should never happen to a civilised people. By the age of fourteen, I have learnt a little history. I know that certain nations in ages past were ruled as Iran is ruled now. I have heard of Timur, who made life a living hell for people within the reach of his armies. I know that the Assyrians met all opposition to their decrees with an iron fist.

But something has gone badly wrong when a sophisticated state like Iran is dragged screaming back into the middle ages. I have seen a man strapped to the roof of a bus being lashed so many times that droplets of his blood rained down on those watching his punishment (he was caught drinking alcohol),

and with each lash a number was called out, 'One...two...
three... forty-two... fifty-eight... eighty... ninety-two... ninety-
nine...one hundred.' By one hundred the suffering man was
unconscious from the pain. And I have seen the body of a man
hanged in public from the hook of a mobile crane displayed
as it progresses through the streets, each bump in the road
threatening to cause a parting of the ways between head and
torso. His crime was said to be making sounds of dissent about
what was happening in his country.

On another occasion, a friend of my mother's lost her son to
the regime's thugs and was left with no body to wash and wrap
in white linen and bury according to Muslim rites. Instead she
was given the clothes in which he was executed. A shirt saturated
with blood and mud and torn to shreds with bullet holes from
a semi-automatic weapon. Security officers told her that her
son had been found guilty of criticising the Islamic Republic
and, whatever trial was given him, was quickly followed by
execution. My mother—to her great credit, for it is dangerous
to show sympathy for anyone executed by the state—visited
her friend's house with Koorosh and me. The poor woman, my
mother's friend, knelt beside the bloody clothing of her dead
son—Mohsen—and cried, clawing at her face until it looked
as though tears of blood were streaming down her hollowed
cheeks. The father of the dead boy sat in silence, his head bowed,
crushed by grief.

Other punishments I have not yet seen and do not wish to
see: stonings, beheadings, beatings that make of a human body
one great, throbbing vessel of pain. All of this in Iran. All of this
in the country that has the gall to fling abuse at Israel.

You might think that the regime would be embarrassed to
have the civilised world know of the medieval executions and
tortures carried out in its name in the streets and public squares.
But no, the regime is proud of everything it does. It is proud to

be thought 'medieval'. The regime is a stranger to shame. Its engine is a monstrous egomania, far worse than the egomania that informed the Shah's regime. What the fundamentalists have created is a truly totalitarian state, where every action, every thought, every utterance of every citizen is scrutinised for 'impurities'.

To the shame I feel over my mother's grotesque love affair with the vile Haji Heydar; and the disgust I feel at the never-ending torments of the regime; and the dread I experience whenever Jews and the state of Israel are abused in the regime's declamatory language: 'I am a Jew,' I think, 'and I will never yield up my faith, but it all may end in my death, and Koorosh's, and our mother's.' To all of these is now added a frantic fear. My father is brewing his own vodka since he can't buy it anywhere. Into my mind comes the image of the man being lashed on top of the bus and I know that if it were my father being lashed I would scream myself to death.

My life is a nightmare and my only solace—now that my pigeons are gone—is to trust and believe and pray that my adult life will be altogether different. Maybe I will flee Iran and live in America as so many Iranian Jews have, or maybe I will travel to Israel itself and raise a big thriving family of proud Jewish children there, in Jerusalem. In my most despairing moments, I cannot remotely imagine that the life I will live as an adult will eclipse in its misery and pain anything I have experienced up until now.

What if I have my fortune read by some seer, and what if he or she tells me this: 'Ah, poor boy, one day you will work assiduously for this regime you so revile, yes it is here in the lines of your palm. Ah, the pity of what awaits you!'

Yes, the pity.

NEW SHOES

I sfahan again, 1982.

My mother's intervention with the authorities in 1980 saves Uncle Abraham's life. To show his gratitude, Uncle Abraham invites us back to his house in Isfahan each year. My mother is especially welcome; Koorosh and me not so much. Our father is Muslim. Our blood is not pure Jewish blood. Koorosh and I are half-breeds. Deep down, our Isfahani relatives despise us.

There was a time when I was too young and inexperienced to notice the condescending looks from my mother's people, too young to see that the smiles—the very occasional smiles—were forced. But I notice now. I am thirteen. The last three years of my life have taught me a great deal. I know a phoney smile from a genuine one. And thanks to Haji Heydar, I know what hypocrisy looks like and what it smells like. Uncle Abraham's family needs my mother's help once again—her help as a Muslim, not as a Jew—and so they don't look down their noses at Koorosh and me quite as much as usual. That's what I mean about hypocrisy.

During the long, long journey from Mashhad to Isfahan by bus, with a changeover in Tehran, my mother explains this new crisis threatening Abraham's family. Abraham had moved from his ancient, rather ramshackle house in the Isfahan ghetto, Mahala, as it was called (a Persian word that simply and appropriately means 'ghetto') to a new suburb of Isfahan. Abraham had worn out his welcome in the ghetto, partly because he was such a bitter and sour old man with never a good word for anyone, and partly because he'd been a retailer of alcohol in the past. Even amongst Jews, selling alcohol is considered a very dubious occupation, and amongst Muslims it is irredeemably wicked. Under the rule of the mullahs you can be lashed almost to death for drinking even a glass or two of rough-and-ready home-made liquor. So the Jews of the ghetto thought themselves well rid of Abraham, while the Muslims of the new suburb he'd moved to detested him for being a Jew. As you might imagine, to a devout Muslim a Jew who also sells liquor is as close to the embodiment of Satan as a human being can become.

In Uncle Abraham's new house, unlike the previous one in Mahala, there is no well in the courtyard and no bucket that descends on a rope to the pool of water below. His new house has hot and cold running water, modern bathrooms, modern kitchen, modern toilets, modern everything. It doesn't have the well-used feel of the old house, and doesn't seem, well, Jewish. Judaism is more than twice the age of Islam. And I associate my faith with great venerability. I don't mean that the paint on your window frames has to be flaking away before you can be Jewish, but the new house at first seems to me more the sort of dwelling that goes with obedience to the regime. But I overcome my initial disappointment. Who can argue against modern plumbing?

Certainly not my mother. Brand new is fine by her. I realise this is probably the sort of place she dreams about. If she were suddenly made rich, she would indulge in every sort of modern convenience. Our kitchen would be full of gadgets, we would have a television set in every room, our front door would be painted red. My mother craves wealth. Given the freedom to do so—not that such freedom exists in the Iran of the puritanical mullahs—she would go about dripping with jewellery, her hair styled by some genius of the salon, she'd wear diamonds on the soles of her shoes, as they say. But she is not rich. Sure, she has a rich boyfriend, but the gifts he gives her are not lavish and her children—me, Koorosh—still get about in shoes distinguished by the many holes they accommodate rather than diamonds. My mother has my promise that I will make her supremely comfortable one day, but that's a long time to wait. Meanwhile, she enjoys luxury only in her dreams.

Her intervention in Abraham's latest crisis exploits certain talents she has always had in abundance: a talent to seduce, to flatter, to manipulate; a talent for making words taste like honey, and a talent to conjure pity in her listeners. She has employed all of these talents to persuade Koorosh and me to do what she wants at various times. I am just old enough now to smile in secret at what awaits the Isfahan Council when my mother addresses them. These councilmen must be thinking to themselves, 'What, let a Jew who has polluted the souls of good Muslims with liquor live next door to those of the true faith? Never in a thousand years!' They don't know what they're in for.

I'm not present when my mother takes on the Council, but I hear all about it later when she is still in the full flush of her triumph.

'Kushi, if you want something from these Muslims you must know how they think. You must know how to play the games they play. Remember what I tell you. One day, it will surely be your fate to make these donkeys dance to the music you make in the way I have done. Listen to me.

'I told the Council that I am a Muslim, a sister in the faith. That was the most important thing I told them. I didn't say, "Oh, my husband made me change my faith." No. I said that

I became a Muslim of my own free will long before Khomeini returned to Iran. I said that I didn't want to be a Jew, anymore. I said that my children have been raised in the faith of Muhammad—yes, you two, raised as faithful Muslims! I told these donkeys that I pray three times a day.

'Then I said that Abraham and his family had done nothing wrong. I said that he had only ever sold liquor to Jews and infidels, never to Muslims. I said, "Good sirs, in your wisdom I pray that you will honour the constitution of our Islamic State. Why are we fighting this terrible war against the Sunni Saddam if not to uphold our Shi'a faith? Why are young men offering up their lives for the Revolution if not to honour Our Great Father Khomeini, who wrote the constitution we live under?"

'Tears came to my eyes, children—yes, real tears, I swear to you! I wept before those greybeards! And then—ah, boys, I wish you had been there!—then I spoke the words of their own Prophet to them! Yes, I spoke the words of the Koran so lovingly that the councilmen wiped tears from their own eyes! Believe me, boys—every word I tell you is the truth! And what did they say, these mullahs and lords? They said, "By God's grace, Abraham the Jew may live amongst us."'

'What do you think, children? Do you think your mother is a genius? Who will say I am not?'

My mother, of course, is hailed as a hero by Abraham's family, but Abraham's son Mansoor and his wife, Nahid (pregnant and with many good reasons to bless my mother's name) still treat Koorosh and me with disdain whenever my mother isn't around. I feel wounded by their insulting condescension and beneath my breath I whisper, 'You think I am not a true Jew, but I am more a Jew than you!' The large coloured paintings of Abraham our Patriarch and of Moses our Great Prophet displayed on the walls of the house thrill me—but at the same time they sadden me. I want to shout my faith from the rooftops. I want to walk from one side of Isfahan to the other carrying a portrait of Moses. I want to declare to everyone I meet, 'Yes, this is Moses, and why do I carry his portrait? Because I am a Jew, and my faith goes back two thousand years, further into the past than yours!'

I smile these days when I think of how indignant I became as a boy denied the public display of his faith. In the life I lead now and in the country in which I lead it, I could, without arousing the slightest protest, walk about all day and all night with a portrait of Moses as tall as myself held before me. People would think, 'A lunatic', or 'So what?' and pass me by. Even the Jews I might meet would say, 'You don't think this is a bit excessive? Calm down!' But even as I smile, I have to acknowledge something I didn't quite grasp back in Mashhad and Isfahan. And it is this: my mother, with all her faults, with all her vanity and egocentricity and duplicity—my mother is the reason that Jews have survived their long and brutal trial.

Let me explain.

All the Jews alive today, gathered together, would just about populate one of the world's larger cities. Even at their most numerous—early in the twentieth century—all the Jews of the world would have been ranked at the very bottom of a table of major faiths. We have never sought converts, we have never proselytised; quite the contrary, we positively discourage those who for one crazy reason or another want to count themselves as Jews. We say, 'You know what? Give it a bit more thought.' Between the era of our greatest numbers and the present day lies the Holocaust, the greatest episode of mass murder in history. One third of the Jews of the world were murdered over a period of six years. Today, Jews live in countable numbers in more than fifty countries and, although the Jews of America outnumber the Jews of Israel, we have our own state, and that state thrives.

I wouldn't wish to boast of Israel's military prowess, and yet I will: surrounded by hostile Islamic states whose populations vastly outnumber the population of Israel, our homeland is secure from invasion.

There is nothing sitting right there in the open that would explain why a people so few in number and so subject to abuse has survived into the twenty-first century. Anti-Semitism perpetuated to the point of murder has been wildly popular for so long—more than two thousand years—that anyone scanning our history for the first time would think, 'But there must be no Jews left, or some hundreds at best.' To some it is explained by nobility of being, which is to say some profound moral advantage of Jews that allows us to rise above tragedy and set our sights forever on a better future. But I doubt very much that nobility of being is any more prevalent amongst Jews than amongst Christians, Hindus, Buddhists, Muslims or fire-worshippers. It's rare, whatever the faith, and in any case, it's more likely to get you throttled or shot or nailed to a length of timber than to benefit you in your struggle for survival.

I think our survival is explained by something fairly distant from nobility of being, namely the stubborn resourcefulness that is defined in the character of my mother. There are better Jews in the world than my mother; Jews who honour our faith more consistently, Jews of a more generous disposition, braver, more intelligent. But when push comes to shove, my mother is the sort of Jew who digs down deep and finds a way to walk out of the burning ghetto. Her motto is, 'Try as you might, you're not going to kill me.' If she has to dress like a Muslim, pray like a Muslim, eat like a Muslim she will. If she has to flaunt her body in front of some Islamist big shot like Haji Heydar in order to keep her cooking pot filled, she will. If she has to quote from the Koran with tears streaming down her face, she will. But she's a Jew in every atom of her being, now and forever.

When Abraham and his family hail her as a hero, they don't understand that her real heroism is the heroism of the Jew down through history who has survived: 'Try as you might, you're not going to kill me.'

If you are to believe what I have written, you would be left thinking that my mother—the woman I have characterised as the embodiment of Jewish ingenuity—has a hypertrophied chutzpah gland. And so she does. But let me tell a story that reveals another side of her, one that is just as important as the whatever-it-takes creature of my portrait.

The story begins with a business enterprise—one that demonstrates that I am the principal beneficiary (if that is the word) amongst the Karimi clan of my mother's resourcefulness.

I have yearned to become the owner of an air rifle for years, just like countless boys all over the world. I am not a violent boy, quite the contrary. But there is something about owning a firearm—even if it's a 'toy'—that spices up my blood. I can't afford one, of course, but then I could not afford pigeons when those birds were my obsession and yet I eventually had the pigeons I had longed for, and I have no doubt that I will have the air rifle I want, too. Or if not the very model I want, then at least one that will do.

By saving the money I earn at the bicycle repair shop, I am eventually in a position to buy one at a discounted price. An air rifle with a crooked barrel. It is only when you study the barrel carefully that you notice the problem. My father has come to the second-hand shop with me to give his approval to the purchase. He says, 'It's fine.' He likes the idea of me owning an air rifle. He is, after all, a boy at heart and he likes to see Koorosh and me doing the sort of things that he would like to do. He had no interest in pigeons so he never felt any deep sense of betrayal in selling my pigeons when the opportunity came up. But an air rifle is different. In my desire to own one, his daydreams from childhood are being enacted.

I show the gun off to the boys in the neighbourhood and naturally I am encouraged to show my marksmanship by shooting cats and birds. 'Kushi, Kushi, shoot that cat in the arse, Kushi, go on, Kushi, let's see you!' Or, 'Kushi, that pigeon on the fence. Shoot the pigeon, Kushi. Shoot it right through the head!' It is normally a day of tragedy for cats and birds when a boy of my age of fourteen comes into possession of a firearm of any sort. What happens? Boys who would not normally exercise their sadism on harmless birds and cats suddenly feel that God Himself sanctions shooting them. Well, not me. I don't have it in my heart. What, shoot a pigeon after the love and devotion I had bestowed on my birds? As for cats—what pleasure would there be in causing such animals pain? So I decline. In any case, the crooked barrel of my gun makes it next to impossible to hit anything I am aiming at. Knowing this, I begin to hire out my air rifle to the boys of the neighborhood for two *tomans*—that's three shots for two *tomans*.

To spare the birds and cats, I build a target of firecrackers. If you manage to hit the firecracker from a certain distance, you get another shot free. Fat chance. I suppose this was a version of Jacob's strategy in the Torah. Jacob, you will recall, shepherded his uncle Laban's sheep, and for payment, Laban promised that any two-coloured lambs born in the spring would be Jacob's. Laban expected that very few of these lambs would be born and he would get away with a perfectly manageable payment to his nephew. But Jacob discovered a way to make many more of the ewes than normal give birth to two-coloured lambs in the spring. His trick would not bear scrutiny by any modern student of genes and heredity—he simply placed before the ewes while they were being mounted by the rams a stick that had been partly stripped of bark while part of the bark remained—a stick of two colours, in fact. And with this two-coloured stick before their eyes while they conceived, the ewes gave birth to lambs of two colours.

Like Jacob, I use what might be termed trickery to thrive. I'm not conceding that it is trickery (and I'm not sure Jacob would call his dodge 'trickery' either) but alright, maybe I am guilty of less than full disclosure. I make money. And the money purchases my mother a new pair of shoes. There is nothing I could think of that would give me greater pleasure than buying my mother new shoes. In my way, I am competing with the parsimonious Haji Heydar, who could have bought her new shoes every day of the week for a year without doing too much violence to his bank account, but didn't. I bring the shoes home from the store, brimming with delight.

I know my mother won't say, 'Oh Kushi, on your tiny income and with the sweat of your brow, you have been more generous to me than the vile and disgusting Haji Heydar!'

But that is my fantasy. Fantasies are what they are—dreams of triumph, dreams of endorsement. So what does my mother say? She opens the box and looks at the shoes.

'What have you got there, you strange boy?...Ah!...Oh!... Dear God! Lovely shoes, Kushi, lovely shoes, dear son, but too expensive. Take them back and ask for a refund. Yes, yes, you must do as I say! Take them back and ask for a refund.'

'*Madar jan*, no! You must keep them and wear them! You must! I can make much more money.'

'Kushi, hear me. Hear what I have to say. We cannot afford the shoes. No, no! Listen to me. Take them back. Ask for a refund.'

She is adamant and I have to give in. I leave the shoes in the basement in their box when I go to bed. But in the night I feel my mother stirring and open my eyes just wide enough to see her slip out of bed. I climb out of bed myself and follow her stealthily. I creep down behind her when she takes the stairs to the basement. And I watch from the shadows as she takes the shoes from the box and tries them on. I see the expression of pleasure on her face as she gazes down at the shoes on her feet. And I hear the sigh as she removes the shoes and carefully places them back in their box, ready to be returned to the shoe store.

16

ULTIMATUM

The life I lead in my mid-teens is in many ways no different from that led by other boys from a poor background. I dream of riches and comfort, I work hard for very little to help my family, I make a conscientious effort at school. I also follow the progress of the war with Iraq, like other patriotic teenage boys, and I hope for the destruction of Saddam's army—but I most definitely don't pray to God to let me become a martyr! I sit in judgement on my parents, finding grievous fault with both of them, just like other children. I like pop culture—even the watered-down version that struggles for its life in fundamentalist Iran. I suppose I am unusual in harbouring plans for a university career; I am more ambitious in that way than the children around me. So a good half of me is a poor boy from a poor neighbourhood in a poor city of a poor country.

But the thing that creates the most emphatic difference between me and other children is my Jewishness. As I have already said, as a Jew I also live a secret life, and in many ways this secret life is more vigorous than my public life. This is probably true of any secret life, whether as a Jew, or as a Cathar, or as a homosexual. The very nature of keeping something of vital importance to yourself will tend to put steel into your spine, it will act as a source of strength in certain circumstances.

The frustration of having to keep this vigorous life to myself is always there, but at the same time it helps to make me a more thoughtful person, and helps me to see the world in greater complexity. As a minority, you are likely to see the complexity of life in a more vivid way than others. Certain people detest you without knowing a single thing about you except that you're Jewish. Having a secret part to your identity and knowing that you will be judged for this part alone is going to force you to draw some pretty uneasy conclusions, and to experience some very queasy sensations.

As I mentioned, one of the people who detests me for being a Jew is Haji Heydar. With the war raging, he wants me to pray three times a day—the Shi'a custom. (It's five times a day if you're Sunni—total madness.)

'Kushi, pray for our soldiers, like a good Muslim.'

'No.'

'Allah will punish you!'

'Fine, let Him.'

He says: 'Fast for Ramadan like a good Muslim boy.'

'No.'

'Allah will punish you.'

'Let Him, and I'm not a Muslim.'

My mother also exhorts me to at least pretend that I am a Muslim, to at least pretend to pray.

'Forget it!' I say defiantly.

'You will get me into trouble with Haji!'

'Who cares?' I retort.

'The war has made inflation sky-high! Without Haji's friendship we will starve! Try to please him!'

And I say, 'Fine. I'll starve!'

But I am very conscious of the need to bring money into the household, even if I do say I am happy to starve. I have a number of jobs. I work in a shop where electronic items are repaired. I keep my scam with the air rifle going. I work in a bicycle repair shop. I sell ice-blocks on hot days in the streets of the poorer neighbourhoods. The old man, Uncle Alaska, who freezes sugar and orange juice to make ice blocks, entrusts me with his batch of frozen treats, and as a bond, he keeps one of my slippers. I walk the scolding hot asphalt of Zed with only one shoe, selling icicles to thirsty children for one *toman*. When my flask is empty in the evening, I go back to Uncle Alaska's shop with all the money. And from the thirty or so *tomans* that I have made, he pays me back with two *tomans* and my other shoe.

I also stitch clothes for a tailor in a squalid basement for a month, and at the end of it I am paid only half of what I am promised. And I work on my father's bus. Nobody could say I don't pull my weight. Nobody could say that of Koorosh, either. We both toil like slaves. But by far my most creative method of acquiring money is selling kites. My kite business requires a lot of stealing, risk and dexterity on my behalf. Often, I am caught red-handed trying to soundlessly tweak the thin rods of reed from Mr. Ahmadian's bamboo curtains, or smuggle a few eggs from my local grocer that I mix with stolen plaster powder to make glue. I am beaten when I get caught but it does nothing to discourage me. Because, spending my afternoons roaming the filthy streets of Zed to find dry pieces of newspaper, having a hundred tiny cuts on my hands from clumsily cutting the reeds that I glue together for the body of my kites, all these things are worth it in the end. I fly my brittle paper kites in the sky and the children of Zed spot them, and they buy them from me for two *tomans*. And business is booming. I can run carefree to the grocer and treat myself to a bottle of Coke. But I don't. I am saving all my coins.

Bringing money into the household is part of my plan to prise my mother loose from the paws of Haji Heydar. Of course it is.

I know it can't happen in a day or two. I know it will take maybe a year. When my back aches from carrying about a great block of ice, when my eyes ache from stitching in the tailor's basement, when I am too tired to walk straight, too tired to think, too tired to stop the flow of tears from my eyes, I always think, 'But we will have our life back. We will be free of Haji Heydar.'

Then something happens that makes me so sick at heart that I can't follow my strategy through to its long-term conclusion. Koorosh and I are playing soccer with a team of neighbourhood boys against a team from another neighbourhood. Our team is good, very good; we're beating the other boys easily. Then, in the way that these things happen, a boy on the opposing team shrieks at Koorosh, 'Your mother's a whore!' I see red and leap onto the boy who has so insulted my mother, pummelling him with my fists. Within a minute every player on either side is involved in the brawl, kicking and punching and scratching and screaming. My fury is so intense that I can't be bothered with possible sanctions against our team for throwing the first punch. A couple of years of hatred of Haji Heydar surge through my body. I'm homicidal.

But when the brawl is over and Koorosh and I are on our way home, I tell my brother that I can't stand it anymore.

'*Madar jan* has to choose between Haji and *Baba jan*. It's not possible to be a wife to two men. If she chooses Haji, fine, I'll live with it. But it has to be one or the other.'

We arrive home scratched and bruised. Our mother demands an explanation. I don't try to protect her. I tell her exactly what's happened, and why. And I give her my ultimatum: one husband or the other, not both.

'*Madar jan*, I'll work day and night, I'll leave school so that I can earn enough money to keep us. So you can choose *Baba jan* instead of Haji. That's not an impossible choice. One way or the other you have to choose. If you don't, I'm leaving home. I'm serious. Either *Baba* or Haji, or I walk out the door forever.'

Given a little more time, my mother would have worked out a way to evade my ultimatum, but she doesn't have time. She can see how determined I am.

'Kushi, I will never see Haji again. Never. Believe me. I tell you this from my heart.'

I should have been sceptical. I should have thought, 'My mother is a very clever woman. She will find a way to keep seeing Haji, no matter what she says.' But I don't. I want happiness to return to my life. So I hug her and thank her with all my heart.

'*Madar jan*, you won't be sorry. Your reputation will come back. People will respect you again. We will have a real family, just the way we used to.'

Two months later, I see my mother sitting with Haji in one of his cars, this one a brown Chevrolet. Haji has parked the car a few streets away from our house to avoid being seen doing whatever he's doing with her. When I glimpse her my heart turns over as if it is trying to escape and fly away. I hurry home, race down the stairs to the basement, uncover my Star of David and pray and weep for an hour. I beg Moses and Abraham and Adonai to make my mother a good woman, but even as I pray I know it's beyond the power of any god to change my mother's ways. Koorosh has a different attitude. I tell him that I've seen our mother with Haji again and he shakes his head as if he can't bear to hear any more about her betrayals.

'I've had enough!' he says. 'If she wants people to call her a whore then they can. Let her do what she wants. If she doesn't care about her reputation, I'm not going to either. She's driving me insane.'

When my mother arrives home I first let her prattle on about her 'trip to see the dentist' and how he'd kept her waiting a long time and so on and so on—utter nonsense.

'You were with Haji Heydar. I saw you with him in his car thirty minutes ago. You were not at the dentist's. That was a lie. If *Baba jan* knew he'd kill you.'

Oh she's full of contrition, and full of excuses, too.

'This is the first time I've seen Haji in months. I swear to you. The first time in months. And it was to do with business, this I promise to you on my life. Business, nothing more. Listen to me. Have you heard me on the telephone to Haji for this past two months? No! Why would I lie to you?'

Then she pauses and at that very moment, switches to a new strategy.

'In any case, what's so good about your father? Tell me that. What's so good about your father? We would starve to death if he had his way. We would go about in rags. He has other wives. He has daughters he cares about more than his own sons. That's the truth. You are second-best so far as he's concerned. Second-best to his beloved daughter in Tehran. Do you want to know the truth? I will tell you. I hate the man. I hate him for making you second-best. I can't stand the sight of him. I don't want his hands on me. Okay, you asked me to choose. I choose Haji. I want to be with Haji. He cares about us. He gives us money. He makes our lives more comfortable. You know what your father does? He makes our life hell. And that is the truth.'

'Alright. You choose between my father and Haji. No more of this two-husbands thing. No more!' I say.

'I choose Haji. I want to be with him. There, you have made me say it. I choose Haji.'

The next day after school, Haji himself arrives in his brown Chevrolet and tells me to get in beside him. I could refuse, I could shout something insulting at him, but I don't. I am approaching a state of exhaustion with the whole issue. In a sulky state I climb into the car and let Haji drive. He finds somewhere to park then turns to me.

'I want to talk to you, man-to-man. You are fifteen now. We can do this. We can talk, man-to-man. Do you agree?'

'Say what you have to say.' I reply, resentfully.

'Good. Listen to what I tell you. Your mother is a fine woman, Kushi. A very fine woman. Do you think I would go to all the trouble I do for just any woman? No, it is for your mother, for Homa that I take such trouble. It is for your mother that I leave my business at this time of day to talk to you. Do you see, Kushi? What do you think this is all about, this relationship between your mother and me? I'll tell you what it's about. It's about you and your brother. I swear on my faith, it is about you and your brother and a good life for the two of you. That's why your mother has accepted me into her life.

'You are such a proud boy; you think there is something sinful about our relationship. Nothing could be further from the truth, Kushi, I swear on my faith. From the first day I met your mother I asked her to divorce Khalil. These were my words, I swear on my faith: "Divorce that man and be free of him." They were my exact words. But your mother said that she was not truly in a marriage with Khalil any longer. She said she stayed with him so that the boys would have a father—the boys, that's you and Koorosh.

'Your mother does not sleep with your father any longer. That part of their relationship is over.

'And listen to this that I tell you now. I have made a *sigha*[9], a special document from a mullah. This *sigha* means that your mother is my temporary wife. So no sin is involved, Kushi. No sin in the slightest. I swear this to you on my faith. Now is the time for Homa to rid herself of this husband who is not a husband. Ask yourself this: who keeps you in food and clothing? Khalil? Never! It is me—I am your father before the eyes of Allah.'

---

9. Sigha: a 'fixed term' or temporary marriage is allowed under Islamic law whereby the man and woman agree to the 'marriage' for any period of time, whether 1 hour or 1 month or for years.

I don't say a thing. What Haji is telling me is just what I expected. Self-justification, self-congratulation. My expression of disdain is meant to antagonise him, and it does. Maybe he wasn't intending to tell me what comes next. Maybe my contempt for him has wrung it out of him.

'Your father knows I am in your mother's life,' he says quietly, not over-playing his hand just yet. 'Do you think he knows nothing? He knows everything. The other drivers at the garage have told him. They say, "Khalil, your wife passes her time with Haji, don't you know that?" Yes, he knows, Kushi. He knows it all. And what does he do, your father? Does he burst into my office and shoot me? Does he punch me in the face? No. He does nothing. Alright, I am his boss, for sure. But would a man who loved his wife do nothing? Your father doesn't want any trouble. For years he has known and he does nothing. No trouble—that is his way of dealing with it. No trouble.

'And Kushi, I have to tell you one thing more. Just one thing. Your father divorced your mother years ago. Not yesterday, but years ago. Years and years. I've seen the papers, I swear to you on my faith.'

This is as devastating to me as it is intended to be. Haji wants to destroy whatever lingering respect I have for my father.

When I return to our house I am sick with disgust for my mother, my father and Haji. Each is a liar. Each has ignored whatever feelings Koorosh and I retain for them. That my father knew all this time that my mother was unfaithful is too much for me to bear. It's sick, it's vile. I resolve to tell my father everything I know. And I do. I tell him that my mother is having an affair with Haji Heydar. This is in the living room of our house, with my mother present. She's sitting by herself in a chair, her head bowed. She knows what I'm about to say. I've warned her. My father listens to my slow, methodical account of her affair with Haji (not the gaudier details—Haji on top of my mother, Haji with his hand inside my mother's chador) then stands with his eyes blazing before striding across the floor to her. He whacks her on the head, on the face. She barely resists his blows.

'You told me it was all over with Haji!' he shouts. 'I begged you for the sake of the children to see him no more!'

Before he can use his fists more fiercely Koorosh and I restrain him. But even as this ugly scene is being played out some part of my mind registers that all the shame being enacted is false.

My father has already confessed that he knew about Haji. What right has he to feel humiliated? What right has my mother to sit there as if she is the chief victim in all this rage and accusation? Oh, I know exactly what she has been saying to my father—exactly! It's what she told me only a few months past, 'It's all over with Haji and me, I won't see him anymore'. My anger begins to abate. I no longer experience moral outrage, only a desire to have things settled in a way that saves my brother and me from being taunted by the boys of the neighbourhood.

Other confrontations follow. Haji comes to our house and faces my father.

'I have been supporting your family for years. Are you going to pretend you didn't know?' he says.

My father shapes up for a fight but allows himself to be talked out of it. My mother sits with her head bowed, not saying a word, just as she did on the night of my intervention. She is not backing either of her two husbands in this showdown. She is keeping her options open.

Watching on, I marvel at her cunning. She knows she will suffer at worst a couple of whacks on the head from my father. She can put up with that. When the dust settles, she will make her move. I think it very unlikely she will stick with my father. But I'm not so sure now that she will give herself wholeheartedly to an open relationship with Haji, either. And it dawns on me as I watch her sitting in her chair, never raising her eyes to the struggle of the two men in front of her, that she may be weighing up a third option. Is that possible? Is there someone else? Or many 'someone elses'? I've had fleeting suspicions in the past. A fellow who runs the tyre place down the road always gives her a special, meaningful look. She sells him the suicide-mission vodka that my father makes. Muslims never look lustfully at a pious woman. But they look at my mother as if she were a succulent lamb kebab.

After Haji's visit, everything returns to the way it was. Unbelievable. The capacity of adults to hold contradictory positions baffles me. It's as if nothing had been said, nothing brought out into the open. In my puzzled state I ask my mother what she intends to do now.

'What do you mean?' she says, with feigned puzzlement. 'Do about what, you strange boy?'

'About the situation! About *Baba jan* and Haji!'

'Oh, that. There's nothing to be done. Don't talk about it.'

And *Baba jan* has adopted the same strategy. He acts as if all is forgiven. Both of them are dissembling.

'I'm talking about Haji,' I tell him. 'Don't pretend!'

'Oh, him. He won't be back.'

'What do you mean, he won't be back? Of course he'll be back!'

'You worry too much. It's all settled.'

I can feel that lulling sensation that comes over you when you yearn to put down the burden of standing up for what's right. You think, 'If they don't care, why should I? Give me some peace and quiet.' But I know what will happen if I don't persevere. My mother could continue to entertain Haji Heydar, and continue to see my father until she is ready to move on to somebody else altogether, maybe the tyre man. Rasool—that is his name. A real loser.

'*Baba jan*', I plead, 'You have to listen to me. I want you to

181

sell your bus and stay in Mashhad. I want you to be with us all the time. Can you do that? Or if you don't want to live in Mashhad, take us with you to Tehran and live with us there. One or the other. You have to decide.'

My father says nothing for a few minutes, instead running his hand through his hair as if he were giving a lot of thought to my new ultimatum. Then he says, 'Son, I can do neither. Do you understand? Not one or the other.'

Now it is my turn to be silent. The words I am about to say will sear my throat and tongue like acid. But I say them.

'Then you have to leave.'

'What do you say?'

'I said, "You have to leave." It's the only way.'

'You think you can tell your father what to do? You, a child, tell your own father how to behave? You think you can do that?'

'It's either me or you. If you don't go, I go. I mean it.'

Even as I speak, I resent the fact that I should need to say the things I have. Why should a fifteen-year-old be compelled to resolve this appalling mess his parents have created? Am I to go my entire life without ever being free of anxiety and distress? They say that the things that dominate your life as a child and a teenager will be with you forever. Oh, material circumstances can change, for sure, but the soul you own will never alter. If you find it impossible to live with what is plainly destructive, what chance do you have of happiness? Because so much of what we live with is destructive. So much of it makes me weep with pity. In the life that is waiting for me years ahead I will negotiate a daily hell as I attempt to rid myself of guilt and remorse. And I will let my head fall to my chest, as I do now, in our living-room, telling my father to leave our family forever. I will be tormented by the thought that some great cosmic power is playing with me, deriving enjoyment from my anguish. This is self-pity of course, but one is permitted a little self-pity. Heaven allows it.

I am learning. Surrounded by liars, dissemblers and hypocrites, I am, without even knowing it, training myself for an adulthood dominated by liars. I will lie myself. I will keep an inscrutable face. I will say, 'I am here to see you, Mr So-and-So, about such-and-such a matter,' when really I have come to spy, to record, to betray. But then, as now, I will believe that there is peace to come, that I will one day be able to forgive everyone, forgive myself too. As I write these words, that day is yet to arrive.

So my father is gone. I have been weeping for weeks, Koorosh has been weeping beside me. But not my mother. Whatever is happening in her mind, in her heart and soul, it is not enough to bring floods of tears to her eyes.

'*Madar jan*,' I say to her, 'Marry Haji, there is nothing to stop you now.'

'Marry Haji?' she says with a sigh. 'How can I marry Haji? He is already married. His wife would murder me. And Kushi, one thing you don't understand is that Haji has no desire to marry me. It would cost him too much. His wife is his cash cow. His success was built on her fortune. If he takes me into his life in an open way, she will destroy him. After murdering me, that is.'

And on the topic of murder, I have told my mother that I will kill her myself if she takes up with Rasool, the tyre man. Enough, already. Koorosh and I have put up with a father who doesn't want to be with us, with a lying, hypocritical, holier-than-thou slug like Haji Heydar sticking his hand up my mother's dress, and with my mother herself living out her carnival of deviousness. And now the signs are that this Rasool wants to hang around exercising his lust on my mother? Forget it.

THE SPY
IN EVERYONE

The great human advantage in the art of lying is our command of language. Certain animals have the knack of playing dead to avoid the onslaught of predators; others can change colour and pattern. But language is a more subtle agent of camouflage than anything nature can offer. The time will come when I will spend most of my life camouflaged, but before that day there is an initiation into the life of disguise.

I am a surgeon at twenty-seven. My studies have prepared me for a life of my own choosing in medicine. I am also a writer. A number of my books have appeared in Iran, including my own translations of texts written in languages other than Farsi. I am a husband, too, and a father. I have completed my twenty-six months of military service. Free of obligations to the state, the world is at my feet. I am working shifts in a Mashhad hospital and at the same time making enquiries that will eventually allow me to open a surgery of my own.

Naturally, my mother expects me to succeed—I have been a clever student throughout secondary school, my results the best the school had ever awarded, not only in subjects directly related to the profession of surgeon but also in the arts. I was my school's golden student of Persian literature. And now, at the time of my release from military service, of my searching for premises where I might set up as a surgeon and begin my climb into the ranks of the well-to-do (thin though they may be in Iran), the prospect of pleasing my mother remains a fixed star.

I have, time and time again, been plagued by a feeling of cosmic ill-favour, a sense that the planets are aligned against me. At this golden moment in my life, I briefly think I am clear of the trials and misfortunes of my childhood and adolescence. However, two events change everything. Two events, both innocent enough in any sane society but highly fraught in fundamentalist Iran, put me into the hands of the state's licensed torturers. And these two events go on to introduce a whole new relationship with physical and psychological pain.

The first is in 1997 with the appearance in my life of a girl by the name of Zahra Sharifi. Zahra is from the village of Torbat, a couple of hours' drive from Mashhad. She has Down Syndrome, and as would be expected is mentally impaired, although not severely. She has been brought to the hospital in Mashhad and is placed in my care. It transpires that she has attempted to end her life, swallowing thirty-five Valium tablets. Why she should take this drastic course is a mystery to me at first. Down Syndrome does not of itself act as a source of profound depression in its sufferers. But as I am irrigating the girl's stomach, evacuating the Valium's constituents, the nurse on duty whispers to me that Zahra had been raped by four boys of her village. The nurse has to convey this information in a whisper not only to spare my patient but because she, the nurse, is herself embarrassed.

Rape in Iran—and in many another countries with a predominantly Muslim population—is a cause of shame, principally for the victim. It makes no sense, it is grotesque and cruel but it is a fact that any woman who endures violation of this sort in Iran is in deep trouble in more ways than one. Zahra and countless other girls and women would be most reluctant to press charges against their violators because the investigation could well end up with the victim facing a death sentence. If the alleged rapists claim that she consented to sexual intercourse, the burden of proof rests on her. If she cannot prove that she was violated—that no consent was given—she then becomes the person under investigation. Even tacit consent would be enough to get her into trouble, and by 'tacit consent' I mean that the men could argue that she (or any other victim) did not actually say 'No!' at any point. This defence would apply even if the victim were unconscious or gagged. In fact, the only reliable defence a woman can provide is suicide. If the shame is so great, the argument would go, why did the victim not kill herself?

I ask Zahra if she wishes to press charges against the boys who assaulted her. She says no, she doesn't want anyone to know, she only wishes to die. My own distress is mounting but I calm myself and tell her what I must tell her, knowing that any consolation I can provide stands like a molehill beneath the towering mountain of her anguish and shame.

'These things happen,' I tell her, as gently as I can. 'You have to be brave. As hard as it seems now, no permanent harm has been done. You can go on with your life.'

From beneath the blanket she has pulled over her head, she cries out, 'No! No! Please let me die!'

But I go on with my futile attempt at comfort. 'Just try not to think about it. I can organise a mental health review, completely confidential. It will help.' It will help? Who am I kidding?

And from beneath the blanket comes the anguished voice saying, 'No! I beg you, let me die!'

I order a pregnancy test then take myself out in the garden of the hospital to smoke a much needed cigarette, thinking all the while, 'Oh, God—the poor child, the poor child!' As I'm smoking and sorrowing for Zahra, I hear a voice behind me, very quiet.

'Dr Karimi?' I swing around, a little startled despite the unthreatening tone.

'Yes. Yes, I am Dr Karimi. How may I help you?'

'Are you the doctor who is looking after my daughter? Zahra Sharifi?'

So this is the father. I gaze at him in sympathy. He is a village man, late forties, dressed in dusty clothing, his face given a leathery look from all the hours he has spent in the sun. But the most striking thing about him is not his ragged clothing or his sunburnt complexion but the deep sorrow in his eyes. I am certain that this is a man who has never had a lucky break in his life, has never known comfort, and now his daughter lies in a bed in the poisons ward, wishing to die.

'I am caring for your daughter, yes,' I answer the man with all the respect he deserves. 'She will be all right. She can be discharged later today.'

The man shakes his head slowly.

'Allah's blessings on you, Doctor. With all my heart.'

Then his hands reach up and cover his face and his shoulders shake with the rigour of his weeping.

I step closer, without actually touching the poor man.

'But why are you so upset? She will suffer no lasting harm.'

The man takes his hands from his face and wipes his damp cheeks with the sleeve of his shirt.

'Are you married, Doctor?' he asks me.

'Yes,' I reply. 'I'm married. Why do you ask?'

'Do you have any children?'

'Do I have any children? Yes, certainly. I have a small daughter.'

'Then you will understand my tears, Doctor.' He shakes his head in sorrow then gives a deep sigh. 'I should kill myself,' he says. 'It is a sin, I know, but I should kill myself.'

I can only listen. Perhaps another, more demonstrative person would have embraced the man, comforted him. As a doctor I see enough to break my heart every day, but a doctor who actually allows his heart to break is a type of cripple. He can't function as he should.

'My daughter has a mental problem,' the father goes on. 'You could say she is retarded, surely. But do you know, Doctor, she sees everything, she understands everything, she feels everything. Even with her mental problems, she knows that something very, very bad has been done to her. I watch out for her all the time. I know how easy it would be for bad people to take advantage of her.

'But this time I was not careful enough. She went out to buy bread and when she was coming back these men caught her—a disgrace to creation, they are!—they caught her, Doctor, and took her to a dark place and raped her. How I sorrow for the poor child!'

Later that day I do my rounds in the ward, checking on one patient then another. The girl, Zahra, is lying on her side, unwilling to meet my eyes. The pregnancy test is negative, and thank God, for that. And yet I know that Zahra can never recover psychologically. In the Middle East, a girl's virginity is everything. You would barely find a girl above a certain age who would not rather surrender her limbs than her virginity, such is the shame associated with its loss. There is a surgical procedure that can compensate for the loss of virginity by restoring the hymen. I know all about it. I have performed it a number of times. But the procedure is illegal and can attract the death penalty.

The plight of poor Zahra plays on my mind. I can easily imagine her attempting suicide again. She will succeed eventually. I am still thinking of her when I leave the hospital in my car at the end of my shift, and so it seems providential when I glimpse Zahra and her father walking away from the hospital, the father looking downcast, the daughter even more so. Without giving myself a chance to change my mind I pull into the kerb beside them and roll down the window.

Mr Sharifi!'

The father turns. Not knowing why his name has been called, he expects bad news. But when he sees it is me his clouded look changes to one of relief.

'Doctor!'

I'm writing my address rapidly on a piece of scrap paper.

'Mr Sharifi, take this. Maybe I can do something for your daughter. Come to this address after five, tomorrow.'

The father knows what the 'something' is likely to be. It is what he had in mind when he spoke to me in the garden, but was too shy to make any such suggestion.

'Doctor,' he says, 'this is dangerous for you. I don't want you to get into any trouble. It would be on my conscience.'

'Mr Sharifi, just come after five, tomorrow.'

He reaches his hand towards me and I extend mine. As I grasp his hand I can feel decades of his life's hardship transmit itself to mine.

Mr Sharifi and his daughter come after five, as I invited them to do. And with my wife Azita acting in the role of a nurse, the operation is completed. It's a painstaking thing to carry out, and even though it can be thought of as folly in certain regards, refashioning the hymen membrane with the expectation that it will one day be ruptured again, it is important to Zahra. So far as she is concerned, she is a virgin again.

And she is happy. It does my heart good to see the joy in her eyes. She wants to give Azita a gold bangle from her wrist, a present from her mother in the days when her mother was still alive. Azita declines, graciously.

'You keep this for yourself,' she tells the girl. 'What could be more precious than a present from your *Madar*? We were pleased to be able to help you.'

The second event contributing to the catastrophe poised above me like the snow of a mountain-side about to become an avalanche (if I had but known) follows only a few weeks after Zahra, newly intact, returns to her village of Torbat. I am still searching high and low for premises in which I can establish my surgery. There is no shortage of places that would serve but some are too expensive, some are in neighbourhoods far too out-of-the-way, some simply give off the wrong feel. I have to feel right about the place I'll be working in day after day for years to come.

I take my search to the old bazaar, Bazarcha Aqajan, not so far from the shrine of Imam Reza, sacred to Muslims all over the world. The bazaar is a densely built area with crooked, slanted shops leaning on one another like old drunken friends. Multi-coloured stalls are jammed in everywhere, people shouting out the virtues of their wares in chants that have kept the same wording for centuries, almost everything on earth for sale if you ask the right questions and your pockets are full of cash. It is many small side streets and alleys, some almost as old as the pagan Persia of pre-Islamic days.

At the gated entrance to one section of the bazaar I look up and scan the arched face of the gate and the walls on each side. My gaze picks out, extraordinarily, a Star of David figured in small coloured tiles. I am flabbergasted. Here, in the heart of the sacred city of Mashhad where Muslim pilgrims arrive in their hundreds of thousands each year, sits the primary distinguishing emblem of militant Islam's most hated enemy. The emblem is built into the oldest part of the wall and underneath, some lines in Hebrew have been scored, as if some of the faithful have taken it upon themselves to deface the script of the Zionist enemy. I think, 'This is fate.' I am essentially a scientist—how can I be other as a surgeon?—but like so many other people I am capable of believing things that completely contradict reason and logic. It's fate, I tell myself. Destiny. The God of the Jews led me here. I am where I am meant to be.

Now I am searching painstakingly for something I'm sure I will find: evidence of a mezuzah having once been nailed to the architrave of the doorway in the wall. And with delight, I detect two nail holes showing where the mezuzah would once have been fixed. Mashhadi Jews in their thousands abandoned the city in waves following successive *koshtar*, or violent attacks, over the centuries. But this building in the bazaar must once have been the home of a Jew, perhaps even a synagogue.

I venture into the nearest shop, a place that sells prayer vestments, ironically enough. The old man who is the proprietor is attending to customers but as soon as we are alone, I ask politely about the Star of David on the wall. The old man, one minute merely indifferent to me and my purpose at once becomes furtive.

'Shush!' he hisses, glancing over my shoulder to see if anyone is eavesdropping.

'Pardon?'

'Don't talk about it,' he whispers. Then he leans toward me. 'Jews!'

'Jews? In Mashhad? Surely not!'

'Not now. In the past. Why so many questions?'

'Just my curiosity. My name is Kooshyar. I'm a doctor.'

I offer my hand and the old man accepts it, with reluctance.

'Why does a doctor take such an interest in Jews?'

'Well, I'm not a doctor all the time. I write as well. Writers are inquisitive. Something like that Jewish star makes me want to know more.'

'You want to know more? Talk to someone else. Talk to Sarabi. The shop on the corner. I have no desire to waste my time talking about Jews.'

I go straight to the shop on the corner—a rug store—and with persistence I'm finally permitted to talk to this Sarabi gentleman. He's old, but not ancient. Abundant grey hair, bright brown eyes full of intelligence. He at first denies that he's ever noticed the Star of David out there on the wall. He says he doesn't know what I mean. Star? What star? A star in the sky? In the middle of the afternoon? But he's not being candid—I can sense it. I keep smiling, remain unfailingly polite. I've already told Sarabi that I'm a doctor, I've told him my name, given him my business card. And just as I can sense something covert in him, he seems to detect something concealed in me. He's naturally suspicious. I could be a spy. I could be trying to inveigle him into telling me things that will land him in strife.

'Are you sure you're a doctor?' he says. 'Pardon me, but I'm not sure I believe you.'

'I'm a doctor and a writer. My books are published in Iran.' I lower my voice a little. 'I have a particular interest in minorities. Persecuted minorities.'

Sarabi studies me in silence for a minute or more. Then he says, 'Sit here. I will be with you in a moment.'

He calls to someone by the name of Mehdi to bring tea. I try my best to look harmless. Sarabi busies himself elsewhere in the shop for a short time before pulling up a chair. 'Mehdi!' he calls. 'Where's that tea!' To me he says, 'You will take some tea, I hope?'

'I'd be delighted.'

Sarabi smiles, then in the most casual way he can manage he asks, 'Are you a Jew?'

This is a question that no Iranian Jew within the Islamic Republic's borders would be prepared to answer in any direct and honest way. It is a question that you would only ask of someone you are convinced is a Jew. To the overwhelming majority of Muslim Iranians, a question like that, 'Are you a Jew?', would be tantamount to asking, 'Are you a child molester?' Or a vampire, or a homicidal maniac. It would be considered a gross insult. And I am no different from other Iranian Jews who become evasive when the query is put. I glance at Sarabi's bright eyes to see if malice has surfaced in his expression. Then I say, without the least compunction, much less shame: 'Me? No! Not at all!'

'That's a very strong denial, I must say.'

'But why do you ask?'

Sarabi says quietly, 'I can see it in your face. I worked with Jews for many years. So I ask you again. Are you a Jew?'

'I might have links somewhere or other. That's all.'

Sarabi shakes his head. 'No, we can go no further unless you are honest with me. And you are not being honest, are you, Doctor?'

By this time a young man has brought us tea on a tray. This must be Mehdi. He leaves the tray and withdraws quickly.

'As I said, I might have links.'

'Well, if that's as far as you're willing to go, I won't press you. Drink your tea.'

He is studiously silent for a minute or more. I wonder if I should have been a little more forthcoming. I think of the sinister themes in *1984*. In Orwell's story, the hero, Winston, and his girlfriend, Julia, believe that they have won the friendship of a shopkeeper who sells second-hand bits and pieces from a time before the tyrannical regime of Big Brother. They reveal one thing and another to him, even rent a room from him for their lovemaking. But the shopkeeper is a spy, an informer. Winston and Julia end up in the hands of the Thought Police and endure terrible tortures. Every single word they say to the shopkeeper is recorded. And every sentence of it condemns them.

Sarabi appears to have forgiven my prevarications.

'There were once many Jews in Mashhad, as you probably know, Doctor. Many. Not now. You, a few others. No, no—no more nonsense, if you please! But many of the Jews who lived in Mashhad also died in Mashhad. Murdered, hanged, shot. They did not always live in this city. They came here about three hundred years ago. Why? Because they were being murdered somewhere else and had to find a new home. For many Jews, life is just the time between massacres. The Mashhadi Jews were clever people. Very clever. Good businessmen. They traded in wool, in precious stones. Then one day someone who was not a Jew said to his friends, "Those Jews, why are they taking up space in our sacred city? It is our duty to cut their throats." And so they did. I surely don't need to tell you this. You know the history of your people.'

'You say they were killed, forced to leave. But who murdered them? Who made them leave Mashhad?'

Sarabi smiles. He puts down his tea glass and pats his lips with a handkerchief.

'Perhaps that is enough for today,' he says.

He knows that I hunger to hear more. He knows I will return. Just look at that shrewd gleam in his eye! A voice within me whispers, 'Kushi! Take care!' But my appetite for more information overwhelms my caution.

I return to Sarabi's shop the next day, and the day after. Sarabi is genial, open, engaging. He speaks of his affection for the Jews he once knew, inviting me to acknowledge my own Jewish heritage. It would be cowardly of me to continue insisting that I am not a Jew—that's what I feel. But really, it's not cowardly at all. It's wise. Taking a risk I know I should have the maturity to avoid, I confess that I am Jewish. As a reward, Sarabi produces from a folder a series of pictures of the Jews he once knew. 'They are in America now. They trade on Wall Street. Important people. This is Daniel, this is Shemoil. Do you know what I mean when I say that Daniel and Shemoil are important? Listen, I will tell you. These two help set the world price of gold. That's what I mean by important. They set the price of gold. Every Jewish New Year, I call them and give them my good wishes. Every New Year.'

'New Year?' I say.

I'm trying to find out if Sarabi knows the name given to the Jewish New Year. Why should this be so vital to me? It is a test, of a sort. If he knows the name Jews give to their New Year, then he is to be trusted. This is what I tell myself.

'Rosh Hashanah,' he says, and instantly I wish to embrace him.

Sarabi explains that the pictures were taken by a friend of his, a certain Mr Sayar. I ask if it would be possible to meet this Sayar, and Sarabi gives me an address in central Mashhad.

'He lives by himself, now,' says Sarabi. 'His wife died a little while ago. His sons are married. But if you are honest and open with him, he will help you in your project, I am sure.'

I express my thanks to Sarabi, shake his hand again, speak of my gratitude. The truth is that I am almost delirious with delight. This quest for information about the Mashhadi Jews has completely eclipsed my original mission of finding premises for my surgery. It is as if the sane, painstaking, adult part of me has gone on holiday. I'm behaving as I did when I was a child and gave all my passion to flying pigeons, ignoring everything else. What pigeons were to me then, the story of the Mashhadi Jews is to me now.

I am by nature an obsessive, inclined to follow my heart when something arouses me. Obsessives, for all the transitory joys they experience, seldom find lasting happiness. At various times each day I tell myself to calm down, but I don't calm down, not at all. I should consider the fate of Winston in Orwell's novel. He convinced himself that he deserved some happiness, that it was his due, his right, something he'd earned by so assiduously hiding his secret life of dreams and passions from Big Brother.

But he underestimated his enemy. What he thought was his secret was no such thing. The Thought Police were watching, listening, waiting.

Sayar is an elderly man, retired, white hair and white beard, a face that has seen enough of life to leave deep wrinkles. On this day of my first meeting with him I am deeply excited by the prospect of advancing my project. I introduce myself, trying to keep my enthusiasm in check for the time being. I say to myself, 'Kushi, listen to me, don't go crazy, don't gush, play it cool.'

'Sarabi, in the bazaar, gave you my address?' he says.

'He did indeed. I am a doctor, Mr Sayar, as you can see from my business card. But I am also a writer. Your pictures of the Mashhadi Jews who used to trade in the bazaar fascinated me, and what I am hoping—if you will excuse my presumption—is that you might tell me more about them.'

Too much too fast, Kushi!

'Is that right? Well, I don't know.'

I can see into Sayar's house from where I am standing in the doorway. It is impeccably kept and beautifully decorated with ornaments and objects d'art. Sayar is now wearing a guarded expression. I should have taken the time to slowly win his trust, fool that I am! What is the matter with me? This is a country in which the very word 'Jew' immediately puts people on the defensive—either that, or it produces apoplexy. Slow down! Fortunately I have a copy of one of my books with me. I offer it to Sayar—a translation of a work on Assyrian history—hoping it suggests that I am a serious man, a scholar. He accepts it with thanks, but he still regards me with a degree of suspicion. As he turns the pages of my translation, he asks quietly, 'Tell me, Doctor, are you a Jew, or are you an intelligence agent? We can go no further until I have an honest answer to this question.'

Even after conceding to Sarabi in the bazaar that I am Jewish

I remain reluctant to come out and declare my heritage to Sayar. This wretched reticence, bred into me by a lifetime of secrecy! But I can see that Sayar is completely sincere. He will close his door on me unless I am entirely honest with him.

'I have some background,' I say, still holding onto a portion of my secret.

'You have some background? Some background of what sort? My question is not difficult. Are you a Jew or a spy? You are one or the other, so which is it?'

I pause as I cast about for some alternative to candour. I have barely known this man for five minutes and now I am to reveal everything? And yet, I must.

'I am a Jew. Yes.'

Sayar nods slowly and a smile spreads across his face.

'You are a Jew?'

'Yes.'

He reaches out and takes my hand in both of his. 'That wasn't so hard, was it? You are very welcome in my house, my son. You are very welcome.'

The relationship I develop with Sayar (that's a sort of nickname, meaning traveller, his real name is Sadeq) over the months is one of the great consolations of my life at this time. He is a one-time journalist who has travelled internationally, taking his own photographs to illustrate his many articles. He constantly warns me to be scrupulous in my dealings with the regime.

'They hate Jews, Kushi. I can't tell you how much they hate Jews. Don't give them any chance to take out their hatred on you. They will show you no mercy, no, not even the smallest amount. Believe me. I know how these people think. They have been to my house stealing pictures, accusing me of being a traitor. I know how they think, and it is very, very ugly.'

Sayar's compassion and intelligence restore my faith in Iran. Oh, he is Muslim, but he's not representative of the majority, I know that, and just being made aware that there are some Iranians who are capable of rational thought and rational conversation on race is such a welcome discovery. Islamic fundamentalism is, after all, the political expression of the ignorant. Anyone who loves the world, who loves life, who has genuine intellectual curiosity and who understands the world in all its complexity can never endorse the primitive frenzies and phobias of fundamentalism—and that would be true of fundamentalism of all types—Christian, Muslim, Hindu. The fundamentalist is essentially a man who fears life, and his fear takes the form of assault. He is like some sort of cave-dweller, terrified of the light outside his cave. His message to his fellow cave-dwellers is, 'If anyone attempts to enter our hole in the ground, kill him!' These people would rather live in darkness than risk embracing the world outside in all its complexity and wonder.

The consolation Sayar provides is much needed. My wife is scolding me for neglecting my professional life for the sake of a project in which she has no interest whatsoever, one that she is positively hostile towards, in fact. She is not Jewish but Muslim, and my obsession strikes her as offensive at best and an abomination at worst. Perhaps, deep down, her real objection simply has to do with home and hearth. If I land in trouble for following my passion, she will suffer, my little daughter Newsha will suffer, and poverty and death will engulf them both.

And yet I persist. The power of my compulsion is not really to do with a profound conviction regarding the beliefs of Jews. If I were to sit down with a piece of paper on which were written ten of the most sacred convictions of Judaism, I doubt I would say 'yes' to many of them, in particular those that invoke the supernatural. It doesn't matter, because my yearning is to belong to the community of Jews; both embodying it in my own experience and sharing the history of the Jews, the heritage. I could not become an orthodox Jew upholding a thousand rituals handed down in the sacred texts. But I am Jewish, nonetheless. It is in my soul. A person must belong in the end. You cannot belong only to yourself.

Sayar tells me of a synagogue that once existed in Mashhad. I hadn't known that the Mashhadi Jews built a synagogue. It is said to be in Arg Street, and Sayar encourages me to seek out the old building. Indeed, my search for the synagogue does eventually meet with success. I find the building off Arg Street, stripped of all insignia but still bearing phantom impressions of the past: the ghost of a Star of David, the nail holes of a mezuzah above the door. I knock on the door and speak with a woman in a black chador, asking if this derelict building she now inhabits was once a synagogue. I go through my usual spiel, telling her that I am a doctor who writes in his spare time, I am interested in the history of the Mashhadi Jews, and so on and so on. I only succeed in frightening the wits out of her. She tells me to come back when her husband arrives home in the evening. But when I return, the woman's husband wants no part of my project.

'If you are a doctor,' he says, 'why are you not in your surgery helping people? We don't want you here.'

Without properly realising it, I am leaving a trail all over Mashhad; the trail of a man who asks questions about Jews. How many people have I asked, 'Do you know where the Jews of Mashhad used to live? Do you know of any houses that Jews once occupied? Do you know where I can find the old synagogue?' If the police wished to, they could thrust before me this map of Mashhad and say, 'Here you asked a woman the way to the Jews' house. Here you asked an old man the same question. Here, on this street, you stopped and studied the letters of Hebrew script on a wall. Here you met Sarabi.

Here you met Sayar. Your questions are those of a traitor. Your project is that of a traitor.'

What I believe protects me is something that many other Iranians also relied on for protection in these days, just as ill-advisedly as me. It is 1998. Mohammad Khatami is our president. He is a reformist. He wants to open a dialogue with the West. He is an intelligent man and encourages the Iranian people to enjoy their freedom of speech. Many have taken him at his word. They do not know, and I do not know that Mohammad Khatami is President of the Islamic Republic of Iran in name only. The people with the real power make up the Council of Guardians, and the office of the spiritual head of the republic, Ayatollah Khamenei. It suits the people of real power to permit Khatami to go about encouraging people to enjoy their freedom of speech because those who do speak up for human rights, individual rights and freedom of expression identify themselves publicly and are easy to pick off. Khatami is like a stalking horse sent out in advance of the real army in ancient times to draw the enemy out.

What I know now I did not know then. With Sayar's blessing I put more and more of my energy into this plan to reveal in a book the history of the Mashhadi Jews. I already know that they did not come to Iran from Mesopotamia, as most Iranian Jews did. Some of them came here from Russia. What a book this will be! And what a tribute I can construct for these people who suffered so much but never abandoned their faith, never exhausted their ingenuity. I have so many questions I would love to ask those Jews who fled Mashhad for other places. Did they find safety in their new home? Did they miss Iran? What dangers did they face in their flight from this city? Did they have relatives still living secretly here?

Sayar speaks of a book that will help me in my project. The title of the book is, *A History of Iranian Jews*, written by a certain Dr Kohen Sedq who lived in Iran under the regime of the last shah, Mohammad Reza Pahlavi. Sayar doesn't have a copy of the book himself but he thinks I might find one if I search diligently. Would I be interested to undertake such a search? What a question! Of course, certainly, absolutely, immediately!

'My son,' says Sayar, 'Remember everything I have said. Be extremely cautious and circumspect. Let me tell you something. Are you paying attention?'

'Yes, yes,' I say. 'I am listening.' Sayar can see the fever of desire in my eyes to own this book of which he has spoken.

'What I want to tell you is this. Many Iranians in the past have tried to help Jews who were being persecuted. Not all Iranians accept the horror stories that the regime spreads about them. Those of us who have known Jews, personally, remember them with great affection, as I do. But those of us who have helped our Jewish friends have suffered for it. Look at this.'

Sayar lifts his shirt and turns around so that I can see his back. The flesh is criss-crossed by the scars of a whiplash.

'They tortured me for days,' Sayar says, lowering his shirt again. 'The most horrible experience of my life. They knew that I'd had Jewish friends. They wanted me to confess that I was a Jew myself. The most ignorant and stupid people in the world were demanding that I answer their questions. The humiliation, Kushi!'

After the publication of a number of my books I had made many friends amongst booksellers in Iran. I now rely on them to hunt down this book by Kohen Sedq that I so covet. It is the underground press that will come up with the book; it will not be for sale openly; the regime would have banned it, since it was written by a Jew, just as they have banned or censored almost all books written before the Islamic Revolution.

The book is eventually found, but the price is prohibitive. It is ten thousand *tomans*, which is to say about five hundred dollars. Nevertheless, I agree to the price. The book is actually three books, or three volumes of the one work. I open the packaging in a state of almost manic excitement and caress the blue cover of each volume with a reverence, as though it holds the answers to every question I have asked and not asked. I think that, except for Newsha, this is my most treasured possession. I open the pages of the first volume and let my eyes feast on the table of contents. The record of Jewish settlement in Iran goes back to the days of the Persian Empire, of the Babylonian Captivity. I turn the pages greedily, devouring sentences like a famished man falling on a loaf of bread. But then I think, 'Do this systematically, Kushi!' and almost immediately I turn back to the start and begin to read the story of my people in Persia, making notes as I go. I read of arrivals in the west of Iran, of the building of synagogues, of the destruction of synagogues, of Jews flourishing under an enlightened ruler and of Jews being put to the sword or hanged from ropes under a different one.

It is inevitable that Azita should see me with Kohen Sedq's blue volumes. It is inevitable that she should notice the fevered gleam in my eye as I dash down notes. And it is inevitable that she should lose her temper and demand that I stop pursuing this folly and concentrate on my family.

'Azita, you don't know how important this is, this book I'm writing. What it means to me I can't describe. We are in no danger. Khatami himself has told Iranians to open up, to explore their freedoms. Azita, this is my soul. Do you understand? It is my soul.'

Azita is full of scorn. Talk of 'my soul' always inflames her. She thinks what soul I have should be placed at the service of the family. She wants another child, a companion for Newsha. The idea appals me: how could she not see that there's no future to our marriage?

'Khatami knows nothing!' she says. 'Khatami is nothing. Khatami will get you hanged, fool! I tell you this, if you will listen. If you keep on with this book of yours, I will divorce you. Is that clear enough? You treat me as if I am stupid. Don't deny it—I know you think I am stupid. You are the famous intellectual! I am the poor stupid woman who stays at home and cares for your daughter and cooks your meals and washes your shirts. Well, I have had enough! I will divorce you, I promise you this. And one more thing you need to know. I am pregnant.'

My heart sinks. I think, 'Oh God, no!' I hate myself for not having the sort of feelings that should accompany news of this sort. Feelings of joy, of gratitude, feelings that would make the baby in Azita's womb know that he or she is welcome.

There is, I can see, a contradiction in Azita's two messages to me. The first, a threat, 'I will divorce you' is rendered hollow by the second, 'I am pregnant.' But for the sake of peace, I agree to stop working on the book. In my mind, however, I continue crafting sentences. Maybe I will put the book aside for a week or two or three weeks. I will never abandon it, though. Never.

It is the month of February, 1998. Very cold. The nineteenth anniversary of Khomeini's return to Iran has been celebrated with enormous fanfare in every Iranian city. I am on my way home from the office of a publisher. I'm wearing my thick woollen jacket to ward off the bitter wind from the north. My head is full of my project, notwithstanding my promise to Azita. It is what I live for. I'm imagining the way the chapters will unfold, I'm thinking even at this point of how beautiful the book can be made to appear. This might be the most important book of my professional life. It might be the book that I will look back on many years from now and say, 'Kushi, you were right to be stubborn, you were right to keep that book in your heart, you were right to honour the Jews of Iran in that way.' Overhead, the last few yellow leaves of a plane tree are torn from a bough by the fierce wind and carried away.

I turn into the lane that runs down to the back gate of my house, my hands thrust into the pockets of my coat and my head bent low against the wind. A car passes me, not at any great speed, a black Peugeot with four men inside. It's odd that the car should turn down such a narrow street. And isn't it true that the state security service uses black Peugeots of this sort? A little shudder, not caused by the cold wind, runs up my spine and a slightly sick feeling settles in my stomach. I slacken my pace, suddenly wary. The car stops a little way ahead of me, the passenger doors open on each side of the car and two powerfully built men step out. They are young men in identical grey suits and white, open-necked shirts. By this time I have stopped walking altogether, but now I take a few slow, hesitant steps towards my back gate, no more than a hundred metres further down the narrow street.

The two young men walk towards me, without any great haste. The focus of their eyes is directly on me. Their expression is not entirely impassive; some hostility towards me is detectable. This is it. This is what Sayar feared would befall me. This is what a thousand Iranians a week experience: sudden arrest, interrogation, torture, maybe death.

As the two men reach me, I stop still. They stop in front of me.

'Mr Kooshyar Karimi?' one of them asks, not too loudly but with authority.

'Yes. Is there some problem?'

'Come with us.'

I resist, but not too forcefully. I ask again, pointlessly, 'Is there a problem?' One of the men says in a metronomic way, 'Intelligence. We have a few questions. You'll come with us.'

My arm is held and I am marched towards the black car. One walks ahead and opens the rear passenger door. The two men in the front don't bother to turn and look at me, although the one driving glances into the rear vision mirror.

'Get in,' says the man with a grip on my arm.

'Some mistake has been made,' I say. 'I haven't done anything. Some mistake.'

I am utterly terrified. My throat closes up. I can't breathe. I think of the illegal operation I performed on Zahra. That alone could get me shot in the back of the head. I think of my confession of being a Jew, to Sarabi and Sayar. Being a Jew is not a capital offence in Iran, so far as the constitution goes, but in reality it means that the security people can do anything with me that they wish. Anything. I already feel that I will tell my interrogator everything. I don't need to be warned. It is different for each person, the thing he or she fears most. I don't know what I dread most. So many things. Seated between the two young men in the back seat, my heart racing, I sense that I am about to find out more about pain than I ever wished to know.

RITES OF PASSAGE

In Iran each year, as in many other countries, students completing secondary school sit for exams that will determine their academic future. University admission will depend on one's results. It's a rite-of-passage experience, an ordeal that you must survive if you want to play your part in the affairs of the tribe—in this case, the whole vast tribe of adult Iranians. And I do want to play a part in the affairs of that tribe. I want to play a part that rewards me financially, maybe permits me to travel beyond the borders of Iran, or at least permits me to establish a nice, comfortable nest for my mother to occupy and where she can preen her feathers all day long and croon, 'Kushi, oh Kushi, you are a good boy, you are a treasure. I need only you, Kushi. I don't need any other companions, you are my darling.' Something as sentimental as that.

I want to get into medicine. I am also a writer, even at the age of eighteen, and it is the writing that will sustain me intellectually, the writing that will become more and more the great source of my delight in living. So...lots of money, a contented mother, a book each year, a contented Kushi. That's the plan.

But there is an obstacle in my path. Who is more likely to become a doctor or a lawyer? The student whose father is himself a doctor or a lawyer with his own handsome bank balance, or the student whose father sells watermelons in the market-place, or works in a panel shop taking dents out of automobile fenders, drives a taxi for fifteen hours a day in Isfahan, cooks take-away *kofta nakhod* and *bouranee*[10] for a few cents a serve in a grubby little restaurant in Tabriz, or runs a bus back and forth between Mashhad and Tehran? It's not that the rich father simply buys his son a career in medicine or law (although that can happen, now and again), it's that the rich father can afford to send his son to one of the best secondary schools and can afford private tuition on top of that.

My secondary school is a school for paupers and misfits. Mirza Koochek is the school of last resort for the ragged people of Mashhad. You are sent here when no other school will accept you because of your unruly behaviour, or your laziness, or indeed your stupidity. Or you are sent to Mirza Koochek because you have hardly a penny to your name, which is why I am enrolled there.

I'll add a little more about the sort of school Mirza Koochek is. High schools are ruled by a principal, in most cases. The principal keeps an eye on everything, tries to make sure that the school's reputation is safeguarded, listens to problems the teachers might be experiencing, maybe even takes the time to encourage the boys directly, one-to-one, or if not one-to-one, can be counted on to get you all together and give you one of those big rousing speeches about school spirit and playing the game and striving at all times to do your best. Well, we have a principal who's a bit like that, but he's not the boss. No, the boss of our school is a twenty-two-year-old bully by the name of Asad. He's in Year 12, he's big, and he is, as I say, a certifiable moron. He's taken two or three years to complete most of the year levels and this explains why at the age of twenty-two he's

10. Kofta nakhod: meat balls; Bouranee: vegetable dish.

still in Year 12—he'll probably be a grandfather by the time he graduates from Mirza Koochek—unless he's recruited by the intelligence services while he's still at school. He's the perfect type to operate a torture chamber.

Asad makes all the teachers nervous. There's his size, as I said, but on top of that he's fearless. If a teacher disciplines him, he makes that teacher pay. So the teachers try to leave him alone even at the cost of their own humiliation. One day in class, he is demonstrating what an impressive guy he is by reading a pornographic magazine inside the textbook we are supposed to be studying. He makes sure all of us sitting nearby can see what he is doing, lifting his book with the magazine open inside so that we can share the scenes of threesomes and foursomes going at it. Every time the teacher tells us to turn the page, Asad turns the page of his magazine, grinning like a lunatic. The teacher knows what he is doing but tries to ignore him.

Then all at once, an explosion. Asad had earlier dropped a distilled water capsule into the old oil heater at the back of the classroom and now his jest comes to fruition when the increasing pressure inside the capsule causes it to go off like a hand grenade. Oh, hilarious! This the teacher can't ignore, and he knows exactly who is responsible. In a fit of temper he grabs Asad by the collar of his jacket and hauls him out of the classroom, probably realising even as he ejects him that he would pretty soon regret it. And he does regret it, within minutes, because Asad begins bombarding the roof of the classroom with snowballs—it is winter—and each snowball lands with an echoing crash. Then he begins jumping up and down outside the window so that his grinning, idiotic face appears with each leap. Finally, he holds the magazine up at the window so that all of us can see the pictures. Whatever we think of Asad—and mostly, we loathe him—we can't help giggling and snorting, making it impossible for the teacher to continue. He strides outside and tells Asad to come back in.

So that's Mirza Koochek. Amongst the people of Mashhad, this school is referred to as The Jungle. The troublemakers, the 'no hopers', the boys who get expelled from every other school, they all come here as the last stop. But, it has one thing going for it, and it's this: if you can survive six years here, you can survive anything.

We are both good students, Koorosh and I. If I may be permitted to boast a little, I am the best student Mirza Koochek has ever known. But to pass the end-of-year exams requires the specialist tuition I spoke of, coaching of a sort specifically targeted to the type of questions in the exam. One-to-one tuition is out of the question for me—far, far too expensive—but there is a less expensive alternative: after-hour group tuition. I ask my mother to enrol me, but she is reluctant. The expense of group tuition is still far beyond what we can afford, she says. I encourage her to think of the future.

'*Madar jan*, this is an investment. Look at my marks. All I need is some coaching and within a few years you will be living in splendour!'

She finds excuses. She dawdles. She hums and hahs. She doesn't want to spend the money. She thinks I'm clever enough to win my way into university without the group tuition.

I remind her of another reason to get me out of circulation for a few years, that is to say, to get me out of the huge pool of young Iranian men without a penny in their pockets—the war. All Iranian males of seventeen years and above are compelled to register for military service, with the exception of those enrolled in the nation's universities. Everyone knows what 'military service' means. It means death or disfigurement. In every town and city in Iran, even in the tiny remote villages of the

Dasht-e Kavir Desert or settlements of three or four houses in the Zagros Mountains—everywhere!—you will come across families who send their sons off to war with prayers and kisses, and receive them back in plain wooden boxes, maybe only a few weeks after departure. Or families who send off a son with the normal complement of arms and legs, and receive him back missing one limb, or two, or more; or missing one or both eyes, missing their faces, missing lungs lost to phosgene gas. The dead are hailed as 'martyrs', the maimed are provided with a miniscule pension and maybe a wheelchair. It's hard getting about in a wheelchair along the goat tracks of the Zagros.

But why should I have to remind my mother of the war? It's advertised everywhere. Huge, gaudy wall paintings and posters depicting Saddam armed with American bombs casting covetous eyes on Tehran, other posters encouraging us to sing the praises of the nation's 'martyrs', Islam's martyrs, Khomeini's martyrs. Amongst the rural poor, the war is still considered a holy crusade against the wickedness of the Saddam/Uncle Sam creature depicted in the posters and paintings; but elsewhere, particularly amongst the middle class, people think of the war with misgivings. Propaganda can only hold you in thrall for so long. 'You go off to the front upright and come back horizontal,' is the bleak saying going around.

At last the hideous prospect of seeing me in uniform persuades my mother to take me along to the group-tuition classes. These classes are conducted in one of the more affluent suburbs of Mashhad, just the opposite of the suburb in which I live. My mother and I travel across town in two buses then find ourselves wandering about in search of the address in a part of the city as remote from our experience as the Rue de Madeleine or the heart of Venice. We locate the building in time, only to be turned down by an old man at a desk in the antechamber.

'Too late,' he says, not unkindly. 'Where have you been, son?

Classes started five months ago.'

I shoot an accusing look at my mother. She tries to make up for her tardiness in getting me here by suggesting to the old man that I start the tutorials immediately, paying half of the full fee.

'Ah, but you see,' he says, 'the classes are over. They're just doing quizzes now.'

I jump in right there. I'm desperate. Well, I've been desperate all my life but now I'm particularly desperate. 'Sir,' I say, 'I must go to university. It's very important. Very, very important.'

'What can I do?' He shrugs and holds his hands out palms upwards in the universal, 'Such a pity!' gesture.

'But look at this, please, sir. Just look for ten seconds!'

'At what?'

'At this!'

I'm displaying a copy of my Year 12 results, my marks in all their shimmering glory. The old man pushes his spectacles down his nose and reads over the top of them.

'Hmm!' he says, and, 'Well, what can I say?' and then finally, 'I'll tell you what I can do. I can let you into the Maths quiz and if the teacher thinks you're worth it, you can do all the quizzes free of charge. How about that?'

'Oh, yes, sir! Thank you, sir! I am so grateful to you, sir!'

These tuition schools trade on their success in getting students into the elite faculties of universities, such as the medical schools. The old fellow knows that I won't last ten minutes unless I can demonstrate some sort of brilliance. But he's at least willing to give me the chance. He didn't have to.

The Maths class starts after recess. My mother has gone home, experiencing the deep satisfaction of having got something for nothing. I'm intensely self-conscious sitting amongst these well-to-do boys in their expensive tailoring. Maybe thirty, in all. I slink to the very back of the room and take a vacant seat beside a boy who glances at me as if I were the school cleaner.

He's courteous, however, and instead of asking me if I might be more comfortable outside sweeping the corridor, he offers his hand and we exchange names. He's Majid, and he wants to know what high school I attended. I murmur the name of my infamous school and Majid says, 'What?'

'Mirza Koochek,' I repeat, and Majid raises his eyebrows as if I'd just confessed that I was raised in a brothel.

'Mirza Koochek?' he says. 'Is that a fact? And what does your father do?'

This question is always asked in Iran to establish the particular prejudice that will guide the questioner's opinion of you from that day forward. You *are* your father's occupation. My intensive and lifelong training in evasion—set to become an essential tool of survival within a few years—allows me to defer answering the question just for the moment by asking Majid what *his* father does for a living.

'My father is a doctor,' says Majid, very pleased to have been asked.

I turn to the boy on my left and ask him what his father does for a living. This boy, Yahya, answers promptly that his father is also a doctor. And he goes further, informing me that his father knows Majid's father and that he and Majid are best friends. Well and good. I'm left with the awful prospect of telling the plain truth—'My father is a bus driver, but I don't see him at all these days because I told him to go away so that my mother could continue her disgusting relationship with a grotesque individual by the name of Haji Heydar'—or I can tell a brazen lie. After consulting my conscience, I decide in favour of the brazen lie.

'You know what?' I say, striking a cheerful note. 'My father is a doctor too.'

Yahya and Majid study me sceptically. I'm preparing myself for an interrogation—'In what branch of medicine does your father specialise?' 'At what hospital does your father work?' 'Does your father have a private practice?' 'If your father is a doctor, how come you attend the worst high school in Mashhad?'—but at this moment the teacher enters the classroom, informs us that his name is Mr Moqadas (this is for my benefit—everybody else in the classroom knows that this is Mr Moqadas, a man with a reputation as the best algebra teacher in Mashhad) and immediately sets a difficult algebraic problem. I have the answer within seconds and shoot up my hand, but Moqadas signals to me to wait—he doesn't know my name. Two minutes later, another student puts up his hand. Moqadas says, 'Yes, what's the answer?' The boy gives his solution, and it's wrong. A second student attempts the answer, and he's wrong, too. Moqadas reluctantly points to me and asks me for my solution. I respond with the right answer. Moqadas frowns and puts one hand to his chin.

'You came up with the solution in twenty seconds?'

'Yes, sir. Twenty seconds, sir.'

'Okay, now tell us how you did it.'

I explain my process rapidly, knowing perfectly well that the only person in the room who can follow me is Moqadas. I'm not showing off—well, maybe a bit—but rather fighting with all my wits for the future that will save my own children from ever having to lie about what *I* do for a living. Moqadas is impressed.

'What's your name?'

'Kooshyar Karimi, sir.'

'From which high school, Karimi?'

'Sir, from Mirza Koochek.'

'From Mirza Koochek?'

'Yes, sir. Mirza Koochek, sir.'

'Astonishing!'

At recess, Moqadas tells the man on the registration desk to enrol me. 'The boy's a genius,' he says. And he adds, 'Mirza Koochek! Extraordinary!'

I travel to my tuition quizzes each day after school. By this time, my ramshackle bicycle has been replaced by a ramshackle motorcycle. Just as my bicycle needed to be repaired every day to keep it on the road, so my motorcycle needs daily First Aid, and sometimes surgery. Owning a motorcycle such as my wreck of a machine is a spur to fantasies of wealth. Your hands are covered in grease and blood because the spanner you are using to remove a nut is not the right tool and it slips and you whack your knuckles, you're constantly employing bits of wire to hold your machine together, you have to teach yourself to ride the wreck in a certain way because the brake pads are worn down to the rivets. And you dream, between your curses, of walking into a showroom and buying a new car—not even a new motorcycle, but a proper car, one you will never do a day's work on, one you will hire a mechanic to fix, if fixing becomes necessary. That is the pauper's dream—not of palaces and banquets but of a car that can always be relied upon to get you from A to B. Or of a pair of shoes without holes in them. Or of a shirt that you don't have to wear in such a way that the frayed hem is concealed.

I have to hide my motorcycle from my new friend, Majid. My father is supposed to be a doctor—what would I be doing riding such a clapped-out machine as mine? Always with Majid I'm playing a part, concealing my origins, pretending that I go to the movies regularly, that I buy records, that I am never hungry, that my father takes me and my brother and mother for holidays to the Caspian seaside in summer and to the Alborz in winter for skiing. It's all training for my future life as a spy, and just as I am a brilliant student of Maths and Physics and Persian literature, I'm also a brilliant student at pretending to be someone I am not.

Today I've been invited to visit Majid's family, and I accept the invitation as I must (what reason could I give for declining?) but I leave my motorcycle around the corner from Majid's house in his salubrious Mashhad suburb. Majid greets me, introduces me to his mother and sisters, and to his father, the doctor. He's a pleasant man, almost bald, clean-shaven, maybe forty. He is one of those men who enjoys complete authority within the household, respected by all the members of his family. But he wears his authority lightly, no growling, no shouting. This is what it is to have a father you have loved and admired all your life. This is what it is to be Majid.

Dr Vahedi greets me courteously. 'My boy has told me so much about you, Kooshyar. So much. He says you are the best student in the class. So maybe you can help Majid with his Maths and Physics, hmm?'

'Of course, sir. We are friends.'

'And you father is a doctor, Majid tells me?'

'Yes, sir. A doctor.'

'In which branch of medicine, Kooshyar, if I may enquire?'

'He is in General Practice, sir.'

'Is he, then. In General Practice. And where does he practice?'

'In Zed, sir.'

'Is that so? I used to practice in Zed many years ago. What's his name? Perhaps I have met him.'

'Oh, I don't think so, sir. His name is Dr Karimi.'

'No, I can't say I've heard of him. Still, I haven't heard of every doctor in Mashhad, so that's no mystery. Kooshyar, you are welcome in my house. Very welcome indeed.'

This conversation, and Dr Vahedi's good-natured acceptance of me in his household, leaves me with a squalid feeling. I hate deceiving him. I have pointed out again and again in these pages that many events in my life prepared me for the years I spent spying, but one thing I haven't made clear is that I am not a pathological liar. I do not enjoy it, nor do I relish some sick feeling of power it might be thought to impart. I know what a lie is, I know when I'm lying, and I hate it. Like most other people who try to get away with a lie, I desperately want it to be accepted and never spoken of again. I don't want to be forced to embellish the lie, to reinforce it, to repeat it. When I tell Majid that my father is a doctor I think that he may accept it, maybe with a few doubts, then leave it be. And so now, as we head upstairs to Majid's room, I give him a censorial punch on the arm and say, 'Majid, why do you do this to me? Why did you tell your father that my father is a doctor?'

Majid faces me with a puzzled look. 'What are you talking about?' he says.

'You told your father that my father is a doctor!'

'Of course. Why shouldn't I? He is a doctor, isn't he?'

'No!'

Majid is looking back at me as if it were an equation he was suddenly required to solve, but an equation that leaves him baffled.

'What do you mean?' he says.

'Majid, my father is not a doctor. My father is a bus driver. He hasn't even been around for the past four years.'

Now Majid's expression deepens from bafflement to disappointment.

'Then you lied to me?'

'Yes, I lied to you. Or it wasn't really a lie. I didn't expect you to take me all that seriously. Don't you see? Yahya said his father was a doctor, you said yours was a doctor, so I just said, "Okay, my father's a doctor, too." It was...sort of...a joke.'

'It wasn't a joke. It was a lie. Did you see me laughing? Did I look as if I'd just heard a joke?'

'I'd better go,' I say. I pick up my bag and make my way downstairs, the tears in my ears blurring my vision. I'm out the door and almost on the street when Majid calls my name. He's come hurrying after me.

'Kushi, I'm sorry. Don't worry about it.'

In my humiliation all I want is to be somewhere far away, somewhere by myself. I keep walking.

'Kushi!'

I turn, reluctantly. Majid catches me up.

'Don't worry about it,' he says. 'Alright? We're friends, yes? And you know the crazy thing? My father really likes people like you. He comes from a poor family. He likes people who try to make something of themselves. He's not a snob.' And, he adds, 'I'm not a snob, either. Alright?'

So I stay, and Majid and I become closer than we were before the revelation of my impoverished background. I take on the role of Majid's tutor, unpaid. And he needs my help because he's not brilliant, and he's lazy. Well, when I say lazy I'm being a little too harsh. He's laid-back is what I should say. His father is a renowned surgeon with excellent connections so Majid has never had to struggle. For me, it's different. If I live to be a hundred years old I will never forget the sheer wretchedness of growing up poor. I will never take comfort and security for granted. But for Majid, life is a stroll in the park.

When we're not studying together at his place, we chat about the future, and Majid's vision of the future is as full of rose petals and sweets as the present. He says he wants to marry a beautiful girl and raise a number of beautiful children. (Might be a problem there, because Majid is dead ugly with a huge bugle of a nose. I hate to say it, but it's true. But if I hate to say it, why am I, in fact, saying it? Forget I mentioned it.) When Majid asks me what I think my future wife is doing at this moment, I say:

'Oh, I don't know. Living it up with some tough guy in Zed.' And we laugh.

By the looks of it, I'm going to go to medical school to become a doctor. But the truth is, I'm not attracted to medicine. I've only adopted medicine as a career because my mother wants me to become a doctor, and for the sake of the income. I've fought the battle to go my own way, and I've lost.

'So you want to be a writer—something like that?' My mother says. 'In other words, an absolute fool. You think you're going to find a girl to marry you? You think some nice girl is going to say, "Oh yes, I always wanted to marry a loser and live on bread and rice?" Is that what you think?'

I try to explain to my mother that I'm temperamentally attracted to art and culture, to literature, to philosophy, and not at all to medicine. My passions are roused when I read Dostoyevsky, Tolstoy, Chekhov, Nietzsche and Sartre, or Rumi, Shams, and Nima, not when I read a medical textbook. With medicine, I think 'Yes I can do this', but there's no thrill, no quickening, no tumult in the blood. And my mother responds in that way people always respond when there is not a syllable you can say that will make the slightest difference to their prejudice. You know the expression, falsely patient, frankly bored, and accompanied by the unspoken comment, 'Tell me when you're finished.' My bargain with myself is to practise medicine and please my mother while I live a private life, maybe even a secret life, devoted to literature and philosophy. This will be my second secret life, living side-by-side with my life as a secret Jew. You see what's becoming of me? I'm turning into a creature of compartments. And soon there'll be a third secret compartment, for my life as a spy.

19

THE GENIUS

I sit the exams with fluctuating confidence. Maths and Physics—fine. English—not so good. Amongst the other subjects, some are a breeze, some a bit awkward for me. Koorosh, who has attended a different secondary school from mine, one that caters more for the study of science subjects, remains entirely calm as the day approaches for the publication of results. He's rejected my mother's demand that he apply for medical school and is hoping only for a good enough grade to enter a science course at a polytechnic. I need a stratospheric result to get into medical school—in the top two percent of students nationwide—which is to say within the first ten thousand out of three hundred thousand students—otherwise, forget it.

When the results are published I'm astonished to find my name in the top one percent. My aggregate mark gives me a university entrance score of 99.9 percent, practically a guarantee of a seat in medical school. The relief is like being transported to paradise and bathed in warm honey. I think, 'I've arrived,' as if my whole life with all of its trials and ordeals has undergone a radical conversion to comfort and security—and yes, as if the God of the Jews, Adonai, has lifted me out of squalor and whispered in my ear, 'Kushi Karimi, you are my favourite person on earth, so pleasing to my sight...'

My mother is ecstatic. She makes excuses to wander about the neighbourhood so that her opportunities to run into people and brag about my results are multiplied. 'Oh, he studied so hard, yes he did, day and night he studied. I was worried that he would wear out his eyesight with such studying. Oh, but now his dedication has been rewarded, ninety-nine point nine percent, the highest result in the whole of our city, and of half a million students he is ranked eighty-seven. Can you imagine? Eighty-seven in the whole of Iran! He is a genius, of course. I knew from the instant of his birth that he would become a genius. All my sacrifices have been repaid. Ya Allah! I cannot tell you how much I sacrificed for that boy!' I'm happy to let her carry on in this way, although I pretend I'm embarrassed.

'Please, *Madar jan*, don't boast so much. There's nothing special about my results.'

And it is important that I let her soak up the sunshine while she can, because I am about to tell her that I intend to make Tehran my first preference for medical school.

'*Madar jan*, it won't be Mashhad. Koorosh is going to Sharif University in Tehran, and I'm going to Tehran Medical University. Alright?'

I'd anticipated histrionics but not quite on the scale that unfolds.

'Oh such a nightmare I had! Such misery came to me! I thought you told me that you were going to leave me to my loneliness and sadness and go to Tehran!'

'It wasn't a nightmare, *Madar jan*. I *am* going to Tehran!'

'Aiee! There it is again! Aiee! No, he would never do this. Kushi would never do such a thing! Tell me this is just a nightmare, God! Oh, strike me dead, now! How can I live if this is true? Both my sons ten thousand kilometres away! It might as well be a million! Aiee, kill me now! Spare me the pain! Put a knife to my throat, Kushi! Don't make me suffer every day you are away!'

'*Madar jan*, calm down for God's sake! I have to go to Tehran. Tehran is the best university. Don't you want me to have the best?'

But I know it's futile. My mother can't turn off the melodrama once it starts. She has no shame. She knows if she keeps wailing I'll succumb. And she does keep wailing, and yes, I do give in.

'I'll go to Mashhad university, then. Whatever you like.'

Now there is a special, burning pain in my stomach when my mother goes about telling people of her 'sacrifices'. I say to myself, 'Kushi, have you learnt nothing? Did you really believe she would let you go to Tehran? Did you think that for once in her life she would let you do what you truly want to do? Wake up, idiot!'

I am about to do something that I know I will regret—something that will spoil my day and leave me feeling sick-at-heart. I am about to phone my father in Tehran and tell him of my exam results—not just me, Koorosh and I together. What is the matter with me? Why can't I accept what stares me in the face? First I convince myself that my mother will behave in a way that she has never before behaved in her life and permit me to study something other than medicine. Now I convince myself that my father will be proud of me, proud of my results, that he will say, 'Kushi, my dear son, what joy you have brought me! I bless you with all of my heart!' So I'm on the phone. Koorosh has already spoken to him and told him that he will be coming to Tehran to study. Now it is my turn.

I say, '*Baba jan*, guess what?'

'I don't know. You tell me,' he replies.

'I got a result of ninety-nine point nine in my exams!'

'Really? What does that mean?'

'It means I can go to university and study whatever I like. Medicine, it will be. I can study medicine and become a doctor.'

'Well, that's good.'

Is he even interested? He doesn't sound it. He sounds as if he'd rather be somewhere else, or asleep.

'*Baba jan*, I'm the only one from Mirza Koochek with a place at university.'

'Good. Good to hear.'

And that's it. Hanging up the phone, I promise myself that I will never again look to my father for any sort of support whatsoever. Why do I bang my head again and again on this brick wall of my father's indifference?

No more. Never again. I swear.

My application to enrol at the Medical University in Mashhad is now undergoing the scrutiny of people in the Ministry of Intelligence. Every application for university enrolment has to face this scrutiny. If you ever wondered what a society that makes no distinction between the priorities of Church and State, or Mosque and State might look like, Iran gives you that opportunity. In Iran, Islam *is* the State. To attend university, you must demonstrate that you have been a pious Muslim, which is to say that you have exhibited the sort of behaviour that the Council of Guardians has established as the standard of piety. You must show an established habit of prayer, for example, three times a day is the regulation for those of the Shi'a branch of Islam. If you only pray twice a day, you would have to explain the discrepancy. And you must proclaim that all the tenets of the Shi'a faith suit you just fine. In other words, your faith can take the form of objective subscription. If you follow the rules and regulations of the faith, you are, by definition, a pious Muslim.

In *Notes Towards the Definition of Culture*, T.S. Eliot argues that in a community of shared faith, the great majority of citizens need only exhibit their belief through their behaviour. He is talking about a Christian society, of course, but the point I'm making holds true for a Muslim society as well. He is suggesting that most people will get along fine by doing what they are told to do, and if they are told that a good Christian expresses his faith in a certain way, that is all they need to know. Eliot's suggestion is at the opposite pole to Kierkegaard's argument on the subjective nature of faith. For Kierkegaard, faith can never be truthfully expressed by following a blueprint. A Christian is a Christian when he *is* a Christian, not when he acts like a Christian.

This is at the furthest possible extreme from the dogma of the Iranian mullahs. But we go even further in Iran, for piety also means obedience to the state in every particular. There are no laws established outside the scrutiny of the mullahs. Nothing is secular. If you were to complain that you are not paid enough in your job, that would make you impious. If you were to say that Iran is a backward country, that would be impious. If you were a woman and you expressed a wish to study law and become a judge—a subject that only male Iranians are permitted to study—that would be impious. In Iran, piety is obedience and obedience is piety: faith-based totalitarianism.

But the state does not know every little thing about every single citizen, as much as it may wish to. The state does not know everything about me, for example. It doesn't know that I am a Jew in my heart, it doesn't know that I don't pray three times a day to Allah, nor twice a day, nor even once a day. It doesn't know that I consider the Supreme Leader, Khamenei, an evil old man with the intelligence of a house-brick. It doesn't know that I despise Haji Heydar, the sort of Muslim that the regime adores. The regime, embodied in those scrutinising my application for enrolment, doesn't know a single thing about me. Or so I think at the time.

When the acceptance notices for university enrolments are printed, my friends and I join thousands of other students feverishly scanning the lists of numbers. We're like flocks of pigeons descending on scattered birdseed. Chatter and groans and shrieks of joy fill the air. Majid is on the list (although his mediocre examination result does not get him into medical school, his first choice) and Yahya is there, Koorosh is there. But I'm not there. I enter that state of profound denial that overtakes you when a fact, that every atom of your being rejects, persists in staring you in the face. How can someone like Majid, whose result left him a hundred-thousand places behind me, read that he has been accepted into a polytechnic while I do not even exist on the lists? I read through the numbers again, and a third time, and a fourth time. My friends gather around and make sounds of astonishment and sympathy. Finally, accepting that destiny has once again made an utter fool of me, I find an alcove on the street where I can be alone and hang my head in despair. Why? Why? I say to myself 'If I don't get into university I will kill myself.' Then I say 'If I don't get into university, I'll go to Israel.' I say 'Enough is enough.' And I say, yet again 'Why? Why?'

The person who attempts to find out *why* is Majid's father, Dr Vahedi. He is appalled at my failure to win a place at university. He has a lot of influence, and many connections, but it is doubtful than even he can fix things for me. With Dr Vahedi's encouragement I lodge an appeal with the authorities, knowing that such appeals rarely produce much of a result and are usually ignored altogether. The scrutiny of university applications is conducted under the auspices of the Revolutionary Court, and the Revolutionary Court is a law unto itself. In the days of waiting, I walk about in a daze, returning again and again to my promise to kill myself, and then to my other promise, contradicting the first one, then I change back to killing myself, then change again—to escaping to Israel.

My appeal does elicit a response, surprisingly. The ruling from the Revolutionary Court is this: I have been denied a place at university because I'm a poor excuse for a Muslim. That is what the letter says, in its own hackneyed phrases. I am not a good Muslim. The Revolutionary Court knows what a good Muslim is, and I am not one. But what about my brother? He's no better at being a Muslim than I am, and yet he was accepted into his polytechnic in Tehran. Why me, especially? Dr Vahedi says that medicine is regarded as one of the elite disciplines, and for this reason the scrutiny of the Revolutionary Court is particularly severe. My brother's computer studies are not considered all that vital.

Dr Vahedi vows to persist in having the rejection of my application overturned. I remain dazed and depressed. I am likely to be forced into military service, likely to be transported to the war front, likely to be killed within days. My fantasies of self-annihilation and escape to Israel afford me little relief. I know I won't kill myself. And I know that I will never see Israel. I will put on the uniform provided for me and march into the swamps on the Abadan front and die within minutes. My body will be returned to my mother, a Muslim burial will be arranged, perhaps my coffin will be carried through the streets of my slum, people will cry out, 'Poor Kushi! Poor young man! He gave his life for the Revolution! He died a martyr!' How blackly ironical—I am denied a place at university because I am not a good Muslim, yet I will be buried as an Islamic martyr.

I have no more hope. But Dr Vahedi has. He's a very stubborn man with an enduring sense of justice. He will not put up with it. He will not have a brilliant student like me denied a place at medical school because some fanatic in the Revolutionary

Court, who probably can't add up two and two, thinks that I am not a good Muslim.

'Don't worry,' he tells me. 'I'll get this sorted out. What, one of the best students in the whole country refused a chance to become a doctor because of some bureaucrat? Never!'

He persists. He pulls strings. He swears he'll have this rejection overturned. I sit at home, my mood swinging between bitterness and despair. I talk to no one.

Then a month or so after the letter arrives explaining that I am a sub-standard Muslim and unworthy of a place at the prestigious Mashhad Medical University, Dr Vahedi calls on the telephone and tells my mother that I am to come to his place immediately. Not just me—my mother too.

'Sir, it is late. We will come tomorrow,' she says.

'Come now,' Dr Vahedi insists.

When we arrive, he is waiting for us in his study with Majid. He asks us to sit and offers us tea. Offering tea to visitors is such an ingrained custom in Iran that you would probably still be asked if you would like tea even if your host had invited you to his house to cut your throat. Majid is gazing at me in a puzzled way. When Dr Vahedi is ready, he leans forward in his chair and rests his forearms on his thighs.

'Two revolutionary guards came to visit me today. They came to my surgery. As you know, I sent a letter to the head of the investigation bureau. He is a friend of a friend. In my letter I requested an explanation for the university refusing to find a place for you. My letter was very polite. But it was firm. I didn't want them to fob me off with the usual excuses. So these two visitors, these revolutionary guards, they asked me what I knew about you, Kushi. And I said, "What do I know about him? I know that he is one of the best students I have ever met. I know that he is an honest boy, and very hard working. I know that he will make a brilliant doctor." They listened to me, and then one of them said, "Do you know he is a Jew?"'

Silence.

I had, of course, never mentioned anything about my Jewish heritage to Majid nor to his father. Not a word. And I have nothing to say now. Keeping quiet about my Jewish heritage must seem like a betrayal to Majid and his father, but I had no intention of deceiving them. I never tell anyone that I am a Jew. It's an ingrained habit of many years' standing. My mother is on the verge of saying something, and I know exactly what she is going to say. She is going to deny that we have ever been Jews. That would be a mistake. Dr Vahedi would know in an instant that it is a lie and he may come to the conclusion—the perfectly correct conclusion—that my mother is prepared to lie at the drop of a hat if she sees any advantage in it.

'They said that you had changed your religion,' Dr Vahedi continues, forestalling my mother's ill-advised deceit. 'I felt they wanted me to say that you are now a true Muslim. And that is exactly what I said. I told them more than that. I said that I will take personal responsibility for you. And so I will. You are free to take up your studies, Kushi.'

Do I have any right to make such an issue of my mother's predilection for lying considering that I am now about to tell a flagrant untruth myself?

'Dr Vahedi, I thank you with all my heart,' I say. 'I will not let you down. I am a true Muslim now.'

'Good,' Dr Vahedi says. 'Remember this, Kushi. If they see any reason to doubt that you have adopted our faith, they will throw you out. Believe me, they are looking for an opportunity. Don't give it to them.'

Perhaps when I promised Dr Vahedi that I would be a good Muslim I wasn't actually lying. Maybe I believed that I would take his advice and stick to the rules. If I did in fact believe that I'd behave myself, it would have only been for about

227

two minutes. Because when I get to university a month later, I couldn't care less about pleasing the authorities. The very idea disgusts me. You have to understand how completely religious fanaticism has corrupted the student body of a university like Mashhad's. Students are encouraged to inform on other students who show the slightest deviation from the prescribed behaviour of a 'patriot'. You see a girl wearing lipstick—or even just the traces of lipstick that she has rubbed off before appearing in public—and you go running to the university authorities to tell them all about it. Some fellow shrugs when the Spiritual Leader of the Republic is mentioned—off you run to dob him in. Somebody with a little less sleep than he needs yawns during Friday prayers—*Namaz Joma*—and you scamper away like the good little stooge you are and bleat to the bosses. Iran in 1988 is George Orwell's *1984*. Faith is obedience.

And these people are serious about it. The students have a 'Discipline Committee' charged with investigating lapses in religious observance. The Discipline Committee can have you arrested, removed from the campus, lashed. I take very few precautions, but why is that? I am not especially brave. I am certainly not about to lay down my life in the name of freedom. So why don't I keep my head down and stay out of trouble? Why do I take the risks I do? Arrogance, maybe? Pride? Or it might just be the conviction that I earned my place at university through hard work and high marks and deserve to be here. Why should I bow down to a bunch of zealots?

The peculiar thing is that even under a totalitarian regime where half the people you meet are perfectly capable of informing on you to the police, people still give cheek. Because that's what I'm doing—I'm giving cheek, like a naughty boy bored by the oppressive supervision of his parents. I should know better, but I can't help myself. It's an expression of individuality in a society that despises individuality. If I had to endure being lashed like the man I saw being lashed when I was a child, I would swear to heaven that I would never misbehave again. From what I have seen and from what I have been told, a single lash produces such overwhelming pain that only a madman or a martyr would court such punishment. And yet that's what I'm courting, that's what awaits me if I continue in the way I'm going. I don't know where it came from—my mother, my father—but I just can't adopt the sort of complacent manner that would make me safe and secure. I go about looking for trouble.

Here's an example. I get tired of the clapped-out wreck of a motorcycle that I ride to university each day and begin looking for a clapped-out wreck of a car. At least in the car I can remain dry when it rains. Also, I need a car to attract girls. How can I ask a girl to share my old motorcycle with me? Impossible. In Iran that is just not acceptable. I've been able to save forty thousand *tomans*—about eighty dollars. Not so many cars sell for this amount. Hardly any. But I find one on the premises of a shonky mechanic on the outskirts of town, an ancient VW manufactured in 1945. It looks as if it has barely survived the bombing of Berlin in the last year of World War II. I ask the mechanic if I can take it for a test drive.

'Test drive? Fuck off! Test drive? You can have it for forty thousand, kid. Take it or leave it.'

The doors can't be opened from the outside. It's necessary to leave the driver's side window wound down so that you can reach inside and open the door that way. That's fine. I can live with that. I can just about live with the ramshackle interior, too, I suppose, although chickens and goats may have been living in it for the past twenty years. I drive it home without bothering to inquire about the paperwork—the registration, transfer of ownership. I'm ecstatic just to have a car to get around in. Oh, and the brakes. No brakes. Not even a hand-brake. That's alright. I can live without brakes. I develop a technique for stopping the car that involves changing down gears to reduce speed then sticking my foot outside the car and digging it into the road surface. A tiny bit dangerous, but what else am I to do? I also discover, over the first weeks of driving, that the engine is inclined to burst into flames. I have to jump out of the vehicle and beat the flames out before resuming my journey. It's a difficult car and I wouldn't trust anyone other than myself to drive it. A very difficult car, but I feel the sort of affection for it that people sometimes bestow on bad-tempered little dogs they keep as pets—somehow lovable in their unlovableness. In my fondness for the little VW, I give it a name: Jafar. The worst car by far travelling the roads of any Iranian city: Jafar.

My car, my ancient VW, has a part to play in this example of the lack of political caution I've spoken about. Driving home from a jog in the park one day with my friend Masood as a passenger, I notice a mullah waiting on the roadside for a taxi. It's a custom in Iran—particularly in post-revolutionary Iran—for drivers to stop for mullahs and offer them a ride. A type of courtesy, if you like. There is no love in my heart for mullahs, but I stop and pick him up just to tease him. Teasing mullahs is also a custom in Iran, if you can get away with it—a much more fraught undertaking after the Revolution, of course, and best avoided if you have anything to hide. But I can't resist.

I stop and call to the mullah, 'Hop in, Haji!'

Masood climbs into the back seat and the mullah takes the front passenger seat. I look into the rear-vision mirror once we head off again and catch Masood's eye. I give a wink.

'Sir,' I say to the mullah, giving every impression of respect, 'May I ask your advice on a sensitive matter?'

'My advice? Of course you may.'

'Sir, it's like this. My friend and I went to the Imam Reza shrine last week for prayer. It's something we do every chance we get, isn't that right, Masood?'

'Certainly,' says Masood. 'Every chance we get.'

'Well, Allah bless you boys. A very good thing to do. Allah will reward your piety.'

'Thank you, sir. But this is my problem. On the night before I went to the shrine I experienced a strange dream. And this dream, sir, caused me...well, it caused me to ejaculate in my sleep, sir. A great volume came gushing from me. I must have been dreaming of naked women, sir, I am ashamed to say. And the emission came pumping out of me—whoosh! Like that!'

The mullah glances across at me in alarm.

'Whoosh!' I repeat for the mullah's benefit. 'Now does that mean that my prayers were polluted when I went to the shrine in the morning? If I am correct, a man must not go to prayer if he has ejaculated in the previous twenty-four hours, just as a woman must not go to prayer if she has her period. You understand what I mean by her period? Her menstrual flow?'

By this time, Masood is almost killing himself with laughter and the mullah can see plainly that he's being toyed with.

'Infamy!' he hisses. 'Let me out!'

'But, sir, my emission—can you tell me if it polluted my prayers? I am desperate to know, sir!'

'Let me out, you pair of Satans! You lovers of America! Let me out!'

I stop the car but only after going through my entire braking procedure—changing down gears, sticking my foot out of the car, putting the wheels into the dirt on the roadside and finally aiming for a small hill.

The mullah leaps from the car as if running from victims of the plague. 'Devils!' he shrieks. 'Both of you! Devils!'

I call after him, 'Sir, please, my emissions—what am I to do?'

Now, this is madness. Great fun, in an undergraduate way, hugely entertaining to Masood, and cathartic, in its way, for me, since it allows me to release some of the seething scorn I carry with me every single day. But madness. The mullah, if he wishes to, can report me; maybe the police will eventually locate me if the mullah can recall the number plate and make of car—not easy, but possible by tracing the car through the mechanic I purchased it from. Or the mullah might demand that we drive him to a police station, where he would make a complaint against me. I would refuse to drive him to a police station, but he could easily resist being dragged out of the car, and the whole struggle might attract sympathetic attention (sympathetic to the mullah, that is) from other people, ending up with me being marched off to the police. As I say, madness. I am a man with a Jewish heritage likely to exacerbate any complaint made about me to the police. I should behave like a perfect angel if I know what's good for me. But the risk excites me. It's part of me, the hunger for subversion, the urge to give cheek, in the phrase I used earlier.

Then there is the matter of the counterfeit dollars. One fine day my friend, Masood, shows me a small pile of American dollars he keeps concealed in his house.

'Masood, what is this shit!' I exclaim.

'Calm down.'

'You crazy bastard! Where did you get them?'

'They're fakes. My brother, Hooshang, brought them back from Pakistan. In Pakistan you can buy anything.'

Fakes. I study them carefully. Five one-hundred-dollar bills. If they are fakes, they're masterpieces. I've seen real American hundred dollar notes and these are indistinguishable from them.

'Only bank tellers can see that they're counterfeit,' says Masood.

'Sell them to me!' I blurt out, not yet sure how I can make use of the notes but deeply attracted to the opportunities they will doubtless provide. 'How much?'

Masood shrugs. 'Five hundred *tomans*.'

Five hundred *tomans* is nothing. One dollar! Chicken-feed. I agree to pay the one dollar right there on the spot, before Masood gets more grandiose—and greedier—ideas.

Mischief is like a genie dwelling in a lamp. You let it out of the lamp when something you crave becomes too urgent to resist. Of course, the original genie could fulfil the wishes of the one who released it, but the genie of mischief, once released, pleases itself. My fake five hundred American dollars had been sleeping restlessly in the lamp, calling to me each day: 'Kushi! Kushi, my master! Set me free!' And I had responded, 'A time will come. Be patient.'

A time does indeed come, and my patience could not be better rewarded. For the person on whom the mischief is released is none other than Haji Heydar, the person on earth I most detest. And why would I not attempt to fool him? He keeps my mother as a sex slave, holding her in his thrall with a few *tomans* here and a few *tomans* there, gobbling his meals at our table like a fat white slug that leaves behind a trail of slime. He mentions at the table on one occasion, crouched over his food, that he intends to send his wife to Mecca where she can exercise her piety. He says he will furnish her with five thousand American dollars for the trip so that she can buy gifts and souvenirs. He intends to buy the US dollars on the black market, this grotesque champion of the US-hating regime.

I remember my fake dollar bills and ask casually, 'How much do you pay for a US dollar?'

'Seven hundred *tomans*,' says Haji.

'You know what?' I say. 'The university permits medical students to buy five hundred American dollars so that we can purchase textbooks overseas. The bank has to sell us the dollars at the official rate of five hundred *tomans* per dollar. I can get you five hundred American dollars for twenty-five thousand *tomans*. It's up to you, of course.'

Haji's greedy little eyes narrow as he studies the proposition.

'Five hundred *tomans* per dollar?' he says.

'Five hundred.'

'Do it for me!'

'You want me to?'

'Do it for me, please.'

'Sure.'

The whole story of the textbooks and the five-hundred *toman* rate is a spur-of-the-moment thing. It just comes to me. I don't know what it means about me that I can concoct these lies so quickly, but I can. And a couple of days later I hand over my fake dollars to Haji and take possession of his genuine twenty-five thousand *tomans*—a clear profit of four-hundred and ninety-nine dollars. And if Haji discovers that my dollars are counterfeit? No problem. I'll think up something when and if that happens.

Once again, the risk-taking. It's compulsive. And thrilling.

The time does come, as it must, when Haji realises that five hundred of his five-thousand dollars are forgeries. And the time comes, as it must, when I have to come up with a plausible story to get me off the hook. No problem. I ask him where he purchased his other four-thousand five-hundred dollars.

'Where? Where do you think? In the market.'

'But who did you buy them from in the market?'

'Who did I buy them from? How do I know! Crooks. Who do you think?'

'You see,' I say, 'you have to be really, really careful, Haji. Really careful. Those fellows deceived you.'

'And who says it wasn't you who tricked me? Who says?'

'Haji, you are like family. Why would I cheat you? And where on earth would I get five hundred fake dollars? Think about it.'

Haji's suspicions are impossible to act on. He can't be sure that I am the one who cheated him, but deep down he believes it was me, all right. But look at the way I carried it off! Never a blush, never a stammer, never a false step. Should I not be worried about the condition of my immortal soul? For all the stories I tell of my mother's duplicity, the truth is that I am just as accomplished a liar as she is. Maybe I inherited this talent from her. But there is a difference between my lies and my mother's. My lies spare those I care about. Haji—he's a legitimate target. But I have never lied in a way that would land my mother in strife, or Koorosh, or even my father. A time is coming when my mother's duplicity will take me almost to the scaffold. So there is a difference between her lies and mine.

My facility with untruths saves me from any dangerous repercussions of the fake dollar affair. But once again—what a risk! If Haji had been able to prove that I'd duped him, he would have had no hesitation in turning me over to the police, and that would have been the end of my university career. I go out looking for trouble. It's chutzpah. It's insanity. And it's also very, very enjoyable. It never occurs to me, even with *my* imagination, that in the near future I will be repeatedly rushing to his bedside, with my doctor's bag, in order to save his life.

20

MAHSHID

I have opposed my mother in her plans at various times. I have argued with her passionately many times. I have complained of her disregard for my feelings, for my father's feelings (when he was still living with us), and for Koorosh's feelings. I have issued ultimatums. I have said, 'I intend to do such-and-such and you will not stand in my way!' But all of my ultimatums, all of my arguing only confirms to my mother her importance in my life. She might make a strategic withdrawal once in a while. She might pretend to be listening to my point of view, but she knows, as all tyrants know, that when the matter is of great significance, she will prevail. And of course, what is and is not of 'great significance' will be decided by her and her alone. I am nineteen years old and before I am much older, my mother will decide that my heart should be broken for my own good.

My second year of medicine at Mashhad University has been a golden year in the calendar of my life. I have had two books published—translations of medical textbooks from English to Farsi—and have been handsomely rewarded for both. The translations were arduous, calling for me to sit over English dictionaries for long, long hours, but those long hours had the secondary benefit of improving my English. And just as important as the improvement in my financial status is the increase in my appeal to the opposite sex. I have grown a beard and I look startlingly like the pop hero, Dariush (based in the United States, but spectacularly fêted in Iran), so find myself in the enjoyable situation of being attractive to the girls of Mashhad. Oh, happy man!

In the midst of all this delight and excitement and titillation, I receive a phone call from someone who is a stranger to me. But not a complete stranger. His name is Mohammad, he lives in Tehran, and he is (as he explains) my stepbrother, which is to say the son of my father with his first wife. He has seen my medical textbook (he himself is not a doctor but a scientist with a degree in agricultural industry, gained in Italy) and wants me to come to Tehran and pay him, his wife, his two daughters and his son a visit. 'Do you think you might be tempted to come?' he asks. I say, 'Of course!' and what I'm thinking is, 'Just try and hold me back!' I'm thinking, naturally, of all the girls in Tehran longing to run their fingers through my hair and beard and exclaim on my fabulous resemblance to Dairush. Oh, and I'm enthusiastic about the prospect of meeting Mohammad, too, and of catching up with my brother Koorosh who's studying at university in the capital. Of course I am.

I have enough money at this time to fly to Tehran, and so within days of Mohammad's call I'm standing in his living-room embracing my half-brother, who looks very like me, same height, very handsome! Then I meet his son and his lovely sister, my half-sister, Katayoon. Over tea and biscuits, Mohammad tells me that he is proud of me, that I surprised him by emerging from an impoverished background in the way that I had. Would Mohammad have bothered to contact me if I had failed to find a place at university, if I hadn't published those textbook translation? No. Success wins you admirers—it's shallow, but

Iran and Persia's four thousand years of civilisation have not made us any wiser than other peoples of the world.

My days in Tehran give me an opportunity to do this and that. To meet my wonderful half-sister, to visit my brother Koorosh, to chat with Mohammad's wife, Soheyla, and his daughters. But I am itching to speak of someone else, because it is in Tehran on this visit that I meet the love of my life and feel my heart swell with a type of love I've never known before.

We are going to the movies. Katayoon has invited me. In the taxi on the way to the cinema, Katayoon says, 'Oh, I should have mentioned that we're meeting a friend of mine. Actually, she's the cousin of your father's wife here in Tehran. Her name's Mahshid. I think you'll like her.'

The taxi stops on a street corner and there waiting for us is what appears to be the most beautiful girl on earth. Though, perhaps that is not accurate. Because Mahshid is not earthly in any way. She is like the moon, glowing and beautiful. I feel like the tide, drawn to her.

'It's Mahshid,' says Katayoon. 'Remember I said we'd be picking her up on the way?'

'What?'

'I said it's Mahshid. What's the matter with you?'

'What?'

Mahshid gets into the taxi, and immediately glances at me. Her eyes are so dark, deep and silent. I feel as if I am once again gazing upon the tranquility of the Lut Desert. Her cheeks are sheer, her complexion immaculate, her lips perfectly defined. A fringe of black hair sits on her forehead, exposed by her scarf. She smiles at me with such intimacy that I think, 'If I can't marry this girl, I will die.' And then I think, 'Idiot! Don't even think about it! She is the cousin of your father's wife!' But it is a tiny bell of warning to myself that goes unheard, drowned in the booming symphony of desire bursting within me.

'Mahshid, this is Kushi,' says Katayoon. 'Kushi, say something.'

What I want to say is, 'We've only known each other for two minutes but I must tell you that you are the most beautiful woman in the world, the most beautiful woman in the history of the world and I dare to hope—please!—that you will simply sit still and permit me to gaze at you hour after hour until I die.'

What I actually say is, 'I'm pleased to meet you.'

Throughout the movie I sit in a state of intense arousal, but not sexual arousal. This is the arousal of every sense to a receptive pitch that is an agony to endure. Without looking at Mahshid, I am aware of her as a force that exerts an overwhelming tactile attraction. I want to plait my fingers in hers, to lay my hand against her cheek. This yearning is to mere sexual need what great poetry is to gibberish.

This is something I must say now, before I lose my courage. I have written this book, this life story, not to explain myself, not to justify myself, not to make the world acquainted with a thousand things I did and a further thousand things I failed to do, not to tell tales of despair and triumph. No, I have written this book for one reason: to relive this time with Mahshid in the cinema when something came to life in my heart that I was not to experience again until the birth of my children. It is as if you have become special to God at such times, as if His shifting gaze has settled on you, of all the people on earth, and that His gaze will remain until you have either embraced the love that has come your way, or found some way to squander it. Even God in His omniscience does not know the outcome, and so He waits and watches this story of Kushi and Mahshid unfold.

After the movie we wander down to a park, the three of us, and spend hours talking about music (Mahshid and I share a passion for Pink Floyd) and art (Sohrab Sepehri) and philosophy (Nietzsche). Mahshid is at university, studying English, intending to read the great classics of English literature. The two of us are in a zone that all but excludes the rest of the world. Even Katayoon, seated with us, barely interrupts the flow of sympathy between Mahshid and me. Every story Mahshid tells invites a complementary story of my own, so that we are constantly exclaiming, 'Oh, but that's amazing, the same thing happened to me!' Or, 'But that's exactly what I think! I didn't know anyone else thought that way!' This coincidence of interests deepens my conviction that destiny is involved in this meeting with Mahshid. We are the male and female sides of the one soul.

For the rest of my stay in Tehran the sole study of my minutes and hours is Mahshid. We talk on the phone each day and meet as often as possible, always with Katayoon as chaperone. Mahshid's parents are enlightened and would quite likely agree to us meeting without a chaperone, but the reign of the mullahs means that boy and girl cannot be seen in public together (unless they are brother and sister) without another person present. With Katayoon present, we can say, quite truthfully, 'We are all family.' Katayoon knows full well that her role is merely to facilitate the romance that is thriving between her cousin and her guest and she gives us as much liberty as we need. Although not the liberty for anything intimate.

In a Western country, a boy and girl with the enthusiasm that Mahshid and I have for each other would already have slipped into bed. But not in Iran. In its way, the taboo on premarital sex serves to emphasise the seriousness of the courtship. Any girl you want to marry would feel badly insulted if you were to say, 'Shall we make love?' An exquisite current of sexual desire runs between Mahshid and me, yes, but it is only one of the sympathetic currents that enliven us, and in fact is not to be distinguished from the broader flow of feeling. We don't spend our time struggling to keep our hands off each other. But for many Iranian girls, including Mahshid, a fair bit of caution and astute judgement is exercised in those rare unchaperoned times with a boyfriend.

On the last night of my visit I am invited to the house of Mahshid's father and mother for what might be called a farewell party. The prospect of leaving Mahshid behind in Tehran leaves me sick at heart. Mashhad seems to me a place of endless boredom, of tedious study and of friends in whom I no longer have any interest. I eat and drink this evening as if it were the feast a condemned man eats before mounting the scaffold or facing the firing squad. Every time I glance at Mahshid a sheet of flames runs over my skin, succeeded by a hideous ache in the pit of my stomach. I think, 'What is the point of love if it is accompanied by such awful pain?' And the insane thing is that my love for Mahshid may be unrequited. I know she likes me, I know she enjoys my company, but maybe she likes everyone, and maybe this time we've spent together is for her just an amusing way of passing the hours.

Late in the evening when it is time for me to return to Mohammad's house, Mahshid seeks me out as I'm gathering my things and putting my shoes on. She seizes my hand and draws me into a corner, whispering urgently that I must not go yet, I must stay longer.

'Can you do that?' she asks. 'Please, can you stay just a few more minutes?'

What Mahshid has in mind is a walk to a nearby park in the balmy air of this autumn evening. This is to be an unchaperoned walk, apparently—so hard to believe! We find a bench in the park. We're all alone, the wind is barely moving the foliage of the trees. And now look—Mahshid has taken my hand and is urging me to settle beside her on the grass. What in God's name is going on? This is an extraordinarily daring thing for Mahshid to do, but then she is daring, very, not only in her deeds but in her thoughts.

'Mahshid…' I murmur, preparing to warn her that we are on risky ground. Mahshid in her daring is bolder than I am, myself.

'Shhh,' she says, and then with a deft movement plucks the scarf from her head and shakes her long silken hair free. She says not a word. She simply lets her gaze engage my own.

'Our last night,' I whisper.

'It looks like it—I'm very disappointed! But, I'm getting used to disappointment.'

'You'll miss me?' I coax.

'What do you think?'

'I don't know.'

'Yes, of course, I'll miss you! How can you ask?'

'Ya Allah! I'm so relieved!'

'Are you? I'm not relieved. I don't want to be attracted to someone. I hate it. It's just pain and disappointment, pain and disappointment.'

'Then—you're attracted to me? Is that what you're saying?'

Mahshid says nothing for a minute or more, perhaps thinking me stupid for asking for it to be spelt out.

'I'm falling in love with you,' she says then. 'There. Is that what you want to hear? I'm falling in love with you, beautiful man that you are. Have I made it clear enough?'

This is why there is a world to begin with—moments such as these, precious moments when love stirs our feelings of immortality. And do you know, immortality has nothing to do with time? Immortality can exist within a moment. All that has come before in time is gone, all that will be is gone, there is only the present, and the world dwells in that present, and the present is forever.

I reach out and press the palm of my hand to Mahshid's cheek. Her skin is as tender as a whisper. The scent she is wearing, like the ether that rises from the perfumed garden of an antique Persian king, makes me drunk with joy. I kiss her. Never such a meeting of lips, never such happiness—never in history, never before.

When love comes your way, it will flourish or wither depending on your courage. It's a pact. You can have love, but not if you fail the test of courage. Why this should be I don't know but if you consider the literature of love you find again and again that courage is the medium of success. That test of courage is waiting up ahead for me and for Mahshid. She will pass the test. She will demonstrate all the courage in the world. I will fail.

Back in Mashhad, I can think only of Mahshid. I call her every day, I make three trips to Tehran in two months. She is in my mind every waking instant.

My mother knows that I am in love. I have not confessed anything to her, but she knows. And she is intensely jealous. She does not want a daughter-in-law, she wants only a son studying hard for his medical degree, making money as a writer. But her jealousy goes much further than resenting the prospect of her son slacking off in his studies and perhaps threatening her comfort. She is jealous of whoever I am in love with primarily because she wants me to love her before every other woman in the world.

'Who is it?' she demands.

'No one you know.'

And she seethes.

Every visit I make to Tehran, Mahshid seems to me to be more beautiful in her physical form and in her intelligence. Every visit confirms my belief that in all of creation, she is the only woman I will wish to marry. On one such visit, Mahshid's father takes me aside in his house.

'Kushi, you are a good man and an honourable man. I know you would never cause my daughter shame. And as you know,

I am not one of those parents who runs to a mullah every time I want advice. I take my own advice. But this is Iran, Kooshyar, and a boy and girl cannot conduct a romance in the way that couples do in the West. You have to consider the future. Are you understanding me?'

'Of course, sir.'

Knowing how deeply I love Mahshid, I should tell my mother immediately. But I don't. I am terrified of her response. She knows that I am in love but she thinks that I will merely amuse myself with whoever it is and then tire of her. She doesn't yet imagine that I would wish to marry. And she doesn't know that the girl I love is a relative of her husband's hawoo—that would be utterly unbearable for her.

So this is it. Either my love for Mahshid is stronger than my dread of my mother, or I fear my mother more than I love Mahshid. There is no way I can put it that is kinder to me, no way I can qualify the equation: either Mahshid's love or my mother's wrath.

At the same time as I maintain my secrecy about Mahshid (I spend so much of my life in secrecy, so much so that it is an ingrained habit) events are conspiring to show my love to the world—or at least to my mother. On what is to be my final visit to Mahshid in Tehran, I am permitted to take her out in her mother's car, unchaperoned once again. And we are stopped by a couple of Basiji (religious militia) who have noticed a young man and a young woman in a car together. In other countries, the police might stop a car with a half a dozen suspicious-looking boys in it, all looking as if they were about to commit a burglary; or they might stop a car with a defective brake light. But in Iran, what the Basiji are looking for are boys like me alone in a car with girls like Mahshid. They will want proof that we are related—brother and sister, something like that. When I pull over and roll down the window, I can feel a cold trickle of sweat running down my back.

'Ya Allah, Kushi! What will we do?' Mahshid exclaims.

'Pull your scarf over your hair. And don't worry. It will be fine.' I feel no confidence at all in the message of my own words.

Two boys our age, with rifles over their shoulders, are at the car window.

'What's happening?'

'My sister has been to her English class. I'm driving her home.'

'Your sister?'

They peers closely at Mahshid.

'Your sister, my arse,' one of them says.

'Sir, I swear to you, she is my sister.'

'Is that right? Okay, does your mother have a sister too? Your aunt, that would be.'

'Yes, she does.'

'And what's her name, this auntie of yours. Whisper it to me.'

An aunt—why did I say I had an aunt?

'Her name is Maryam, sir. Maryam.'

Maryam is one of the most common female names in Iran.

'Maryam, is it? I see.'

The Basiji goes around to the passenger side of the car and asks Mahshid to whisper her aunt's name. Mahshid, having no talent for deceit, will certainly tell him her aunt's real name. He comes back to me.

'She didn't say, Maryam,' he says, and immediately I break down and confess that we are not brother and sister.

'Oh, but sir, she is a good girl, very chaste, and we are to be married, please believe me, sir. We've done nothing wrong.'

The upshot of all this dread and panic is that I have to pay a bribe. That's why we were stopped. It's revenue for the religious militia. Pay a bribe, the whole thing will be forgotten. Since I have money in my pocket after selling my beloved old car, my Jafar, back in Mashhad (I hated to sell it but I needed the money for my bus fare to Tehran), I pay up with relief and Mahshid and I are permitted to return to Mahshid's place.

This incident, which could easily have ended in a far worse way, catapults Mahshid and me back into the real world. I wouldn't say that we had been living a fantasy, but it is not in the nature of love to give space to all the tedious aspects of existence. Love is the antithesis of all that. It wishes to soar above the world, not trudge along its squalid streets. In the real world, Mahshid is compelled to tell her mother of the incident, and her mother is compelled by custom and duty to tell her husband, and her husband is compelled by duty to tell me that the courtship I have been conducting cannot go on in the way it has.

'I have spoken to Mahshid,' he says. 'She loves you, Kooshyar. It is true love. She loves you and she wants to marry you. You are a good man with a prosperous future ahead. The two of you must become engaged, surely you see that. You must become engaged, and when you have graduated from medical school to your internship at a hospital, you can marry. With a little patience, the two of you will find great happiness.'

Mahshid's father tells me all this on the phone, as I have returned to Mashhad. Even as he speaks, my dominant feeling is not clear to me. Is it a great joy in the knowledge that this beautiful and intelligent girl will be my wife? That my dreams of meeting someone with whom I can share for life everything in my soul, are about to be realised? I should be ecstatic, shouldn't I?

I should reply to Mahshid's father with these words: 'Oh, I thank you with all my heart! Yes, we will become engaged. Yes, we will marry! I am the most blessed man alive.' But these are not the words that I stammer out. No, to my eternal shame, I am thinking not of Mahshid and the future that awaits us, but of my mother and of her fury when I tell her that I am to marry, and who I am to marry. I am more terrified of my mother's response than I was of the Basiji who pulled us over in Tehran.

'I will think about it,' I say. They are the words I use. 'I will think about it.'

There will come a point in any scheme of existence when the matter of 'the trial' is raised. We know what we should do (never mind how we know, we just do) and we are free to make a choice between the alternative that will enhance our humanity, or at least confirm it, and the alternative that will diminish us as human beings. Sartre speaks of a colleague in the French Resistance during World War II who has lived a quiet life, has never handled a gun, has never conceived of a violent response to the German invasion of his country. He is terrified of his situation, terrified of taking part in raids on German installations in Paris. He shakes with fear when he picks up a pistol. Despite his dread, he fulfils his role in the Resistance. He attacks German soldiers, he fires his pistol, but the dread never leaves him. He knows what he is risking. He knows what awaits him if he is captured. He will be tortured, even to the point of death. But something worse awaits him if he fails to do what his conscience—his moral being—tells him he should do. He will have to live with the betrayal of his own soul. What Sartre is suggesting is that once our conscience whispers to us and makes us aware of our moral being, we can only refuse to listen if we are prepared to live with betrayal.

In Sartre's writing, courage is the issue. We can maintain our courage even as we tremble with fear. The trembling and the fear don't matter. They are expected. But what does matter is that the trembling and fear do not overwhelm us and make us turn away from the path we know in our hearts is the right path. Here I stand, the telephone in my hand. Mahshid's father says: 'You must marry.' And I say, 'Let me think about it.' As soon as I utter those words, I have betrayed Mahshid and betrayed myself. My mother is the equivalent in my story to the Gestapo in Sartre's story. 'Let me think about it' in my story would be the equivalent in Sartre's story of the quiet man who so feared what he was doing, that he says, 'No, I cannot do this, I am going back to my wife and children, I am leaving the Resistance.'

I do not give up immediately. No, I first resolve to tell my mother about Mahshid. But before I take my life in my hands and reveal my secret, my brother Koorosh pre-empts me. Yes, my brother has a secret of his own that he has decided to share. He intends to marry, and the candidate is a divorcee by the name of Maryam. She lives in Mashhad, and Koorosh has been making regular trips back to Mashhad from his university in Tehran to court her. When he tells my mother, she hits the roof. 'A divorcee? You want to marry a divorcee? Are you insane? An intelligent, well-educated boy like you marrying a divorcee? A woman who has already passed through the hands of another man? Over my dead body! And why is she divorced? What is the matter with her that her husband has no use for her anymore? Have you asked yourself that?'

My mother is forgetting, in her convenient way, that she herself is a divorcee. She puts every obstacle she can find in the way of Koorosh's plans, and what does my brother do? He quietly persists. He says that he loves the woman and will never abandon her. He finds the courage to keep to the path he has chosen. And he marries her, he marries Maryam, the divorcee, he finds a job locally, and he and his wife set up house in Mashhad.

I find an opportunity to speak to my mother in good time. I ask her into the privacy of my room where my textbooks are scattered about, and tell her that I intend to marry and leave home. Her initial response is chilly, but she remains under control. She and Haji would, in fact, like me to marry and move out so that they have the house to themselves. But my mother (I know this) wants me to marry a girl of her choosing, one who will be her ally in keeping me at her beck and call. She wants a daughter-in-law who is an extension of herself. But she is prepared to listen, at least. So far, so good. Then I begin to introduce the prospect of me marrying a girl in Tehran, not a local Mashhadi girl. My mother's eyes flash, she holds onto her temper, though. And now the really problematical information.

'I visited the relatives of *Baba jan's* first wife in Tehran, you know, Layla, that one...'

And before another syllable escapes my lips, my mother has transformed herself into a screaming harpy.

'That bitch! You dared to visit that ugly whore! You know the misery she caused me and yet you dare to speak her name to me!' Then more rage, denunciation, hysteria. 'You care nothing for me. You care only for yourself. Do you know how much I have sacrificed for you and for your brother? Aiee! Why did I waste my life for you when you wish only to kill me? Kill me now! Don't wait for me to die of sorrow! Take a knife and cut my throat now! You and your brother, such ingratitude! Both of you can take a knife and kill me now!'

I back off. And I haven't yet told her that it is Mahshid, her hawoo's cousin I wish to marry. I think of my brother, of his calm endurance of all the threats and accusations, and I ask myself where my own courage has gone to hide. Then I rationalise and say this to myself when nobody else can hear, 'It is because I love my mother that I strive to spare her pain.' But that's not true. I know that my mother is manipulating me. I know that she is, in her way, a tyrant. It is only for the sake of my pride that I tell myself that it is my devotion as a son that prevents me standing up to her. I am not yet ready to accept that it is not devotion to my mother that stops me from claiming the woman I love, but fear.

My studies fall away. I am in a state of desolation. My friends laugh at me as I assume more and more of the comic aspects of the lovelorn fool. I don't call Mahshid. My mind is like some storm-wracked landscape that barely survives the devastation of one hurricane before another comes roaring in. All I am good for is sitting with my head bowed, rehearsing again and again the arguments for and against standing up to my mother. I think, 'She will say that she will kill herself if I marry Mahshid, and I will tell her not to be so melodramatic, then she will remind me once more of struggling through the snow to give birth to me all those years ago, and I will say that I have the right to choose my own destiny, and she will say that the destiny I have chosen is one that ignores her suffering, then I will...'

And so on, and so on.

I finally tell her, but even as I speak I'm sick with fear.

'*Madar jan*, the girl I love, I must speak to you about her. The girl in Tehran. Her name is Mahshid...'

She screams, she weeps, she tears at herself with her fingernails, she implores the God of the Jews to strike her dead, she unleashes a shrill stream of invective aimed firstly at my father's first wife, then at Mahshid, then at me. Struggling to get a word in edgeways, I wish with all my heart I hadn't mentioned a thing but had taken my misery and gone into the desert to live out my life as a hermit.

'And what of your future?' she shrieks. 'Have you even begun to think what getting married at this time would do to your career? You, the most brilliant student at the university, a doctor, an author, the world is waiting for you and all you can think of is how to destroy your own happiness. Tell me one thing, idiot: are you mad? Are you insane? After all your hard work, you throw it away. Once you are married, where will you find the time to study? Tell me that. Where will you find the time?'

'I'm sorry, *Madar jan*. Maybe you're right. I'll think about it.'

God forgive me, they are the words I use. I know that my life is the sum of the choices I make. I know that I cannot blame circumstances, the structures of society or anything else. I stand here with my own free will with which to fashion my life, and of my own free will, I disown the love of my life. I could say, 'Oh, but this is the Middle East, children are raised to honour their parents' wishes, I was forced to betray Mahshid, it's not my fault.' That sort of excuse might do for someone who lacks the ability to work out their own choices in such matters. But I have a good mind, I know right from wrong and I know that what I'm doing is wrong.

Meanwhile my mother is having a heart attack, or so she says. She clutches at her chest, gasps, writhes. In a panic I call for an ambulance and have her taken to hospital. In the back of the ambulance on the way to hospital, she gestures for me to come closer. In a faltering voice she whispers: 'Promise me you will never talk to the girl again. Never again. Not in your life. Promise me or I will die now.'

'*Madar jan*, I promise. I won't talk to Mahshid again.'

'Don't say her name!'

'Sorry, *Madar jan*, sorry. I promise I won't talk to the girl whose name I can't mention.'

Is it necessary for me to say that my mother was not suffering a heart attack, and was in no danger of dying? I am at her bedside when she greets Haji, who has heard the news of her near-collapse. He wants to add his criticisms and censures to those of my mother.

'What have you done? How could you be so stupid? This poor woman who has given you everything and given herself nothing. That Tehran girl, don't you see, you fool? You were her target, she was hunting you. A clever student you may be but about life you know nothing, about women you know nothing!'

I live a sleepless life, walking the city streets at night, chain-smoking, sorrowing, suffering, wishing I were dead.

Three weeks after my betrayal of Mahshid, I arrive home from university to find that my mother has commenced the process of finding a wife for me, a wife of whom she approves. I'm certain that she thinks my declaration of love for Mahshid is all to do with lust and that I only imagined I was in love with Mahshid. She thinks, 'He's a young man, he has urges, I'll find him a pretty girl to marry and he'll soon forget about that stupid little harlot in Tehran.'

I'm a broken man. My mother has destroyed me and she knows she can do what she likes with me now. Her companion in crime is Dr Vahedi's wife, Parvin, (a fateful coincidence, in hindsight, considering the harm my father's wife of the same name visited on me). I walk in from university one evening, exhausted and heart-sick, only to find Parvin at home with my mother. She tells me we are going out and insists I change into better clothes.

'Please, Mrs Vahedi, I'm so tired and, to tell the truth, I don't feel very well,' I say.

'You'll feel better soon. Get dressed,' interjects my mother.

I can't refuse Dr Vahedi's wife her request and do as I am told. She has come in her Mercedes and when I am dressed to her satisfaction, and to my mother's, she tells me that she wants me to drive. I take the keys from her like an automaton, sit myself behind the steering wheel, pull out onto the road.

'Where are we going?' I ask.

'Where are we going? Very simple, Kooshyar. We are going to the house of one of my closest relatives. I want to introduce you to the daughter of this household. A very attractive young woman. Who knows? In time the two of you might feel you can be very happy together.'

I stop the car immediately, open the door and try to escape. Mrs Vahedi reaches across and grasps my arm—a most unusual thing for a woman to do in a culture such as Iran's.

'Get back inside,' she orders.

For almost a minute I remain half in and half out of the car, tears stinging my eyes. Then I get back into the Mercedes and sit crumpled behind the wheel.

'What's going on with you!' says Mrs Vahedi.

My mother, playing her part in this emotional blackmail, begins praying aloud in Hebrew, invoking the God of the Jews to intervene and show me the duty a Jewish son owes to his mother. This is a very clever tactic of my mother's. She never speaks Hebrew before a Muslim unless she is very, very distressed. She intends me to understand that she is on the verge of a new 'heart attack'.

'I'm not getting married,' I mutter, trying to look as if I mean what I'm saying.

'Marriage?' says Mrs Vahedi. 'Marriage we don't even mention. Ya Allah! What is wrong with you? It is a nice visit with my relatives. We meet a very beautiful girl, we drink some tea. What harm is there in that?'

For a further minute or so, I pretend to myself that I have the courage to make my own choices in this matter. Then my mother raises the volume of her prayers and I start the car again and drive.

Azita is the name of the young woman I am delivered to, like a sacrificial offering. She is beautiful, as promised, tall and willowy with jet-black hair and the complexion of an angel. Azita is the name of the young woman my mother has chosen as my bride, with the complicity of Mrs Vahedi. She is very courteous to me. For a few days. But before much time has passed, Azita has this to say:

'Do you smoke? I hope not. I don't want my husband to smoke.' And, 'What is that dreadful music you are listening to? Pink who? Pink Floyd? Never heard of them. Why don't you listen to Persian music? You should listen to Persian music. Please, no more of this Pink rubbish.' And also, 'Jeans? Are you wearing jeans? I don't like jeans. Dress in more stylish clothes. Not jeans.' And finally, 'Do you pray? I hope so. It is very important to me that I have a husband who prays at the correct times. I could never be happy with a man who doesn't pray. So I ask again—do you pray?'

'Yes, I pray.'

'At the correct times?'

'Yes, at the correct times.'

'This business of your Jewish past. No more of that. I hate Jews.'

'Alright.'

'Good,' says Azita. 'Then I will tell Mrs Vahedi that we can be married.'

What do I think about this interrogation? I think, 'Dear God, what have I done to deserve this?' And the answer to that question? *Kushi, you betrayed Mahshid.*

We are engaged. As tradition demands, an engagement party is held. Music, dancing. It is customary amongst sophisticated Iranians to provide a room after such a party where the bride and groom can enjoy some private time. Some intimacy. And sex. Azita and I are shown to the room. Many ribald jokes are made, or mildly ribald jokes. People wink. People say, 'Have fun!'

Azita slips out of her gown and climbs under the bedclothes, waiting. I put on a nightshirt provided for me and try to think of ways in which I can avoid getting into bed beside my wife-to-be.

'What are you doing?'

'Me? Nothing.'

'Then get into bed.'

I do, but I am unable to respond to Azita's overtures. How can I? I am broken-hearted, I am sick with longing for Mahshid.

Nevertheless, I am now engaged to this bossy, interfering young woman, Azita. Marriage itself is still some time off. I will be required to save a great deal of money for the marriage ceremony, but I will be required to do much more than that before the event takes place. I will disappoint my fiancée in a hundred ways, I will agree to change my behaviour in a thousand ways, I will sneak about looking for a place to smoke a cigarette in secret, I will listen to Pink Floyd in secret, I will attempt without the least success to get Azita interested in poetry and philosophy, I will endure threats from Azita's father (that's Mr Abdollahian) to burn my mother and me alive unless I mend my ways and make his daughter happy. I will, in short, subject myself to endless humiliations over the next two years, and for what reason? To secure a marriage that my mother arranged for me to a girl who will come to detest her, a girl who will demand that I ask permission of her before I even visit my mother, a girl who will tell me that she doesn't like my friends and who will forbid me to see them again. In short, I will pay again and again and again for having lacked the courage to claim Mahshid as my wife.

And Mahshid?

Do I ever see her again? The answer is that I do not see her again. But I hear news of her, conveyed to me in a note from her father. The note tells me that Mahshid has attempted to end her life and is in intensive care in hospital.

I do not visit her.

A BOX OF
PRAWNS

As I open the door of my Mashhad home in the winter of 1995, I am not prepared for the sight that meets me. There is a woman, probably in her late forties, with her head scarf wrapped tightly around her face to keep out the chill. Behind her, head down, and trembling hands on her chest, stands a young girl sniffling and shaking from the cold.

I open my mouth and close it again, trying to decipher the situation.

'Are you Dr Karimi?' The older woman asks, her voice oddly steady, though her eyes remain downcast.

I hesitate before answering.

'Yes. Is there something I can do for you?'

The woman's eyes look into mine for the first time, and I notice they are red rimmed and blood shot. Tears begin spilling down her cheeks.

'Shafiq sent us here. I...please help my daughter.' Her eyes remain locked with mine.

'I'm sorry, there's nothing I can really do for you here. Perhaps if you come to my surgery tomorrow...'

'Please, doctor!' She breaks down, clutching at my shirt with her ice cold fingers, and weeping.

'She is only seventeen years old!'

I glance towards the young girl; she is cowering backwards quietly, as though she could disappear. Her lips are blue from the cold and her small form is shuddering. I wordlessly step aside, and usher them into my home. The woman is clutching at her daughter's arm as she emits another wrenching sob. Azita appears at the hallway, and we exchange a glance. She nods and picks Newsha up, taking her to another room. I stand hesitantly in the living-room, wondering what to do next.

'She's pregnant,' the woman murmurs, interrupting my thoughts, breaking the silence. 'Twelve weeks. We tried everything.' Her voice is defeated, her head hanging low again. I look to the young girl, so fragile, as though she is a moment away from shattering.

'What's your name?' I ask her, tentatively, but her lips only quiver in response.

'Her name is Hoda,' her mother answers, 'We're from Bandar Abbas.'

I try to hide my shock. Bandar Abbas is on the other side of Iran. How long must they have travelled? And in such a terrible condition? At this, the young girl cries. Her knees threaten to give out, and she holds her mother's hand.

'I'm sorry,' she chokes out, turns to me and repeats, 'I'm sorry.'

I find my voice again, and assure her that everything will be alright. That she has done nothing wrong. Her mother explains the situation once Hoda has calmed down. I learn that Hoda had been seeing a boy in secret despite her mother's warnings, and that the boy had insisted upon having sex with her. Hoda had agreed, assuming she would later approach her parents with his proposal of marriage. She fell pregnant. The young boy vanished. And here she stands, twelve weeks later. I nod in sympathy; this is not an uncommon occurrence. After examining

Hoda, I explain to her mother the type of medicine used, the procedure, and the cost.

'Fifty thousand *tomans*,' she breathes out, her eyes welling up again. 'But I don't have...'

I stare down at my feet. I hate to take money from people in desperation, but the medicine for these procedures is extremely expensive. I have to take money, in order to be able to continue helping other women. The woman is sobbing uncontrollably.

'I don't have any money right now! I have spent hundreds on the hotels we have been staying at and thousands on Shafiq's herbal remedies!' She pulls at her hair, 'Please doctor! Please! I can get you the money in a few months! I promise!'

She tears off the gold chain that hangs around her neck, placing it into my hands.

'Here, this is pure gold. Please. Take it as insurance.'

I look at Hoda, and know that without this, her only option would probably be suicide. I think about the hundreds of girls who must be in her position at this very moment, alone and with no way out. It makes me think of my mother. She would have been praying desperately for someone like me to help her. I shake my head, and hand the gold chain back to her.

'I cannot do that. No. Please take this back. I will do the procedure without charge.'

The woman stands in shock for a moment, before falling to her knees. She holds both my hands tightly, crying in happiness.

'Bless you, Doctor! Allah protect you and your family!'

I lead Hoda to the basic surgical theatre that I have set up in my home. Her mother sits nervously in the living-room. Finally, at 3 a.m., it is over. Hoda is covered in sweat and tears. She runs a shaky hand through her sweat-soaked hair, her breathing is shallow but she cries in relief. The termination is successful. For the first time, I see an expression of relief on her face.

During the recovery days, I insist that Hoda and her mother

stay at my home. Hoda is very weak, and I monitor her until she is back to full health. I also repair her hymen, much to the disbelief of her and her mother. And with that, all evidence of Hoda's nightmare is wiped clean. Before they leave, I hand Hoda's mother an unmarked envelope. Inside it there are two thousand *tomans*. They cry in happiness, clutching onto me. Hoda's mother kneels once more, and prays. Hoda turns to me, producing a small camera from her bag.

'I want to be a professional one day,' she murmurs shyly, gesturing to the cheap camera in her hand.

I smile at this, imagining her future.

'Could I...if it's not too much to ask for, could I get a picture of you?' she asks hesitantly.

I don't know what to say. What I do is dangerous, criminal. It would be unwise to have a photograph revealing my identity. But I see the hopeful look in the young girl's face and, despite my misgivings, I nod my head. Not a second later, Hoda quickly winds up the camera and the familiar shudder click reaches my ears.

'Thank you, doctor!' She smiles, hugging me unexpectedly, 'Thank you so much.'

A month or so later, a large carton arrives at my home. There is a note attached.

Dr Karimi,

I could never thank you enough for what you did. You saved my life, truly. I enrolled for a photography course last week at university. I wouldn't have been able to, if it weren't for you. I developed the photograph of you, it hangs above my bed. And I pray for you and your family every day.

Bless you,

Hoda

I open the carton and find several kilograms of expensive, frozen prawns from the sea that laps the coast of Hoda's town. We eat them for dinner that night, and I could never have imagined in that moment, around the table eating delicious prawns with my family, that I would be sitting in the horror of my cold cell three years later, starving and alone, in the shadow of a noose.

THE INVENTION
OF TORTURE

There is no great shame in succumbing to torture. With enough skill, enough patience and the right implements, a torturer will outlast any victim. Sometimes the victims die before fully revealing what is being demanded of them, but that is a misjudgement on the part of the tormentor. Keep the victim alive, and he or she will tell you what you wish to know. And, of course, not all torture needs to bruise or produce blood or break bones or sear the skin. A skilled tormentor will know how to enhance the dread of the victim, even before he opens his toolbox and displays the instruments at his disposal.

The torture begins at the moment of captivity, but that is only the first psychological stage the victim passes through. When I am forced into a dark grey car by officers of Iranian State Security I am certainly scared, but not scared enough to confess anything. I think, 'This is a mistake. These people will realise their mistake and release me.' This is the stage of denial—one that allows many victims to sustain hope. 'This is a mistake. I am a good person. They will not harm me.' Sometimes this stage lasts for hours or even days, depending on the strategy of the tormentors, and sometimes it lasts for about thirty seconds.

I remain in the denial stage for the whole period of time in the car, sick with fear, though I am forced down onto the rear floor of the car so that I see nothing. I am more occupied with the pain of being held down in this position than with the dread of what might follow. But in brief periods of slight relief from the stress, I think, 'How do I know these bastards are from State Security? Maybe I am being kidnapped. Maybe they will demand a ransom for me. I have no money; they will see their mistake. I will promise them that I will tell no one if they release me.'

The car travels for quite some time—perhaps forty-five minutes, so far as I can judge. Then we stop, and I hear a gate opening. We travel slowly for a further two or three minutes, then stop again.

'Sit up with your eyes shut,' I am told. 'Do you understand? With your eyes shut! If you open your eyes, I'll break your neck.'

Once I'm upright, a blindfold is tied tightly around my head so tightly that the pressure hurts my eyes. I'm dragged from the car and forced forward, one man guiding me with a powerful hold on my upper arm. We are moving rapidly across what seems to be an open area, perhaps a courtyard, then down three steps. I am inside now—I can sense it. I am wrenched left and right, down what must be a long series of connected corridors before we stop again. A door is opened. I hear what sounds like a metal chair being dragged across a concrete floor. I'm forced down on the chair, my arms are twisted behind me and my wrists tethered. I am told to remain in the chair.

'You try to get out of that chair, shithead, I'll break your legs.'

The door slams shut. An iron door, it must be. And now I am, I believe, completely alone in a cell, and God knows where this cell might be. My wrists are manacled, my eyes blindfolded. I am utterly at the mercy of people who would not know the meaning of mercy.

How many people in history have sat running with the sweat of pure fear in a cell just like this one, in a prison just like this one (for my assumption is that I am in a prison), their wrists chained, their eyes wrapped in a blindfold? Millions, over the thousands of years that comprise the archives of torture. Such a primitive science, the science of torture. It is like one of those inventions that never changes because it was complete in its utility at its first appearance. Refinements such as the use of electricity to administer electric shocks are just that—refinements. But the basics remain the same. In Persia four thousand years ago—perhaps in this very city—someone would have been held in a cell and tethered like me. Someone would have been waiting in terror the next move of his captors. This is stage two of the various stages that a man awaiting torture endures. The realisation that nothing can save him. Nothing.

I sorrow for Azita and for my Newsha. In exactly the way that I am in the powerless position of so many others down the centuries, so my wife and daughter are in the same situation as millions of other wives and daughters in history, left knowing nothing, dreading what they might learn of their husband's or their father's fate. For many of these wives and daughters, the next time they see their husband or father is as a corpse.

I try to imagine the crimes of which I might be accused, and there are a number: being a Jew, being a Jew married to a Muslim, being an abortionist, being a man who utters criticisms of his nation's rulers, being a boy (as I was at the time) who swindled the vile Haji Heydar out of five hundred American dollars. I could hang three or four times over.

I can tell you that the fear I am experiencing is not anything that comes into the life of the average person. As a child, you might fear your mother's anger, your father's anger, your teacher's wrath, or the ill will of some bully who could, if he wished, push you into a puddle and kick your behind. But my fear is not like that. Most things you fear leave open the prospect of survival—your mother slaps you hard, your father takes off his belt, bends you over his knee and thrashes you, ten blows, twenty, even more. But the bed in which you will sleep later that day still awaits you, food will still be set before you at the kitchen table. The people who have kidnapped me have no one on earth to answer to, and there is no bed awaiting me once I have endured a period of punishment. It is impossible for me to imagine the time after the punishment intended for me. The future of Kooshyar Karimi has been suspended.

In such a situation as mine, you will most probably do and think as I do now. You will ask yourself if there is anything you might say or do that will save your life. You think of the people you know, people whom your kidnappers might wish to learn about, and you think, as I am thinking now, 'Will I betray them? Is it acceptable for me, under torture, to tell my tormentors what they wish to know about Sarabi and Sayar, for example? Do I have anything to bargain with? Will the information I can provide win me a reprieve?' Because I don't think I will be able to stop myself saying whatever I need to say to save my life.

Whatever problems I face in my married life with Azita seem utterly insignificant now. My home and wife and daughter form a paradise that I yearn to return to. I picture Newsha's face and it seems to be the most perfect expression of innocence and love on earth. Can love such as that which I feel for my daughter be taken away from me so completely? Is that possible?

I hear footfalls outside the cell. I hear voices. I think the people who brought me here are coming back, and I tremble. But then the voices fade away and there are no more footsteps and I experience a paradoxical anger at being ignored. My hands ache. I attempt to make minor adjustments to my posture in order to relieve the extreme discomfort. I think, 'How much time has passed since I was brought here?' It is difficult to estimate.

An hour? More than that? Yes, surely more, surely two hours! I hear voices in the corridor again and I think, 'Come to my cell! Come in here!' But nobody comes and the silence returns.

Is it three hours now? My bladder is painfully swollen.

In a short respite from the longing to piss, I suddenly understand what is happening. I understand the strategy. These people who have me in their power don't think of time limits. If they want to wait ten days before talking to me, they can. And who knows? They might have a queue. I could be number five or six or seven in line for interrogation. It is to their advantage to make me wait. Every hour diminishes my power to resist. Soon I will piss myself, and my humiliation will please them. I've been waiting for the torture to begin, not realising that it began the moment those two guys walked up to me in the street.

Eventually the door to the cell opens and two men—I can tell by the footsteps—walk in. They stand behind me, making me more vulnerable than if they were in front of me. They whisper. I can make out, 'Alright. If you like.' One man leaves. The other takes up a silent position before me. I can smell him, I can hear him breathing. He waits and waits. I don't know what he intends to do. I raise my head blindly and look toward the place I believe he is standing.

Then he is gone. The door slams behind him.

The madness they intend to conjure in me is taking hold. Four hours have passed now. It must be four hours. My bladder is in agony.

I murmur to myself, a type of low moaning such as people chant at a funeral, 'Newsha, oh God, Newsha!'

I hear myself keening, 'Let me go...let me go...'

I say aloud, 'I have done nothing... I am innocent, oh please believe me. I am innocent.'

'Alright, I cheated Haji Heydar... Yes, I'm a Jew, I admit it...'

Surely five hours now. Whenever I hear footfalls I cry out 'Excuse me! Excuse me!'

My courtesy is ridiculous, but I don't want to antagonise anyone, I only want to be allowed to empty my bladder. I hold on and hold on until I can hold on no longer, and piss comes gushing from me and soaks the leg of my trousers. The piss is hot at first, then cold.

'Let me go, dear God, let me go...'

'Newsha,' I whisper. 'Newsha...'

I sit with my head on my chest. Every time I hear a sound I raise my chin. The pain in my hands and wrists is utterly unbearable. I want them to come. I want them to do whatever they intend to do to me. Sitting in this metal chair in my piss-soaked trousers makes me feel as if I am so insignificant to the people who have put me here. Is this their chosen method of torture? Neglect? Will I be left here to rot and be infested by maggots until they finally attend to me? Something in me insists that I be taken seriously, even if that means torture. In medieval dungeons there was often a cell called an 'oubliette', from the French word for 'forget'. A prisoner would be left in the oubliette—and forgotten. Both alive and dead at the same time.

I was told that if I got up from the chair my legs would be broken. I believe the man who told me this but I can no longer sit where I am. I lift my arms behind me and attempt to stand. I fall sideways onto the floor, free of the chair.

Oh, God, the relief! The concrete of the floor is as welcoming to my body as a feather mattress. I lie where I am for hours, or for what seems to me to be hours. I hear footsteps and experience a renewed yearning for the footsteps to stop at the door of my cell. I attempt to get back on the chair, feeling for it with my feet. It's too hard. I lie still, readying myself for a second attempt. If I am found on the floor I will say, 'I fell off the chair.' But they won't believe me.

Then something occurs to me. One way or another, I have commenced a relationship with the people who intend to torture me. A strange type of intimacy has got into my blood stream. I think of what they will say when they see me on the floor, and of what I will say, and I imagine their anger, and their retaliation, and my response. I think, 'Maybe they will see that it was impossible for me to continue sitting on the chair, maybe they will feel pity for me.' This is just what happens in other relationships, like my relationship with my wife. With Azita, I am always thinking, 'What will she say when I tell her such-and-such? Will she be angry? And if she is, what will I say?' I am appalled to realise that the kind of mindset I experience here, I have experienced in the world at large in ordinary relationships.

And another thing. When the torturers see that I am no longer on the chair, they will be pleased. Does that sound strange? That they will be pleased? Let me explain. If I do exactly what they tell me to do, I bore them. But when the prisoner disobeys, a type of excitement enters the relationship. The disobedient prisoner is far more interesting than the obedient prisoner. The disobedient prisoner provides the torturer with the opportunity to shout and use his fists.

As it happens, I am still out of the chair when the door swings open. And sure enough, the response of the man who has entered my cell is that of great excitement.

'Motherfucker, who told you to get out of that chair!'

I am punched on the side of the head and fall to the floor. I develop a vision of a huge ape glowering above me.

'Zionist dog! I told you to stay on the chair!'

Now I am kicked violently, and I attempt to curl myself up to avoid the kicks landing on my stomach, my face. The kicks come so rapidly and with such force that I haven't got the time to scream, or to plead for mercy. Finally I am lifted to my feet and slammed back onto the chair. My arms are wrenched behind me and over the back of the chair. The pain is fierce. My shoulders feel dislocated. The ape is now in front of me, landing slaps and punches on my face. With each blow he shrieks a curse.

'Piece of Zionist shit!'

'Israeli pig!'

'Motherfucker Jew!'

In my whole life I may have been struck forcefully on the face maybe once or twice. Now I'm being pounded ten or more times in a minute. I'm already in a state of concussion, my vision blurred and my wits scrambled. The blindfold is beginning to work itself loose and I can glimpse below me the heavy black boots of the ape. The blows are now aimed at my stomach and chest and they land so rapidly that I try to scream, 'I'm dying!' What seems to be coming towards me is something I've never faced before: the end of my existence. Over the years of my life, there have been many thoughts about what death would be like, but nothing I've imagined is remotely like this. It's as if a mass of darkness has detached itself from the more general darkness and is wrapping itself around me with a dense, even pressure. I think, 'I didn't know it would be like this...'

And then I am unconscious.

The first thing I am aware of when consciousness returns is just that—consciousness. We like to pretend, at times, that we are not sure whether we are dreaming or truly awake. We might say, 'Is this a dream?' But the truth is that we always know when we are inhabiting the real world and when we are experiencing a dream. I have no doubt that I am alive, and that the existence I am now aware of hangs on the same thread as my last recollections of reality. I have been in the hands of a person who had punched and kicked me black and blue, so my assumption is that I am still in that man's hands, that the punching and kicking might recommence any second.

So I lie still.

I am on a concrete floor, on my stomach. The concrete is cold. The sensation of pain floods into my brain from four or five or six distinct sources. My ribs, my legs, my back, my shoulders, my stomach... Utterly excruciating pain shoots through my head, and I expect that I have sustained a fracture to the base of my skull. I have guessed correctly, because seconds later the copper taste of blood invades the back of my throat. My hands are no longer shackled. I try to part my lips but they are so swollen they won't move. My trousers are soaked with urine. I can recall pissing myself, but I seem wetter than I was then. I must have lost all control of my bladder at some stage of the beating. And I can see nothing. I am so used to the blindfold and to lack of vision that it takes me a few minutes to realise that my blindness isn't a normal state. I am still wearing the blindfold. That's why I can't see anything.

I risk moving my hands up to my face to feel for damage. I touch my cheeks, my lips, my nose. Every touch, no matter how gentle, registers pain. I extend one hand, feeling blindly, and my fingers come into contact with the metal legs of the chair. Then I freeze. I have the very strong sense of someone close by. I can hear breathing. Whoever it is takes a step, then another. I think he is standing in front of me. I can't be sure. I can only think, 'If he hits me again, I hope I die.'

A voice says softly, 'Doctor, you are very quiet.'

Why I should think so I can't say, but I do not believe that the voice I am hearing belongs to the man who beat me.

'Why are you so quiet?' he says. The inflection of his speech is ironical, mildly sarcastic.

I think he expects me to reply. I manage to mumble through my swollen lips.

'I don't know what to say...'

'You don't know what to say. Is that right? You are a writer, but you don't know what to say. A sad state of affairs. Why don't you curse the Imam? You could do that.'

He is referring to Khomeini[11] and suggesting, I suppose, that it is my practice to curse the Imam. I detest Khomeini but I have never publicly expressed my disdain. This man probably means that it must be my habit, as a Jew, to vilify the Ayatollah. He is having a little joke.

'Tell me this, Doctor. Why are you here? Is that too difficult for you?'

'No,' I mumble.

'No? You don't know why you are here? It is a mystery, is it? Well, let me tell you that you are in the custody of the Intelligence Service.'

I don't reply.

'This room you are in, Doctor, it's a special room. Whoever is held in this room is considered to be dead. That means you, Doctor. You are already dead.'

Cold dread overwhelms the pain I am suffering. I remind myself to breathe because I am in danger of suffocating from pure fear.

'I have done nothing,' I say. 'I am a doctor. I have worked all my life on Persian culture. I swear to you. I belong to no political party. I am an Iranian citizen.'

Now something even more ugly is unleashed in the man who is tormenting me. I have angered him.

'Shut your filthy mouth. To start with, you're not an Iranian. You're a Jew. You should have been hanged years ago. And your marriage is illegal because your wife is a Muslim. You lie to me one more time and I'll call back my friend. You know my

---

11. Ayatollah Khomeini (1900-1989), Shi'ite Muslim and Iranian revolutionary. Spiritual leader of the Islamic Republic of Iran after its founding in 1979 till his death.

friend? The one who knows how to use his fists? This time he'll get serious. You understand me, Doctor?'

'Yes.'

There is a pause. I don't know what's happening. I think this man, whoever he is, has crouched down beside me.

'Now you listen to me, Jew. Nobody on earth can save you once you come to this room. Nobody. Your Jew god has no power in this room. If you pray, he can't hear you. So this is what is going to happen. Are you listening? Someone will give you a pen and some paper. This is what you will do. You will write down every illegal deed you have committed in the last six years. You understand? Everything. Your secret trips to Israel, write that down. Your connections with Jews. Your writings against Islam, your writings against the government of the Islamic Republic of Iran. Make sure you write everything, Jew. Because we know everything, already. You see? We already know.'

But if this man already knows, what am I to write? Do I have to imagine the things he thinks I have done and concoct fantasies? I can't even ask him what he means. If I ask any question at all, I risk being beaten again and I will not be able to bear it. The whole of my body is like a throbbing bruise. One blow, anywhere, and I will scream myself to death.

'Nobody leaves this room without confessing, Jew. And you will confess.'

'Sir, please, I have a wife and—'

I am trying to say 'a wife and child' but before I can complete the sentence I am punched on my head so hard that I bite into my tongue.

'Don't talk to me about your so-called marriage!' the man hisses. 'Who let you marry a Muslim girl? Disgusting!'

Now he puts his lips close to my ears. 'You write everything, Jew. When you have finished, I will send you to gaol. Otherwise, you go next door. What happens next door, you wouldn't believe.'

I say without hesitation, 'I will do as you tell me.'

'Of course you will. Now write!'

I hear the iron door open and slam shut. A minute later the door opens again and a pen and what seems to be a notepad are thrust into my hands. The door opens and slams shut again. I wait for what I judge to be five minutes before lifting up my blindfold. The flood of light causes me to wince painfully. I gaze down at the ruled notepad and a green pen. Then I look around at the cell. It is much smaller than I'd imagined. The concrete ceiling is very low—barely high enough for a grown man to stand upright without stooping. No windows. The clay-coloured walls are scratched and stained. It has the look of a room in which suffering has gone on relentlessly for decades. The whole cell is illuminated by the soulless white light of a fluorescent tube on the ceiling.

Sitting on the floor, aching all over, I take up the pen and begin to write a confession. But it is not the confession of a Zionist spy. It is just an account of my life. I tell the story of my Jewish birth, of my mother's conversion to Islam, of my education, of my career as an author. I don't know how to lie in the way I am meant to. I don't know how to invent episodes of espionage, episodes of attacks on the Islamic Republic. All I can do is tell the truth. But I am acutely aware of how unlikely it is that my 'confession' will please the intelligence officer. I am quite prepared to tell lies, up to a point, but I simply don't know what to say. And if I write, 'I am a Zionist spy' what is to prevent them from putting a gun to the back of my head and pulling the trigger?

I am finished in about half an hour. I put the notepad and pen on the floor. Then I replace my blindfold. It is a wait of an hour or so before the door swings open again.

'Finished?' says a voice—not that of the intelligence officer.

I remain motionless on the chair. The guard takes my notepad and the pen, and the door slams shut. No more than three or four minutes pass before the cell door opens again. This time it is the intelligence officer.

'Lift your blindfold,' he says, harshly.

I do as I am instructed and find myself gazing at the face of the man who had been a disembodied voice until this instant. He is deeply unattractive: overweight, balding, with a straggly beard, perhaps in his forties, some evidence in his slightly laboured breathing of incipient heart disease. Just his appearance is enough to make me cower, let alone the knowledge of his unlimited powers of coercion. He is holding before my eyes a Torah, and also a copper plate showing in relief our patriarch, Moses.

'So you are not a Jew?' he shouts. 'That's what you say, isn't it? You are not a Jew. You signed papers in the hospital saying that you are a Muslim. You remember that?'

'Yes,' I say. What point in denying it? I had to sign those papers.

'Then what is this? What is this?'

I know exactly where the Torah and the Moses plate come from. They come from my house. The Intelligence Services must have sent men to my house to search it. What I don't know is whether I am expected to answer the question I'm being asked. It's not really a question, is it? It's an accusation. Nevertheless, I give a reply.

'The Torah,' I say.

And that earns me an almighty whack over the head with the book. The interrogator throws the Torah against the wall and heaves the Moses plate into a corner where it crashes loudly and spins on the concrete floor before coming to rest.

'You are a Muslim?' he hisses at me, his face close enough to mine for the foulness of his breath to wash over me, adding nausea to the pain that wracks me.

'You are a Muslim? But you haven't prayed since you've been here, have you? Not once.'

Then he's gone. I don't see him go. Maybe I've blacked out for a minute. The guard strides into the room and tells me to put my blindfold back on. I hear him picking up the Torah and the plate before the door slams shut.

In the darkness I listen to the random sounds of the prison. I hear doors being closed and opened. Muted voices, the sound of trolleys being pushed along corridors, footfalls. And most horrifically, the shrieks of a man who must be enduring a torture session. I could weep for that man, whoever he is, just as I could weep for myself, weep for the predicament I face. The intelligence people have whatever evidence they might require to torture me to death, to hang me, to shoot me, or to keep me here in prison forever. I am a Jew in the hands of people who have been taught all their lives to detest Jews and who believe quite sincerely, that all Jews are agents of Satan and that Jews wish to destroy the Islamic Republic of Iran. I am a Jew in the hands of people who have the power and the skill to keep me alive year after year and make each day of each year a horror beyond imagining.

In my chair, my head bowed, I think of Newsha, of Azita, and send my prayers to them. What I do not know at this time, as I sit on that chair in my urine-soaked trousers, that the pain I have endured in captivity up to the present moment is nothing compared with the pain to come. I do not know that I will scream my lungs out and long for death or that weeks and more weeks will pass in misery and despair, and yes, even in boredom and that I will stink to high heaven before long and will yearn for a shower and clean clothes even more than I yearn for food. And I do not know that on certain days I will experience a type of aesthetic disgust at the way my tormentors act out such stereotypical roles, as if they had all learned to speak and act like the bad guys by watching B-Grade Hollywood movies.

Above all, I do not know that a proposition will be put to me that will, if I accept it, require me to act as a spy every waking minute of every day. An officer of the Intelligence Service of the Islamic Republic of Iran will say, 'It's your choice. If you want to see your wife and daughter again, you will agree to become our puppet. Or perhaps you would rather hang? That can be arranged.' My answer to this proposition will be simply, 'Yes, I will do it.'

23

TURAN

I am again in Isfahan, the city of my mother's birth. My fiancée, Azita, is with me; my relationship with Azita has not improved in the least, but when the call comes telling us of my great grandmother Morvarid's death, she insists on travelling with my mother and me. Why, I have no idea. Morvarid was a Jew, Azita (as she repeatedly points out) hates Jews, yet here she is. Perhaps she simply sniffs out, in her uncanny way, what course of action she could take that would most irritate me while we visit my Jewish relatives in Isfahan.

Morvarid had reached a great age. The age, in fact, at which Death takes up residence at one's side and waits, and waits, politely and patiently. Of all my great uncle Abraham's family, it was Morvarid I felt most drawn to with her kindness, her warm heart. On the two occasions on which we had visited Isfahan in the past, my great grandmother had spoken a special prayer over my head in Hebrew, a prayer of safe journey. I wish Morvarid a safe journey, myself. If there is a place in some Jewish heaven reserved for the righteous and the kind, she will find her way there.

Abraham's house is full of mourners, perhaps more than a hundred, all wearing the black of this sorrowful time. How many Jews live in Isfahan? I don't know the answer, but surely more than a thousand. We may have a representative of every Jewish family of the city here. Hebrew is spoken openly. My mother understands, but I don't. I feel keenly the absence of my brother who cannot attend because of the exams he is sitting in Tehran. We should all be here.

My mother is respected here because of her interventions with the law on behalf of Abraham. But the respect is superficial. She is not rich, she is not genuinely influential, and she converted to Islam. Amongst the Jews of Isfahan, I wish to be considered a Jew myself, but I am not. If my mother converted to Islam— how can I be a Jew? This is odd, because in their hearts Jews do not think it is possible to 'convert' from Judaism to anything. If you are a Jew, you remain a Jew no matter what nonsense might come into your head, or no matter what ploys you might have to enact to escape persecution. And yet, if you claim to have converted, you are thought of as a Jew with some sort of black mark against your name. My mother and I are what you might call 'second-rate Jews'.

Azita asks me questions about my Jewish relatives—or more accurately, she nags me with questions. But I have no desire to answer her in any detail. There is so much I don't know, and in any case, why does she pretend she is interested? She's an anti-Semite. Yes, it has come to this in my strange, not to say baffling, journey through life: I am engaged to be married to an anti-Semite. Can you believe it? What I dread is that one fine day, Azita will inform me that the Holocaust never happened, it is all a fabrication of Israeli propaganda. Dear God, I have done some bad things in my life, I admit it, but did I do anything to deserve this punishment?

The ceremony of farewell to Morvarid is followed in accordance with the traditional honouring of the dead, *Kavod*

Hamet. My great grandmother's body has been taken in hand by the Chevra Kadisha, the burial society of Isfahani Jews, or by the female members, at least. Her body has been washed with warm water from head to toe, taking care not to turn Morvarid face down—that would be considered a sacrilege. The body has been garbed in *tachrichim*, very simple shrouds, plain white, so that there is nothing to show whether she came from the poor side of town or the fancy side. Her body has been watched continually, for that is our tradition, known as *shemira*, and it would be greatly disrespectful for the body to be left alone, unwatched, for even a minute.

I am not considered an immediate relative of Morvarid, even though I have always loved her dearly and honoured her in my heart. But my mother is thought of as a close relative. All of Morvarid's relatives, the close ones, make a symbolic tear in the garments they are wearing before we go to the synagogue, a gesture to show grief. The rabbi is on hand to assist. He recites the prayer, '*Baruch atah Adonai Elokeinu melech haolam, dayan ha'emet*'.[12] I recognise in this prayer, the memorial prayer, the words we recite when we first hear of one of our own who has died. '*Baruch Dayan Hamet*'—Blessed is the One True Judge.

Mullah Shimon, the rabbi, reads psalms in a clear, melodic chant at the synagogue. As I watch, I feel the awe of our faith settle on me. I think, 'It is a blessing to be born a Jew.' And I think, 'Whatever they do to us, they can never take away our blessing.' I listen to the eulogy for Morvarid, and I think, 'Morvarid, if you can hear me, it is Kooshyar. How much sorrow in my heart that you are not amongst us, anymore!' When the memorial prayer, *El Maleh Rachamim* is spoken, I touch my chest where my heart beats. Then the casket is taken from amongst us to the burial site.

---

12. Blessed are you, Adonai, our God, sovereign of the world who is the judge of truth.

At the cemetery, Morvarid is lowered into her grave after so many years of life. I stand by the grave and sorrow and wish my brother was here. My mother leaves the graveside and begins to search amongst the many headstones. I follow, not knowing what urgent matter could make her leave Morvarid's grave. She stops up ahead of me and sits by another headstone. She sees me approaching but remains where she is, her head slightly bowed as if in contemplation. I put my hand on her shoulder and read the inscription on the headstone: Habib Haimpour. The date of death is given as 1326, or 1947 in the Western calendar.

'Are you alright, *Madar jan*?'

'Who asks? My son who spends his days and years breaking my heart? Yes, I am fine. Thank you for asking.'

This is my mother's habitual manner. Not so much self-pity as self-lamentation.

'Who is Habib Haimpour?'

'Who is Habib Haimpour? Habib Haimpour is no one, since he is dead. But when he was alive, he was my father, God rest his soul forever.'

'Your father?'

'He was my father. He died before my birth, such a sorrowful thing. And so Abraham cared for me in his place.'

'You have never spoken of him.'

'No,' says my mother, and that is all.

That evening I find it impossible to relax. My thoughts turn again and again to this man by the name of Habib Haimpour, who was my grandfather. After the experience of the synagogue, of hearing Rabbi Shimon chant the blessing, the desire to know more of my Jewish heritage has become almost feverish. If I were to wait for my mother to tell me the complete story, I would be waiting forever. She harbours a deep-seated reluctance to reveal the truth about her past, about our past. I am certain there are secrets waiting to be disclosed, and like many others who imagine secrets, I believe that I have a moral duty to uncover them; at the same time, I know that secrets are best left alone. Uncovering what is concealed has never been a path to happiness. But I am incapable in my febrile state of taking the counsel of the wiser version of myself. Finally, I make an excuse to go out alone and walk to my Auntie Nosrat's house; Nosrat, Abraham's middle daughter, is by far the most embracing of all my Isfahan aunties. If I am to learn anything about my mother's life in Isfahan, it will have to be through the discreet revelations of Auntie Nosrat.

As it happens, her husband is at the synagogue this evening and I am afforded the opportunity to plead with my aunt for— well, for what, I don't know. But Auntie Nosrat likes to talk. She's had a life dogged by misfortune and disappointment and her only solace is in revisiting all the events that have left her so demoralised. On other visits to Isfahan, I have listened for hours at a time to her tales of woe, and she values me as a good listener. This evening I ask her to go over those tales again, leading her, with a certain amount of craft, to my mother's story. Auntie Nosrat lifts her hand and shakes her head, reluctant to speak in place of my mother.

'Please, Auntie. Please tell me.'

'Why? What makes you so curious about things that happened so long ago?'

'Auntie, at the cemetery today I saw my grandfather's grave. I did not know his name before today. How will I ever understand myself unless I know more about my grandfather and my mother? I beg of you, Auntie. Help me.'

She looks at me with sympathy. Misfortune and disappointment makes some people bitter, but Auntie Nosrat has instead become kinder and more generous.

'Kooshyar, you are a man now. I can tell you things that I could not speak of when you were a boy. You understand?'

'Yes, I am a man now. That's why I ask you to treat me as an adult.'

'And yet I must be sure that everything I tell you will remain confidential. Yes? Confidential. I do not want your mother to accuse me of meddling in your life. Do we understand each other?'

The story unfolds over a period of three hours. I listen spellbound, sometimes asking a question to clarify a fact, mostly silent. Everything Nosrat knows must have come from my mother. My mother would have sworn Nosrat to secrecy. Nosrat has sworn me to secrecy. But who do I swear to secrecy?

Shoshanna, Nosrat tells me, is my great, great grandmother, a lovely young woman (although how would Nosrat know that? I must accept that she has given herself the licence of a storyteller) and the wife of Moses, a merchant of Isfahan. In 1887 by the Western calendar, Shoshanna gives birth to her first child, my great grandmother, whose funeral we have just attended. Morvarid is born a little too early, but she is a striking child, fair-skinned with red hair, and is named for the jewel of the sea, the pearl, Morvarid. This is a Persian name, but so suitable that it is chosen over a Jewish name.

And Morvarid matures into a fine young woman despite the adversity of being a Jewish girl in a society in which a Jew is always in danger of being murdered. At twenty-one, my great grandmother marries a Jewish merchant like her father. Meir is his name. He travels out into the hinterland of Isfahan with a horse and cart selling produce and garments in the villages. Meir, the travelling merchant and Morvarid, his beautiful wife, waste no time in establishing a thriving family that grows to include three boys and four girls; and amongst the boys is Abraham, the father of Nosrat herself—yes, Abraham, from whom so much grief will flow.

Time passes, the children of Morvarid and Meir grow to adulthood in the fraught society of Isfahani Jews. Abraham is the most ambitious of the children, and also the only one of Morvarid's offspring with an unpleasant nature. Even at twenty-one, he is surly, combative, tight-fisted, arrogant. Morvarid is forever in the position of peace-maker, smoothing over the animosity he creates just by being Abraham. She lectures him, he repents, then returns to his more persistent nature and it is not long before his mother has to lecture him again. What his father, Meir, thinks of him Nosrat doesn't say.

Abraham, with little to recommend him as a husband, nonetheless finds a wife in Heshmat, dead ugly (it has to be said) and as repugnant in her manner as her husband. My Uncle Abraham then rolls up his sleeves and commences the task of realising his dream, which is to open a bottle shop—a humble ambition, and dangerous. But this ambition is consistent with my uncle's irascible nature. He could have sold buttons or bicycles or basins, but no, he chooses liquor and opens a shop in Sheikh Bahai Street. In fact the choice of selling booze doesn't come completely out of the blue. Abraham's father, Meir, is also a one-time moonshiner, distilling and brewing in secret off and on, selling his illicit product in bottles hidden in brown paper bags. Abraham, though, wants to carry out his trade in the open, which is asking for trouble. Like his father before him, he brews and distils and makes wine himself, so God knows what sort of poison he's inviting the drinkers of Isfahan to imbibe. But he's making money, which is all that's important to him; so, too bad about the livers of his customers!

Heshmat gives birth over these years to four daughters: Ezat, Nosrat, Aqdas and Soraya—only one of them, Nosrat, as I have said, with an attractive personality. (As Nosrat is telling this very story, I ask her why it is that she turned out so kind and gentle compared with her sisters. She says, 'Who knows?') The liquor store that provides Abraham with his income remains a constant source of trouble in the neighbourhood. The more pious Muslims of the city protest to the authorities.

'Close down this disreputable establishment!' they demand, and often go further.

But it isn't actually illegal to run a liquor shop as long as you are not a Muslim and as long as you don't sell to Muslims. Because Abraham is a Jew, he is thought to be bound for hell in any case. Most of Abraham's customers are, in fact, Muslims, and everyone knows that, but he is able to get away with it by serving Muslims surreptitiously. What is so amazing about this whole liquor business is that Abraham can surely see the time will come when he will be attacked, maybe killed, when a protesting crowd gets out of hand. Of course, a few years down the track I will be in very much the same situation as Abraham. I will be a Jew carrying on a trade that is likely to get me hanged, and in my case that trade will be even worse in the eyes of the law than selling vodka and dreadful scotch. I will be, in a few years, Iran's leading abortionist. You'd think that I might have reflected upon Uncle Abraham's experience as a law-breaker before I became a law-breaker myself. But I hadn't.

Abraham has a partner in his liquor retailing business— his brother Habib—a few years his junior. Habib has been inveigled into signing up as partner. His wiser judgement is certainly telling him that it would bring grief. And it does. For Habib, the worst sort of grief. One evening, warned of a near-riot at his business premises in Sheikh Bahai Street, Abraham hurries to the site and a scene of mayhem and murder. Men are shouting and waving about their arms, women are wailing, the police have arrived—and Habib lies on the floor of the shop in a pool of blood, stabbed to death for the crime of being an infidel Jewish alcohol peddler. Abraham throws up his hands and shouts to heaven, 'Aiee! Aiee! What has befallen us?'

Then he kneels by his dead brother with the crowd and the racket still swirling around him and whispers the prayer of the dead in our Hebrew tongue, but not quite loud enough to earn himself a knife in the ribs. How will he tell his mother, Morvarid? Her despair will be terrible. 'Aiee! Aiee!' cries Abraham, and pulls his coat over his head.

No one is charged over the murder. No investigation is mounted. Morvarid nurses her grief. Habib's wife Batia is now left a widow, but she is not homeless. In our faith it is the obligation of the eldest son to care for the family of any brother who has gone to his death. Batia and her three daughters move in with Abraham and Heshmat and the daughters, Ezat, Nosrat, Aqdas and Soraya. Now there are seven children and three adults in the household, and Abraham has more need than ever to earn an income from his liquor shop. He opens for business again within a week of Habib's death, and his customers return, quite possibly including the man who murdered Habib.

Seven daughters in the household, seven children, and within months, another child is expected. But it isn't Heshmat who is pregnant. No, it is Batia, the widow; Batia, who in her grief and despair, has somehow managed to conceive. She keeps the news of her pregnancy to herself; of course she does. What else can she do? In our faith we do not believe in Immaculate Conception. As Nosrat reveals this new twist in the story, I involuntarily cry out:

'Oh God! Abraham is the father!'

'Be patient,' says Nosrat, with a small tap of admonishment on my shoulder. 'If you wish me to tell the story, don't interrupt.'

'But it *was* Abraham, wasn't it?'

'I said be patient!'

Batia in her distress goes to Morvarid and confesses that she is with child. 'But daughter,' says Morvarid, 'how is this possible?'

'How it happened I cannot say,' says Batia and buries her face in her hands.

'Daughter, whatever trouble comes into your life you can share with me. Do you think you will be deserted? Never, in this world!'

But Batia is not consoled. So deep is her distress, so piercing her shame that she investigates means of killing the child in the womb, or of inducing a birth so premature that the baby will die in a flood of fluid and blood. One possible means— entertained by women for centuries—is to throw herself down a flight of stairs. The sudden trauma to the body and the release of a great deal of adrenalin could cause contractions. Another is even more desperate. Batia goes to the shed where the grain is stored, hoists a heavy bag of grain high above her with a rope thrown over a rafter, places herself prone directly under the bag and prepares to release the rope so that the laden bag will fall with great force on her abdomen and lower belly. Any method of causing a spontaneous abortion is likely to end with the death of the mother in a country like Iran, because even if the woman survives the abortion and makes it to hospital, she might then have to face the full force of the law for attempting such a thing. Nevertheless, Batia is resolved to either kill the baby or herself or both the baby and herself. She lies on the grain shed floor preparing to release her grip on the rope when Morvarid, worried about her daughter-in-law's absence, comes upon her in the shed, seizes the rope, shrieks at Batia, and after lowering the laden bag, takes Batia in her arms and comforts her back to sanity.

To spare Batia the shame of walking about with a swollen belly, she is kept indoors throughout the second and third trimesters of her pregnancy. When the child is born, a baby girl, the story told to the neighbours (who do not believe a word of it) is that Batia has been to Israel and while there, had adopted a baby girl for Abraham to raise. And the child's name? Turan. My mother. Making Abraham not my uncle, but my grandfather.

Listening so closely to Nosrat's tale, I cannot know that the strange, black comedy of the cosmos is at play in what I am taking in. Here's Batia attempting to abort herself of the child who will one day be my mother, and it will be my mother who in years to come, on a day of shame for her, will place my own life—the life of her very own child—in danger by letting the authorities know that Kooshyar is an abortionist. But before you laugh at these jokes contrived by the cosmos, you must first cry for days, or weeks, or even years.

The new-born child is detested by Heshmat, Abraham's wife, for she can guess the identity of the father. And Abraham himself, who has not a word to say about the paternity of the child, never glances at little Turan without disdain. This is my mother's life. Her mother the widow of a man murdered by a mob, and while in the womb, herself in danger of being murdered. She is fathered by her mother's brother-in-law, and how that coupling came about is anybody's guess—seduction, coercion, we don't know. She is raised by a mother mired in sorrow and grief, despised by her father, loathed by most of her family. At this stage of Nosrat's story, I'm thinking, 'No wonder my mother is the intransigent, devious, paranoid, deceitful, scheming, untrusting and untrustworthy, desperate, fearful, manipulative person she is!' I should have added to that list of epithets, 'fascinating', because that's just as true of her as all the other descriptions. But I say nothing. I listen to Nosrat, torn to pieces by grief for my mother, by confusion, by anger and disgust. I said I wanted to know, and now I've got what I asked for.

It is only Morvarid who has any love for the child, Turan. She tries to shield my mother from the scorn of the family. She takes my mother into her own room and raises her as if she were her own daughter. One woman's love and goodwill has come to compensate for the spite and lack of generosity of dozens of others. Somehow, despite all impediments, my mother grows up beautiful, obviously very eye-catching, and her good looks probably contribute to the hatred she excites in her family, none of whom has anything like her physical charms, especially not Hashmet, who (according to Nosrat's account) had all the allure of a rabid she-wolf.

My mother's situation in the family is approximately that of a servant, or perhaps slave, would be more accurate. She is put to work in Abraham's liquor shop partly to act as an attraction for the clients. She is not only a beauty, she is also very clever, very nimble, and her results at school are nothing short of sensational. She has a teacher who recognises her ability, and when Abraham tries to take her out of school so that she can toil in his shop for fifteen hours a day, this teacher intervenes, in fact, comes to the shop to remonstrate with Abraham. 'Unless Turan returns to school,' he says sternly, 'I'll have the law on you.' Abraham is alarmed; the last thing he wants is the law taking a close interest in him. He allows my mother to go back to school, but the intervention curdles his opinion of his niece and daughter even further. At the slightest protest from Turan— that he drives her too hard, that he feeds her too little—he is ready with his fists.

My mother's nightmare takes on a newer, more hideous dimension when a boy employed in the shop by the name of Scion begins to lust after her. Turan is intelligent, but at eleven years old too immature to know what this Scion is after. Yet she knows that it is not something she wants. He attempts to fondle her in the shop whenever Abraham is absent, to force his hand between her legs. She resists furiously, she threatens to scream.

'I will tell my uncle!'

'He will not believe you,' Scion whispers into her ear. 'He hates you.'

'I will tell my grandma!' Turan retorts.

Scion slinks away, prepared to wait and Turan dreads the times when she will be left alone with him. Whatever the urge that so dominates him, it will return. The idea of his hands reaching for her again leaves her feeling ill. She would rather die than submit to whatever it is that Scion wants from her. She imagines the ways in which she might end her life—by hanging herself, by leaping from a great height, by cutting her own throat. She would tell Morvarid but she dreads bringing more trouble, more grief, into that good woman's life.

Scion waits, but he doesn't wait for long. One night when she has locked the shop and is heading home, he ambushes her in an alleyway. He muffles her mouth with his hand, forcing her to the ground. He lifts her garments and thrusts himself at her. She frees her mouth and screams.

'Shut up, whore! No one can hear you!' he hisses.

He is wrong. Two boys passing by, Muslim boys in their teens, stop at the entrance to the alleyway, judge what is being enacted and rush to Turan's aid. Scion is cuffed and punched and chased away. The boys help Turan to her feet and try to calm her.

'He will come back! I fear him. He will come back!'

The boys promise to protect her.

'We live in this area,' one of the boys tells her. 'If he gives you trouble, look for us and we will punish him. This is our promise.'

Scion knows of the threat the Muslim boys have made; Turan has told him. The threat keeps him at his distance. But as Turan grows and enters her teenage years and her body develops, Scion's lust overwhelms his fears and he again attempts to fondle her. Turan enlists the Muslim boys to warn Scion off. They are very willing to help. Turan is well-known at school for her great academic ability, a star of the campus, one might say.

But Scion, in the manner of rats like him everywhere, is also cunning, and he tells Abraham that Turan is now consorting with *goyim* so that when the Muslim boys come to the shop to sort Scion out, Abraham is waiting. Knowing nothing of Scion's assaults on Turan, he takes it that Turan is peddling her wares to *goyim*, and thrashes her. Turan pleads for the intervention of Morvarid, and once more, my great grandmother comes to her aid. Scion retreats. My mother finds ways to negotiate her way around Abraham's tyranny but she continues to serve liquor in the shop on Sheikh Bahai Street.

At seventeen, her beauty has taken on a lushness that excites every customer who calls. One of those customers is Khalil Karimi, who is to become my father. He's many years older than Turan, but still handsome and, even more importantly, an accomplished seducer. One evening as he takes his vodka from Turan, he invites her to sit with him while he sips.

'What harm?' he says. 'What man would not wish for your company?'

My mother does as Handsome Khalil wishes. Her intuition tells her that he is not a brute, not likely to force himself on her. And she likes him. She likes him very much. He tells her tales of his adventures on the road as a bus driver. What a thick and lustrous moustache he wears! How gentle the light in his dark eyes! How tender his words!

'Married? No, I am not married. I was, but now I am divorced. It's a lonely life.'

'A lonely life.' How my mother responds to those words. Is her own life not as lonely as that of a mouse trapped in a cellar living on the crumbs it finds in cracks? Does her own heart not pine, as Handsome Khalil's does, for light and warmth and the touch of a loving hand? Oh, she could run away with this man, with Handsome Khalil! But listen to her—listen to what her loneliness conjures in her imagination! Perhaps Khalil thinks of her only as a silly young girl, someone to talk to while he enjoys his vodka, quickly forgotten when he is back on the road in his bus.

She dreams of him when she is alone in her bed in Morvarid's room. She whispers in the darkness, 'Khalil, oh Khalil, if you knew what dwells in my heart!'

Handsome Khalil invites her one fine summer evening to the cinema. Yes to the cinema. Has she heard him correctly? He wants her to come to the cinema with him? Turan has never been to the cinema, but she can imagine its wonder.

'Will you come with me, dear girl?' says Handsome Khalil.

'Oh, I will, I will. Oh yes, how I thank you for asking me!'

In the darkness of the cinema she finds it impossible to concentrate on the images that dance on the screen. She is too conscious of the breathing form of Handsome Khalil beside her, so close. He lifts her hand, caresses it lightly.

'Are you enjoying this?' he asks her.

He means the movie; she thinks he means the caress.

'Oh yes,' she says. 'Yes, yes, very much!'

His fingers stroke her wrist, glide up as far as her elbow, just a slight caress, nothing too forward, but oh!—the thrill, the thrill! She could almost faint from the intensity of the pleasure. My mother thinks, 'This must be love, this must be what people speak of when they speak of love. This is the most important thing in the world. This is everything!'

Turan has a close friend at school called Shirin, a girl of her own age. They have known each other for years. Turan has told her of all the travail in her life. Dare she speak of Handsome Khalil? But before she can find a way to speak of the love that has come into her life, Shirin has something to tell her.

'We are going to Israel,' Shirin says. 'We must. There is nothing left for Jews in this country.'

And so Turan loses the opportunity to hear Shirin's thoughts on the Handsome Khalil. If she had spoken to Shirin—who knows?—she may have been warned of what men will say and do when their libidos take over. Some, like Scion, will leap on you and tear your clothes in their hunger. Others will talk sweetly, softly, gently, tenderly, and rouse you to such a pitch of excitement that you can no longer think straight, and you will say, 'Make love to me! Oh, please God, make love to me; I cannot bear it for a minute longer! Make love to me!'

Handsome Khalil makes love to Turan. Turan swoons at the fragrance of Handsome Khalil's scented words. And the result is what it has been since time immemorial; my mother becomes pregnant. And at Khalil's urging, she abandons her Jewish faith and accepts the faith of the mullahs, at least superficially. She flees with Handsome Khalil to Tehran, to the big city. And the rest is terrible history: Koorosh's birth, my birth, the discovery of Handsome Khalil's other wives, other children, the grinding poverty, the disillusionment.

Nosrat's story affects me so deeply that even now, recalling it, my eyes fill with tears. My mother has been, shall we say, not the most embracing and generous of mothers, not the most consistent of parents. But the story told by Nosrat reminds me, whenever I need reminding, that her life has been one of endless struggle. If we cannot forgive those who have the history of my mother, what hope is there for us? What hope for me if I say, 'You betrayed me once too often, go your way and never return?' If I cannot forgive my mother, who will forgive me? I have betrayed infamously. I still hope for forgiveness.

24

TASHKILAT

I spend weeks in my cell. The wasteland of tedium I inhabit, in between bouts of dread, makes me realise that I can see time with my eyes. It is the grey of standing water in the gutter of a slum; the grey of a rag used for drying dishes, never once in its years of service washed in clean water; a grey so ingrained by the repetition of the one task that the rag almost sighs when you pick it up. It is the grey of an old woman's face as she staggers home from a day-long shift in a factory where she is paid less than she will spend on the bread she needs to live until the next day, when she will work another day's shift. I come to feel, at such times, studying bleak grey time hanging in the air of my cell, that torture would be a welcome relief from the exhaustion of contemplating nothingness. Torture is at least an opportunity for interaction with another human being.

And it comes to me in the second week of my imprisonment. The bolts to my cell door click open, signalling the arrival of my lunch. But instead my interrogator, whom I am permitted to address as 'Haji', enters my cell. He looms over me, wearing a fitted grey suit, his black polished shoes inches away from where I lie half covered and weak on the ground. One more time he demands my co-operation. And one more time I deny it.

292

He scoffs, adjusting his collar and smoothing out his jacket. He leaves my cell without another word and before the door can click back into place, two men storm inside, wrenching me up roughly by my arms. They drag me down the dim corridor. I want to be sick, except there is no food in my stomach. I think of what could await me. They are taking me to the gallows. They are taking me to the wall in front of which I will be shot. I should have confessed. *I should have confessed.* Newsha's face is in my mind. My throat has seized up completely. We come to a halt in front of a new room; it is empty except for a long metal table with thick leather binds at each corner. They strap me in, and I barely have the strength to struggle. I am pleading, though, in a voice I barely recognise as my own, I am begging for them to have mercy.

I am lying face down on the cold metal surface. One man roughly shoves an old cloth into my mouth and I fear I will suffocate. I take in deep breaths through my nose and I am overwhelmed by the stench of dried blood. *This must be the beheading table.* There is a moment of chilling silence, a horrifying pause. I can see nothing. I am waiting for the axe. I am waiting for the darkness. The man standing beside the table draws in a breath and exclaims into the silence.

'*Allah u Akbar*!' God is Great!

I hear the crack of the whip against my back before I feel it. It's as though a line of fire ignites across my skin. My limbs tug against the binds, but they barely budge. I can hear a voice, counting out each strike. Another crack. And another. It is *beyond* excruciating. The cloth drops from my mouth and my cries and screams drown out the counting for only a moment. Then I am gagged again. The voice remains steady, counting out the lashes. I feel myself getting further and further away from everything, from the smell of blood, from the voice of my torturer. I think I am about to pass away into blissful unconsciousness.

But each time the darkness clouds my vision and I am about to slip away, there is another strike of the agonising whip across my back, and I am grounded in this hell again.

Fifty lashes.

I am given fifty lashes. When it is finished I am hardly breathing. Blackness ebbs at my vision. I am shaking violently. Blood trickles down from the deep wounds in my back. I wish I were dead.

A country's intelligence services will tend to reflect something about the character of those who establish it, those at the top of government. In some countries the role of the intelligence services will largely be restricted to torture and murder because the people at the top reached their exalted status by torturing and murdering; a more effective means of staying in power never occurs to them. The more sophisticated the state, the more likely it is that the intelligence services will exercise greater imagination. The mission of these intelligence services is not simply to hang people they don't like, right then and there, but to anticipate the schemes of people they don't like months or years ahead. A further expression of this sophistication is to make use of the people they don't like, to entrap other people they don't like; enemies they deploy against enemies. Delayed gratification, you might say. Of course, in the long run both the enemies you enlist to work for you and the enemies they hope to snare further down the track will all be hanged or shot or beaten to a pulp. It is just a matter of how to get the best out of the people they hate.

Haji returns to my cell one morning—if it is morning. I have my blindfold on, as I am compelled to have. It has been two weeks since my torture session. I am sitting in my metal chair. Haji stands before me saying nothing at all. Then he says:

'You don't keep your toenails trimmed, Doctor. Do you not have the time? Are you too busy making abortions for whores, too busy fixing up cunts? Too busy praying to your god in Israel? Is that why you don't have time to trim your toenails? Is it?'

'No, Haji.'

Haji likes to illustrate just how much he knows about my private life. He knows everything. He knows, in fact, much more than I know. He has dates and times and places recorded. He can cite the very day, the very hour at which I performed an abortion on such-and-such a girl, the very day and hour at which I switched the number plates on my old car, the precise place, the exact hour that I went to restore the virginity of Majid's girlfriend. I imagine he could tell me the atmospheric conditions at the time I did anything at all. Rain, sunshine, a bit of both, windy, the temperature. I have been an object of study for Haji and his helpers for years. He owns my life so completely that he could, if he so desired, tell me not only everything I have ever done but everything I will do in the future.

'Well, it is very helpful for me that you have not had time to trim your toenails, doctor. Very helpful. Do you know why?'

'I don't know, Haji.'

'I will tell you. Today I am going to send a man, I know, a very strong man, to pull your toenails out.'

I hear the door open. A convulsion of terror runs through me.

'Haji!' I call. 'What do you want me to do? I will do anything!'

I hear Haji's footsteps return. I feel him hovering above me.

'Good,' he says. 'I am pleased to hear it. I will bring you some paper and a pen. Write down everything you have done to destroy the Islamic Republic of Iran. Everything. I want to hear the name of every Jew you have ever spoken to. Can you do that, Doctor? I am not saying that you must do what I tell you, Doctor. I am just advising you. Who knows? Perhaps you don't care about your toenails.'

It is not Haji but a prison guard—so far as I can tell—who waits in the cell with me while I write this newest 'confession'. Prisoners, Haji has told me, are never left alone with a pen, since they might use it to stab themselves to death. But I have no intention of stabbing myself with the pen. No, my only intention is to confess to every bad thing that has ever happened in the history of the world as speedily as I can. If I were told to confess to inventing smallpox, I would, or dropping the atomic bombs on Hiroshima and Nagasaki. I write that I have worked steadily to undermine the legitimate government of Iran for years and years, and that I have met with many Jews to further a conspiracy of Zionist Iranians. I write down the names of Jews I have met over the years, and many I have not. I cover three sheets of paper with my Farsi scrawl and sign the confession, very emphatically, Kooshyar Karimi, MD.

How can I sign such a document? How can I confess to things I did not do or even imagine? Where is my courage? When the Islamic Revolution swept aside the Shah's regime, revolutionaries invaded the prisons of the Shah. Wide publicity was given to the devices of torture found in the dungeons of SAVAK. I will not describe those devices, except to say that SAVAK had found ways to inflict pain that would not have been exceeded in the torture chambers of medieval prisons. And I know that many of the Shah's torturers were allowed to keep their jobs once the revolutionaries took over. The only difference is that now they are torturing the people who had once employed them. Once I become aware of how completely Haji rules my fate, I give up all hope of resisting him. Should I wait until my toenails, my fingernails, my teeth, my eyes and ears have been torn from my body before saying, 'Stop, I can't take anymore?' No, I am prepared to say right now, right here, 'I confess, I confess, I confess.'

With my cooperation assured, Haji now reveals to me my role in the great scheme of things, or the great scheme of things that concern the regime. I am to be an undercover agent, a spy, reporting back to him. I will infiltrate Jewish 'organisations' (what Jewish 'organisations'? The burial societies of various synagogues?) and Jewish households, all over Iran. I will pretend to have a great sympathy for the success of plots to destabilise the Iranian regime, and for the dissemination of Zionist propaganda. I will encourage Jews all over Iran to think of me as their best friend in the world. I will use my mobile phone, given to me by my mother a couple of years earlier, my *dasti* as Haji calls it (he can't bring himself to use a Western term like 'mobile phone') to contact him at frequent intervals. And he will direct me to various Jewish households, various individual Jews in cities all over Iran, since his knowledge of where Jews live in Iran and who they are is so much more extensive than my own.

'You understand everything I am telling you?' he says when the deal is struck in my cell, me in my metal chair once more, still blindfolded.

'Yes I understand.'

'If you try to deceive me, I will know in an instant. Do you believe me?'

'I believe you, Haji.'

'And what will happen to you if you try to deceive me?'

'I will be executed, Haji.'

A thin trickle of laughter escapes Haji, quite close to my ear.

'Execute you? You wish! Execution is what you will pray for, fool!'

'I understand, Haji.'

Haji imitates my faltering words, '"I understand, Haji!" Let me tell you—you had better understand! Now, take off your blindfold.'

'What?'

'Take off your blindfold.'

I do as I am told. The figure of the man I know as Haji is standing directly before me. But I don't look up at his face. I am so keen to follow orders that I don't know if I can take an order to remove my blindfold as permission to look up. What I can see of him is unexceptional. He is wearing brown shoes, terylene trousers, a shirt tucked in at the waist. He is overweight, not yet obese but perhaps heading that way.

'Look at me!'

I raise my eyes and gaze on the man who has taken such professional delight in tormenting me over the past weeks. One sees people of his appearance amongst the faces in the crowd on any given day. His beard is thin and straggly, his lips, at this moment, unexpressive. His age? About mid-forties. In his eyes it is possible to discern some of the brutality that he lives with and employs, but it isn't all that distinct. He could be anyone. He has watched—I have no doubt, as though it were entertainment—any number of victims die slowly and agonisingly, but most of the ugliness and malice in him is obviously on the inside.

'Do you know who I am, Doctor?' asks Haji in the way that people ask a question that is merely part of a longer strategy.

'Yes, Haji.'

'You think you do. But you don't. I'll tell you who I am. I am the most important person in your life. More than your wife, more than your daughter. If you disappoint your wife, maybe she shouts at you. If you disappoint your daughter, she forgives you. But if you disappoint me, Doctor... Can you imagine?'

'Yes, I can imagine.'

'So you can you imagine what I will do to you?'

'Yes, Haji.'

'I don't think you can. But don't worry. Maybe you will never find out. Or maybe you will.'

Then he says, 'Pick up your pen and write down what I tell you.'

I take up the pen and hunch myself over a fresh sheet of paper.

'Do you know why you have been given a second chance, Doctor?'

'Do you want me to write that?' I ask. I am confused.

'No, you idiot. I will tell you when to start writing. I am asking you a question. Do you know why you have been given a second chance?'

'No, Haji.'

'I will tell you something about the government of our country. Our government is very affectionate. Our government loves every citizen of the Islamic Republic. Our government even loves stinking, deceitful Jews like you. So you have been given a second chance to show that you love the government just as the government loves you. Do you believe what I'm telling you, Doctor?'

'Yes, Haji, I believe it.'

'Good. Now you can write. Listen to me and write every word.'

He now dictates what amounts to an agreement between me and the government of the Islamic Republic of Iran, a contract. Before he starts he asks me if I know what *Tashkilat* means. I tell Haji that I know what *Tashkilat* means.

'Now write!'

And this is what I write, taking great care to get every single word down on the paper. I am completely sincere in my promise to do everything I say I will do. I am not merely pretending. I want to show my sincerity in every way I can. But at the same time I am sick with self-disgust.

'I promise to follow the orders that *Tashkilat* gives me and to report anything I do or anywhere I go. I will not leave town without informing *Tashkilat*; I will not share the information I acquire with anybody else and I will not let anybody else know about this co-operation, otherwise I accept the punishments.'

The syntax is not quite to my taste, but I'm not about to complain. And I am hoping desperately that this contract will lead to a little piece of blue sky, to the smile of my daughter, perhaps a hug from Azita, although of that I can't be sure. She is sure to heap blame on my head for all that's happened.

Haji reads through what I've written, with approval.

He says, 'I'll be in contact with you. Keep your *dasti* charged. When you talk to me, you will refer to me as Haji Samadi.'

Then he's gone. The door slams behind him.

Days pass with no change to anything. I am not in the world.

Something I reflect on in these days of nothingness is the way in which I have come into possession of my mobile phone. In Iran at this time, a mobile phone is a rarity. The regime—naturally—is very suspicious of mobile phones. In the first place, mobile phones are not mentioned in the sacred scriptures of Islam, so that makes the mullahs nervous. Usually the mullahs look for an interpretation of the scriptures when some new piece of technology comes along. (Jews of the more rigid sort do the same thing as they seek guidance for a ban.) What they wish to do is to ban everything that was not around when Muhammad was living, but that's not possible. They find passages in the scriptures that speak of the evil of whispering gossip about one's neighbours, and they interpret this as Heaven's disapproval of mobile phones. Of course! People will use their mobile phones to whisper gossip. If it becomes necessary to sanction the use of mobile phones—the mullahs themselves might begin to see the benefits of owning one—then they re-interpret the scriptures in a second, highly tendentious way, to show that the Prophet would have loved mobile phones. But at the moment—no, mobile phones should not be in the hands of anyone whose loyalty to the regime is questionable.

My mother furnishes me with the mobile phone I use.

'Here, use this,' she says one fine day, and presents me with it. I ask her where it came from.

'Oh, a friend gave it to me.'

I know she is lying. But I think, 'Who cares?' It is very useful to me. I make a great many arrangements for terminations with it. And I never receive a bill. Never. I ask my mother about the lack of bills, and she just says:

'Oh, well.'

Once again, I know she is lying. And once again, I think, 'Who cares?' It is during this time in captivity that I realise every call I ever made on the mobile was intercepted. And I also have very, very good reasons to believe that my mother knew that every call I made was intercepted. I think that she gave me the mobile phone on instructions from *Tashkilat*. I doubt that the *Tashkilat* people said to her, 'Give this mobile phone to your son so that we can intercept his calls and hang him.' But I do think they said something like, 'Give this mobile phone to your son, if you know what's good for you.' My mother is highly alert to anything that is good for her.

And in these empty weeks I also find myself thinking in a very acute way about the breadth of this scheme of entrapment that can be traced back to the gift of the mobile phone. As a Jew, I would have been subject to greater surveillance than other Iranians. Something in the surveillance made the *Tashkilat* people think of me as a suitable case for exploitation. Perhaps they became aware that I was performing terminations and were calculating enough to hold off arresting me until they learned more. How did they come to know of the terminations before my mother facilitated such a discovery with the gift of the mobile phone? Somebody betrayed me, but who?

I go back over the steps that have led me into the abortion business, searching for the informer, knowing that it doesn't matter at all at this point but somehow I feel compelled to seek out the traitor. I suppose I want to know, because when you discover for yourself who betrayed you, some tiny bit of your self-regard is salvaged.

Is it Masood, my colleague in the hospital who first tells me about Mohsen, another colleague? Mohsen had been desperately trying to terminate the pregnancy of his wife. She wouldn't let him perform an abortion himself, for some reason, or maybe she didn't want an abortion—it wasn't clear. But one fine day he tells us that the problem has been fixed. He has given his wife an injection of something called Prostadin, a new drug designed to trigger uterine contraction and evacuation which had originally been used in veterinary medicine, mainly for cows. I am riveted, realising its potential to revolutionise women's control of their fertility in this oppressive society. How much less invasive and risky to take a drug to terminate a pregnancy than to have a surgical abortion! It would certainly be much less dangerous for me as well—performing this operation on patients in my own home presents significant problems should complications arise, or for my entire family if the police were somehow alerted by neighbours, patients' relatives, or others—who knows.

Thousands upon thousands of unmarried women and girls become pregnant each year, often enough in the aftermath of rape. For a girl or a woman to become pregnant out of wedlock in Iran is a death sentence in certain cases, and at the very least the beginning of a life of appalling poverty and disgrace. There is very little sympathy amongst the mullahs for victims of rape. The automatic assumption is that the girl has seduced the inseminator. The police might find the girl beaten black and blue, but they will still prosecute her. Thousands of traumatic conceptions constitute maybe a third of the undesired pregnancies amongst Iranian females. Many married women I later encounter seek to abort their fifth or sixth or tenth child if they can, where they don't have the means or resources to care for yet another child.

So is it Masood who informed on me? Is it Mohsen? Or is it Abdo, the *sepahie*, the name we gave to those government stooges who wander about Mashhad's hospitals, doing next to nothing other than snooping out subversives amongst the doctors? Most of these *sepahies* are corrupt, willing to take a few thousand *tomans* to look the other way if a doctor wants to plunder the pharmacy. Once the idea of obtaining abortion drugs and supplying them to the many desperate women who come to me, has taken root in my imagination, I am in a constant state of fevered desire to get the whole thing on the road. It is whispered that this Abdo has a stash of Prostadin ampoules. It is illegal in Iran, but this Abdo has a brother in the national police or somewhere who supplies him with ampoules that have been seized in drug raids. I saunter up to him on the ward one morning and make friendly overtures.

'I'm Kooshyar Karimi.'

'So what?'

'I've got what you might call a problem.'

'Really,' he replies.

He is cautious, as he has to be, but one way or another I get to know him better and am permitted to purchase a couple of ampoules from him. This is in his apartment. Because he is more or less above the law with this big-shot brother protecting him, and because he's begun to trust me, he lets me see his cache of pilfered ampoules in his refrigerator, about two hundred of them, at least two hundred. As soon as I glimpse them I know how many girls and women whose lives could be redeemed if I could somehow acquire them.

Then comes the heist. I can't afford to buy two hundred ampoules from him but I could perhaps appropriate them, somehow. Yes, extricate them from him. I think, why not? They weren't his until his brother stole them, so why shouldn't I steal them in turn for a good cause?

So what I do is this: I pretend to Abdo that I have found a man who wants to buy his whole stash for a bit under four million *tomans*, which is to say maybe five thousand US dollars. Abdo is immediately hooked. I arrange for a friend of Masood's to play the part of the buyer. Amir is his name, a TV salesman, as crooked as they come, but shrewd and a superb actor. My idea is to switch the Prostadin ampoules for ampoules of another, much cheaper sort containing a sedative usually administered for shaking and mild seizures. These Akineton ampoules are identical to the Prostadin ampoules in every way except one: they have a small blue spot at the top. It is very, very difficult to remove the blue dot, but I find a way, of course I do.

I am now equipped with a couple of hundred of these Akineton ampoules. I make an appointment to meet Abdo at his apartment with Amir, where I persuade Abdo to accept a cheque from Amir for the ampoules. The cheque is worthless, but Abdo doesn't know that and would never find out. Abdo insists on providing a short lecture on the correct employment of the Prostadin before he lets us go.

'You can expect severe lower abdominal pain from cramping before the bleeding, also vomiting and diarrhoea. Don't give any painkillers and don't give an anti-emetic. The cramps and pain help the process.'

'Sure!' I say, then I dash off with Amir to make the switch. I store the Prostadin ampoules in my refrigerator, then race back to Abdo's apartment with Amir and the Akineton ampoules.

'Oh Abdo, Abdo, we have a big problem!' I say. 'My friend, here, has just been contacted by a supplier in Tehran. He can get the Prostadin for half of what you're charging! Such a shame. Sorry. But here are your ampoules, so no harm done. See you another day!'

Isn't it likely that Abdo has come to see that he's been tricked? Especially when the one hundredth customer for the Prostadin had come back and screamed at him, 'It didn't get rid of the baby, you bastard! It just put my girlfriend to sleep!' And isn't it likely that Abdo would have let his brother, the well-known Revolutionary Guard and well-known thug, know that he'd been diddled? *Tashkilat* may have been on my case ever since.

So now I am a signed-up informer, willing to turn in Jews across the Islamic Republic in return for my life. But I don't even have a life anymore. Once the *Tashkilat* thugs have wrung from me every scrap of information they can, they'll slip a noose over my neck, and Iran's greatest entrepreneurial abortionist will dangle and strangle for maybe a minute before he gives up the ghost. I'll be in the informing racket for maybe a couple of years, then I'll be a corpse. Shouldn't I simply recant right here and now and accept my inevitable fate? Two more years of a wretched, ragged, dread-ridden life. Why bother?

And yet I know I will not recant. I know I'll do exactly what I'm told to do. I think of Raskolnikov in *Crime and Punishment*, prepared to spend a thousand years clinging to a ledge over an abyss if that is the only life he can have. Or Claudio in Shakespeare's *Measure for Measure*—Claudio, who can only save himself from a sentence of death by encouraging his virtuous sister Isabel to sleep with the judge who can lift the death sentence. Isabel visits her brother in prison and tells him to prepare for death, for she will not yield up her virtue to the vile judge. She tells Claudio that death is nothing compared to loss of honour. And Claudio speaks of his dread of death, and how unwilling he is to yield up his life. Because even this eternally stretched horror that is now my being, even the weariest and most loathed worldly life that age, penury and imprisonment can lay on nature, is a paradise compared to my fear of death.

25

THE CONTRACT

The child that was me, the adolescent, the young man, the lover, the physician—here they all join with what I am now: the spy. My clothing is returned to me. I am permitted to dress myself in what I wore when I entered this place. I have been through so much that I scarcely recognise myself as the person who once dressed in this shirt, these trousers, who once fastened this belt, slipped his feet into these shoes. I have reached into corners of my heart and soul that I have held sacred in the past; reached in and ransacked them. I am not who I was before this ordeal. I have discovered the limits of my courage, the depth of the fear within. I have pleaded for my life, begged for forgiveness from people who don't know the first thing about forgiveness. I am Kooshyar Karimi, yes, but a new version of me, a diminished version. People must feel like this once they have taken another man's life, people who have crossed a frontier.

I am filthy underneath my clothes, and I can tell by touch that my beard has grown a great deal. And I have lost so much weight! My clothes hang on me like those of a giant. I yearn to be clean again, clean in body and soul. I will have to settle for cleanliness of body, since the other is no longer possible.

When I am dressed, I tie on my blindfold and strike the door with my fist to alert the guard. Then I stand at the back of my cell and wait.

The guard enters and takes me by the arm. I am led from the cell, my arm held just above my elbow. We walk a long way, negotiating steps, turning left, turning right. Now I am aware of being in a long corridor. I can hear the echo of my own footsteps and those of the guard. I know the corridor is long because we keep to a straight path. Every so often, I hear whimpering, groaning, as if the cells open onto this corridor. God knows how many are imprisoned here. Gates open before me, gates close behind me. I climb more steps, then I'm told to stop. I have a sense that the steps have taken me up to an outdoor area. A car door is opened. I'm told to get into the car, told when to stoop. Someone opens the other rear door and sits beside me on my left. I'm nudged by another man who takes a seat to my right.

Everything that's happening seems like some strange ritual that I have to go through to transition from the world that I have inhabited for two months to the world that I am about to inhabit. As the car starts up and begins to move, my hearing, my nerves, begin to recall what it was like to be in the world. A trickle of the familiar returns. I can hear the sounds of other vehicles, I hear voices in the street. But I don't allow myself to experience anything even vaguely like relief. I don't trust the man to my left, I don't trust the man to my right, I don't trust whoever is driving the car, I don't trust the man who has told me to call him 'Haji Samadi'. This might all be an elaborate joke, a cruel joke.

When I last lived in the real world, I was known for a certain bravado, I took risks, I gave cheek, I was just a little bit arrogant. No more. All that swagger is gone. I feel now like a little person, powerless, pitiable. I can't even begin to imagine myself doing some of the risky things I was once known for. Dread has taken the place of that bravado. If these thugs each side of me stopped the car and told me to get out and sing and dance and whistle and bark like a dog, I would do it unhesitatingly. I am theirs, they own me, and they know it.

We drive for what I judge to be a bit less than an hour. The car is travelling smoothly, as if along a paved highway. The three men guarding me don't talk much, and certainly not to me. Now the car slows and turns onto a much less even surface, a dirt track. The climax of this transition back to the big world is drawing to a close. What I imagine is this: the three guards take me out of the car, take off my blindfold, let me look at the sky, then shoot me through the head. If I am given a minute before being shot, please God, please Adonai, let me die with a little dignity, please God let me not piss my pants, let me not sob and plead, let me not grovel on the ground.

The car comes to halt. The man on the left of me gets out and tells me to do the same. I am standing on the roadside, so far as I can tell. I can feel the breeze on my face.

'Count to fifty, then take off your blindfold. Do you understand?'

'Yes, I understand.'

Whoever it is who gives these orders gets back into the car. I hear the sound of the engine fading. I don't begin to count until I can no longer hear the car. But it occurs to me that the car and the thugs may still be waiting with the engine turned off—waiting to see if I am obedient, if I count to fifty. So I count, moving my lips. When I get to fifty, I continue on. I count to one hundred. I count to one hundred and fifty. I count to two hundred. I listen with great concentration, and my hearing is better than it has ever been in my life, sharpened by these months of being blindfolded. I can hear the breeze. I can hear, distantly, the sound of an engine, not the engine of the car that brought me here, maybe a truck engine on the highway some distance away. I hear the cry of a bird a long way off. I hear the distant barking of a dog.

I know I am alone, but I don't believe it. I believe this instead: that the instant I remove the blindfold I will see the grinning faces of the thugs, and they will cry out, 'Surprise!' Then they will shoot me between the eyes, and laugh and laugh, and say, 'Did you see the look on his face!'

I remove the blindfold with trembling hands. The light of day floods my eyes and makes me wince.

I am…nowhere. Nowhere. I look around at wasteland, let my gaze follow the dirt track disappearing into the sand and rock of some desert place.

I say, 'I am not dead.'

I stuff the blindfold into my pocket and walk back along the dirt track in the direction that will, I think, bring me to the highway.

I can see a town in the distance. I know the town. I know where I am. This is Abobargh, a new development on the far outskirts of Mashhad. Yes, this is Abobargh. This is the world. I am not dead.

I walk into the town; I find a shop with a pay-phone. I know that I still have my wallet in my pocket, but I don't know if the money I had in it when I was first arrested is still there.

But it is.

I take a note to the man behind the counter and ask for change. He looks at me as if he wants to suggest that I might like to think of cleaning myself up when I get the chance. I thank him for the change and dial my home number.

No answer.

I dial my father-in-law's number—Azita may well have moved back to her father's house.

And, indeed, it is Azita who answers.

26

FIRST MISSION

In that drifting state you reach when you wake in the morning and, still only semi-conscious, review your dreams, I lie beside my wife three days after my release and ask myself if my arrest had really happened or if it was all an expression of the anxieties that emerge in sleep. So much of what I've experienced has all the hallmarks of the melodrama of dreams. But as the light in the bedroom grows fuller and the real world becomes more distinct, this fantasy of having dreamt it all disappears in an instant.

'Why are you awake?' Azita asks. 'It is too early. Go back to sleep.'

'I'm getting up,'

I slip out of bed and walk to the kitchen.

I pour a glass of water and stand holding it, waiting to see if the slight trembling of my hand will subside. A surgeon cannot have shaky hands. Gradually, the trembling stops. I sip the water then walk to a window and stare out at the bleak morning light. I think, 'Whatever you wish fervently to be true always turns out to be a dream.' I don't know how much more of life I will see. I don't know if I will see Newsha grow into adolescence, into womanhood. And I think, 'I am now a slave. I am like one of the Jews held captive in Egypt, forced to do the bidding of the Pharaoh.' Then I think, 'But maybe Haji Samadi will never ring. Maybe *Tashkilat* will just watch me but never ask me to spy. Maybe they have a thousand Jews they're blackmailing and will forget about me.'

I entertain this desperate fantasy for a couple of hours further into the day, but then the phone rings and the voice on the line is that of Haji Samadi.

'Is this Kooshyar Karimi?'

'Yes, Haji, this is Kooshyar Karimi.'

I am to meet Haji Samadi in the centre of town—that is his instruction. And I obey.

He picks me up in a white Toyota, just him. I get into the front passenger seat, not knowing whether to say, 'Nice to see you,' (which would be ridiculous) or 'Where are we going?' (which would be risky and might earn me a slap across the face). So I say only, 'Hello, Haji.' He doesn't reply, but continues driving. We leave the precincts of Mashhad and head out into the open country. Just as I feared being shot on a similar drive three days ago, so I fear being shot now. I feel like saying, 'Haji, listen, if you intend to shoot me, do it now, for the love of God!' But I say no such thing. Slaves don't issue demands to their masters.

We stop in a small village such as are found everywhere in rural Iran. The walls hemming in the yards of the houses are mudbrick, the houses themselves are mudbrick. Apple trees with dust covering their foliage grow on each side of the road.

'We get out here,' Haji says.

I follow him along the deserted street to a small house with a green door. Haji takes a key from his pocket and unlocks the door and allows me to enter first. This seems oddly like courtesy, but I will come to realise that it is not manners but strategy: Haji never enters a building or a room first, probably to avoid the possibility of the person being escorted suddenly slamming the door on him and running for his life.

Once we enter the building we stand in a cobble-stoned courtyard, two cherry trees growing in the centre. Haji finds a second key in his pocket and opens the door of the building proper. Again, he ushers me in first. The house is sparsely furnished, two rooms and a kitchen, a bed in each room. The only concession to homeliness is a rather expensive Persian rug on the floor. Other than the beds and the rug, it's just the utilitarian minimum, including a couple of chairs. Why we had to drive all this way to this simple dwelling, I can't imagine. Maybe these *Tashkilat* people are creatures of habit and can't function unless they follow a routine, such as driving pointlessly for almost an hour.

In one of the two bedrooms, Haji tells me to take a seat in a wooden chair. When I am seated, he takes the other wooden chair, facing me. Haji is at ease in his wooden chair, I am exactly the opposite. I'm leaning forward a bit, as if to demonstrate how ready I am to listen, to obey.

'Listen to me carefully,' says Haji. 'This is your first mission.'

Mission? The word alarms me. The idea of me undertaking a 'mission' makes it sound as if I have taken on spying of my own free will. I am much more comfortable (if that's the word) thinking of myself as being coerced. This uneasiness with the word prompts me to, well, complain, astonishingly enough.

'But Haji, I am not an agent of *Tashkilat*. You said that I—'

I stop. Anger has overtaken Haji's expression like a storm coming down from the mountains. He leans towards me.

'Listen to me, idiot! You don't ask me questions! Where did you get that idea?'

'Yes, of course. I am sorry, Haji.'

He sits back in his chair, but with his eyes narrowed.

'This is your mission. You will gather information on Jews. First in Mashhad.'

'I understand.'

'Do you?'

'Yes.'

'No, I can see in your eyes that you want to ask another question.'

'No, Haji.'

'Are you certain?'

The fact is, I do want to ask another question. What is the matter with me? Is my natural inquisitiveness so strong that it can overcome the threat of punishment? Am I insane? And look, just look at me—I'm doing it, I'm asking a new question!

'Only I was wondering, Haji, why are Jews so important to *Tashkilat*?'

'Will I cut out your tongue, idiot?'

Dear God, the look on his face makes me certain that the cutting out of tongues would be all in a day's work for him.

'I am sorry, Haji.'

'Then shut up.'

He looks away from me and shakes his head, as if he finds it difficult to comprehend the full depth of my stupidity. Then he looks back at me.

'Okay, I will answer this one question. And then keep your filthy mouth shut.'

He fixes me with his Asiatic gaze.

'Jews,' he says, 'are vermin. They are the worst enemy of Iran, the worst. Do you know why the revolution has lasted for so long? For two decades? Because we keep a very, very close watch on Jews. Very close. Jews are a disease. Jews are AIDS. Do you know how AIDS kills people, idiot? It gets into their blood and destroys the healthy parts of the body. You are a doctor. You should know this. It gets into the blood and little by little it destroys everything. Jews are a disease that attacks Muslims. *Tashkilat* is the doctor. *Tashkilat* kills Jews. Have you ever seen

313

a Jew hanging from a rope, Dr Kooshyar Karimi? Have you?
I have. Many times. When I watch them hang I know that Allah
is rejoicing. You should be happy to help me kill Jews. Because
you are not a Jew anymore, are you, Dr Kooshyar Karimi? You
are a Muslim now. Isn't that right?'

A very small smile lifts one corner of Haji's mouth.

'Isn't that right?' he repeats.

'Yes, Haji.'

'You hate Jews now, don't you Dr Kooshyar Karimi?'

'Yes, Haji.'

'Are you ready to help me kill them? Are you ready to be the
doctor you are supposed to be and destroy AIDS?'

'Yes, Haji.'

'That's very good to hear. That's very reassuring. You know
Sayar, the photographer? You have been to his house.'

'Sayar? Yes, I know Sayar.'

'You go back to his house. You get all the information about
him you can. Everything.'

And so it begins. My first 'mission' is to deceive a good
man who extended the hand of friendship to me. A man who
has already suffered horribly. Even as Haji Samadi explains to
me all the tricks of the trade—how to completely dupe my
victim—I feel my conscience rebelling. It is as if some part of me
that has far more ambition for my soul than the part responding
to Haji is imploring me to listen. But I won't listen. I know what
I will hear: 'Kooshyar, there are far worse things than death. Are
you going to carry through life a bag of skin and bones empty
of purpose? Kooshyar, if you fear the slow death that Haji has
threatened, then stand now and run and die in an instant with
a bullet through your back. You say you are thinking of Azita
and Newsha. What use are you to them when your soul is being
eaten up with guilt?' I won't listen. I refuse. Because what is
the use of another martyr in the Middle East? So I trick my

conscience, and invent the mantra that numbs my very loud sense of judgement. I tell myself that this, fighting against my own soul, is another brand of courage entirely. The courage to survive.

'They will lie to you, these Jews', Haji says. 'You must see when they are lying. When you get back from seeing Sayar, write down everything on paper. Make sure your lines are double-spaced, and leave a broad margin on each side of the paper. When you have finished your report, call me on the number I gave you. What is the number?'

I recite the number without hesitation.

'So this is what you do. You telephone Sayar. You tell him you want to see him. Why? Because you desire more information about Jewish history. He will be flattered. Then you visit him and you talk and talk and fill him with confidence. You ask him a question such as this: "Sayar, my friend, how I hate the Islamic Republic. The only relief I can find is when I talk to Jews who hate the Islamic Republic as I do. Do you know other Jews who hate the Imam?" Okay, not exactly those words, but something like that.'

'Yes, Haji.'

The rest of the conversation is all 'This is what you do' from Haji, and all 'Yes, Haji' from me. Then Haji drives me back all of that long distance to Malek Abad Square. Once again I ask myself what the purpose of the drive to the village has been. I could have sat in Haji's car in Malek Abad Square and heard everything he had to tell me. One possibility is that he could have beaten the daylights out of me in the house in the village if I'd given him any grief. That wouldn't have been possible in the car. Another possibility is that Haji wanted to increase my sense of insecurity by transporting me to a strange location. God knows, *Tashkilat* probably has instruction manuals for interrogation techniques.

Two days later I ring Sayar and make an appointment to see him in the evening. He greets me warmly, offers me tea. We settle into a conversation that turns to the history of the Jews of Mashhad. I ask him question after question, and he answers each question with evident pleasure. I ask to see photographs. He shows me one after another and provides an explanation for each. This is such-and-such a person who left Iran and settled in Italy, this is the same man in the bazaar at Mashhad. He talks at length in a scholarly way about the origins of Jewish settlement in Iran. On the surface, I give the impression (I hope!) of avid interest. 'Hmm. fascinating, is that a fact? Interesting! Extraordinary!' And so on and so forth. Underneath, I'm furiously making mental notes to transmit to Haji Samadi. The deceit doesn't, at first, distress me as I'm too absorbed in trying to remember everything to feel sickened by my 'mission'.

But I am conscious of the great difference between my first visit to Sayar and this present visit. On my first visit, I was a free man, a genuine scholar, full of gratitude for the time Sayar was giving me, for the trouble he was taking. We were colleagues, then, in a fashion. Two free men, with a shared passion. Now, Sayar remains sincere, but my sincerity has gone. I listen with my ulterior motive uppermost. If Haji Samadi were to walk into Sayar's house now and say, 'This man, this Kooshyar Karimi, he is our man,' I would say, 'Yes, I am his man.' Sincerity is such an easy thing to feign.

Back at my own apartment, I tell Azita of the meeting with Sayar. I tell her that I must now write down everything and give the notes to Haji Samadi.

'Do it,' she says.

'It makes me sick.'

'Just do it.'

I write seven pages. Then I dial Haji Samadi's number.

27

CIGARETTE

My report on my visit to Sayar does not please Haji entirely. We are sitting in the front seat of his car off a square in Mashhad. Haji keeps looking up from the report to glance at me.

'Is this all?' he says.

'Yes.'

'He didn't give you any documents? He didn't give you any photographs?'

'Haji, he doesn't trust me enough yet.'

'Then go back. Make him trust you,' he threatens, with his eyes narrowed in warning.

I feel sick to my core. It's midnight. Azita and Newsha are sleeping soundly, but I'm being plagued by wide-eyed consciousness, by guilt. Visions of Sayar invade my mind. I picture him strapped to the metal chair, in Room 113, blindfolded and scared to death, wondering why such a thing is happening to him. Who has betrayed him? His bloodied face, his split lip, his agonising cries. For a second, I falter in my resolve to survive. I tear myself from the clinging sheets of the bed and stumble to the balcony outside. Can I do this? Where will it lead me? Where will it lead Sayar? Who will be my next victim? And through this deafening remorse, I almost fail to hear the timid, mumbled cry of '*Baba?*'

317

from within the house. I walk to Newsha's room to find her murmuring in her sleep, an expression of unease on her face. I realise she is having a nightmare as she calls out to me in her sleep again. At this moment I am struck with a love so deep in my core that I actually fall to my knees beside my sleeping child. Because I, too, am in a nightmare, the nightmare of reality. I will do what I have done my whole life. Survive. Because whatever hope remains, whatever future awaits me—it is held within Newsha's tiny, sweaty hands.

The next day I call Sayar and ask if he will see me again. He agrees readily, and once more I am received like a friend. Warm smile, warm handshake. I find that at the start of my visit, I can almost convince myself that my motives this day are pure because I think, what does it amount to? I chat with a person I like very much, he tells me about the Jews and their travails in Iran, I listen with interest (recalling everything, of course) we chat a little more, we drink a second glass of tea, we shake hands and part. Where's the harm in that, after all?

But then, further into the conversation, Sayar hints that there is another man, another Jew, who might be able to give me even more detail for my book—the book I'm meant to be writing about the history of the Jews in Persia. Haji has told me to let Sayar know that I have government approval for the book, in order to encourage him to tell me more. I am, in fact, beginning to enjoy the thrill of unearthing new material about the Jews of this country—not for Haji's benefit, but for mine. Maybe, just maybe, I can make my career as a spy work for me. Maybe I can gather all this stuff for Haji and build up my own store of information at the same time. I have begun to feel that *Tashkilat* is perhaps not all that clever. It is, after all, my conceit—almost ungovernable—that I am smarter than many people I meet. That's my hubris. Kooshyar Karimi, born genius. I think, 'You know what? You've got yourself all worked up over nothing.

Nothing! Trust yourself a bit more. Outwit these people. In a year's time, you'll have satisfied these thugs in *Tashkilat*, and you'll just about have a book finished.'

'Who is this man who knows so much about us Jews?' I ask Sayar.

'Who is he? Well, I don't know if I should tell you.'

'Please! You can trust me.'

'Can I, Kooshyar?'

'Absolutely. No one will know. Believe me.'

'Believe you?'

'I swear!'

'The thing is,' says Sayar, leaning close and whispering, 'this man is a friend of mine. I think he has some dangerous ideas. Much more dangerous than any ideas of mine. The security people, they would love to know about him.'

Then he whispers a name.

I write up my report for Haji Samadi very thoroughly. It runs for ten pages. I am very conscientious. I include small details, such as the pattern on the glasses from which we drink our tea. I leave out the reference to the Jew in Tehran with the dangerous ideas, even though I know perfectly well that Haji would love to be told of this mystery man. The patterns on the tea glasses mean nothing to Haji. A subversive Jew—yes, that was what my notorious 'mission' is all about. I think, 'Too bad. They will never learn his name from me.'

I phone Haji then drive to meet him in the heart of Mashhad. He picks me up in a different car—how many cars does he have?—and drives me to a construction site out of town. It's a desolate looking place. We sit on the step of a half-completed building while Haji questions me about my most recent meeting with Sayar.

'And this is all he told you?'

'Yes.'

Haji looks at me sidelong. His eyes narrow. 'You're quite certain about that, Doctor?'

'That's all he said.'

Haji nods. Then he stares away into the distance.

'Right.'

He drives me back into Mashhad in silence. I think, 'Well, what does he expect? Does he think I'm likely to give him the entire directory of Mossad agents in the world? Does he think I have the plans for nuclear installations in Israel? I'm just talking to a nice old man about his photographs.'

I'm summoned to a meeting with Haji a couple of days later. He'll pick me up, he says, from the corner of Hasani and Bani in the Ferdowsi area of town. And I'm there on time, as I always am, but Haji is late, as he always is. Waiting on him arouses resentment in me. Why should I be at the beck and call of this half-educated thug? I'm a scholar, and what's he? Damn him. It's an extraordinary thing, isn't it, the persistence of egotism? All he has to do, Haji, is look at me in anger and I'm down on my knees grovelling for forgiveness. But at the same time, I'm thinking, 'Hah! That ignoramus! It's beneath my dignity to so much as glance at him!' It's a class thing. I'm now of the intellectual class, and he's of the ignorant class. I feel disdain for him, even while I fear him.

It's not Haji who picks me up but one of his underlings in a white Toyota station wagon.

As he pulls up beside me, he shouts, 'Get in!'

'Who are you?' I ask the driver, confused.

'Sent by Haji Samadi. Now get in.'

I obey, but I'm very uneasy. The driver certainly has the thuggish look of someone who would work for Haji Samadi. A couple of times I'm on the verge of demanding some sort of proof that this person has been sent by Haji, but I think better of it. The fellow's expression is one of intense impatience—I don't want a slap across the mouth. We head at high speed out of the city, leaving the paved road for a dirt track that leads us to a ramshackle motor repair place. The driver pulls up abruptly in a cloud of dust outside the open doors of the garage and tells me to get out. Another man is waiting inside the garage.

'Okay, Ali, go and get them,' the driver says.

Get who? By now I'm not a shadow of the man who stood waiting for Haji with such haughty contempt. I'm trembling all over.

'W...w...where is Haji?' I manage to stutter.

'Shut up and sit down,' the driver says.

An old metal chair stands at a battered wooden desk. I sit warily, glancing about at the chaos of the place, broken glass in the windows, greasy engine parts on the dirt floor. What sort of response would I get if I asked for a glass of water? And where would this man find a glass of water for me in any case? I desperately need a cigarette.

Ali returns with a great brute of a man carrying a length of steel cable and another mean-looking man, just as menacing.

'Asad, say hello to Dr Kooshyar Karimi,' Ali says.

Asad takes a stride toward me, swings the cable and brings it down across my chest with great force. I scream and half-rise from the chair. My chest feels as if a hoop of red-hot steel had been strapped around it. The three men seize me and throw me down on my back across the wooden desk. I'm struggling with all my strength, thinking of nothing but my need to escape further pain. I'm pinned down, an elbow digging into my burning chest, hands grasping my arms, my legs. Ali tears off my shoes, then my socks. My shaking legs are held firmly. Ali rains rapid blows with the steel cable on the bare soles of my feet, and my mouth hangs open in a silent scream as the shock takes over. Merciless, unrelenting slits and slices of agony are

321

lashed onto my damaged flesh until I feel my consciousness slipping away from me. As Ali rears back with the steel cable for each lash I have perhaps a second in which to hope for a miracle because I know I will not be able to bear one more blow, not one more, but the blow comes and I scream again, and once more I hope for the miracle. The more I writhe on the desk top, the more force the other two men use to hold me down.

Now the whipping stops. Ali lets his hand holding the steel cable hang at his side. His chest is heaving with the effort he has put into the torture and his face is running with sweat. The man who drove me here leans over me.

'Do you know why you are here, shithead?'

My screams have been succeeded by sobs, racking sobs. Then a strange thing occurs: I would do anything for these men who are torturing me, anything in the world to suddenly be their friend. I want to be on their side of the torture business, not on my side. I feel that I want to implore them to take me into their fraternity of torturers, to accept me as a brother. I no longer want to be part of the world that despises these men. I want to be in their world.

'Please,' I whisper through my tears, 'I have done nothing, please believe me.'

'I asked you a question!' says the driver. 'Do you know why you are here?'

'Please, please…'

The driver slaps me hard across the face and I scream once more. I want to say, 'Please don't hurt me anymore. Anything you want me to do I will do,' but all I can get out is 'Please…'

'I'll tell you, little doctor. You are here to have your memory refreshed.'

He clamps his hands around my throat and squeezes tight. I can't draw breath and my body arches in the rigour of strangulation. On the point of fainting or dying—I don't know

322

which—the driver releases his grip on my throat and he and Asad lift me bodily from the desk top and slam me down in the metal chair. Gasping and wheezing, I try to raise my hand to fend off any new assault on my throat.

'Look at the moron!' he says and laughs. Then, 'Go and get him.'

Go and get who? A new dread leaps into my breast: that someone with even greater expertise in torture has been called for. I glance about desperately in the way that all those enduring torture glance about, hoping to see some quick path to death—a blade I might plunge into my throat, a pistol I might seize and fire through my head.

An old man walks into the room and stands in front of me. He looks down at me in a kindly way, shaking his head as if in disappointment and sorrow.

'My son,' he says quietly, 'I told you to be cautious.'

I do not recognise him at first, my vision still distorted by the wetness of my matted lashes. But it is Sayar, the kind old man with the photographs, with an interest in Jews. It is my friend Sayar.

'Sayar?' I murmur in a sort of mad wonder.

'Yes, Kooshyar. Yes indeed.'

He reaches into the pocket of his jacket and brings out a white packet of Bahman cigarettes. Does he intend to offer me one? Even in the midst of my fear and pain and confusion, I want one of those cigarettes. But he doesn't offer me one. He lights one for himself only.

'Open his shirt,' he says, and Asad reaches for my collar and rips open my shirt to bare my chest.

'Hold him,' says Sayar.

Asad, the driver, Ali—they all take a firm grip on my shoulders, wrenching my hands behind me to the back of the chair. Sayar leans over me, holding the burning cigarette close to my chest.

'This is necessary,' he says, and he puts the burning tip of the cigarette against my skin. I strain with all my might against those holding me in the chair, screaming for mercy.

'Yes, it is necessary,' says Sayar again, and he deliberately puts his face right into my field of vision so that I can see the cruelty in his eyes, the rage.

He draws on the cigarette, turning the tip bright red. He holds the tip close to the flesh again, on the other side of my chest, then settles it below my right nipple. I am screaming something that I can't understand myself, screaming it again and again. What is it? What am I shrieking?

It is, 'Not me! Not me!'

Sayar heats the tip of the cigarette once more, it's down to half its length now. He leans close to me, holding the cigarette as if it were an instrument. I'm pleading hopelessly.

'Not me, not me!'

I can hear the grunts of effort coming from Ali, from the driver and Asad. Sayar probes my flesh with the burning tip and my scream this time feels as if it is tearing the inside of my throat away.

Sayar draws on the cigarette one more time then drops it to the floor and extinguishes it with the toe of his shoe.

'Next time, it will be your eyes,' he says.

An hour later I am being dropped off in my street by the driver who had picked me up. He hasn't said a thing all the way, but before he lets me out of the car he tells me to mention nothing to anybody about anything.

'You talk,' he says. 'Next time, it's worse. You understand?'

I realise that he's not threatening me, just warning me.

Once in my apartment I bathe my feet and treat the burns on my chest. Azita stands watching me, attempting to conceal her retching horror at what has happened. There are tears in her eyes, and she is biting onto her knuckle. She looks at me as though she is looking upon a man on death row. I try to explain to her the mistake I made.

'I left out something in my report for Haji. They knew.'

'Sayar works for them?'

'Yes. He works for *Tashkilat*.'

'You should have told them everything in your report.'

I look at Azita, not knowing whether to scream or laugh like a madman. I think to myself, 'Of course I should have told them everything! How much more obvious could that possibly be? I underestimated them. I thought I could outsmart them. But they know everything. They are probably listening this very minute. Dear God, I've been stupid! More than stupid. There are people who are stupid, but they know it, they know they're idiots. But I am the sort of idiot who thinks he's a genius. That's the worst sort.'

Two weeks pass before I hear from Haji Samadi again. Two weeks of stumbling about in agony on the raw flesh of my feet, of applying antiseptic and bandages to the blisters on my chest, two weeks of listening to more gratuitous advice from Azita concerning the necessity of making the fullest possible reports to my handlers. And two weeks of feeling sick at heart over the extraordinary mess I have made of my life. I mean, really, what a catastrophe. Out of the gifts I was born with, look what I've created. I'm a doctor, but a doctor living with a death sentence hanging over his head. I'm a Jew, but a Jew who is expected to betray his own people to a Jew-hating gang of barbarians. I'm a son, but the son of a mother who has made some kind of deal with fundamentalist thugs I can't even think about without wanting to weep. I am a husband, but a husband who turned his back on a woman of incomparable intelligence, gentleness and beauty in order to marry instead a shrewish and intensely annoying woman chosen by his mother. I am a father, but a father who will never see his beloved daughter grow into womanhood.

Two weeks later I sit beside Haji in his car at the usual meeting place in the centre of the city.

'I sent you a message a couple of weeks ago. Did you receive it, Doctor?'

'Yes, Haji, I received it.'

'Good. Would you like another message?'

'No! Please, Haji, no.'

'I didn't think so. Now, little doctor, you are going on a holiday. To Tehran. I want you to find the Jew whose name you left out of your last report. Talk to him. And take this with you.'

Haji hands me a parcel and tells me to open it when I get home.

'It's a voice recorder,' he says. 'Very sensitive. You can hide it on your body or in your clothes. Also twenty tapes. When you talk to your Jew friends, you turn on the recorder before you meet them, then turn it off five minutes after you leave them. It can record for two hours. You transcribe everything on the tape, then you give me the tape, and your transcription, and your report.'

I'm thinking, 'I'll need assistance...'

'How do I find this man in Tehran?'

Haji shrugs. 'You're a Jew. You can find another Jew.'

And so begins a new stage of my life as a spy: My Professional Spying Life. Now that I am required to record everything, any opportunity to leave out incriminating details about the Jews I talk to has disappeared. The information I gather will certainly put other Jews in a chair like the one I sat in while my flesh was cooked with a burning cigarette. My information will cause hands to close around the throats of Jews, will cause those hands to squeeze and squeeze. I had hoped to become a sort of super-brilliant triple agent, counterfeiting information for *Tashkilat*. But that was all vanity, all stupidity. Now the only alternative for me is to do my job as a spy professionally and conscientiously and attempt to block out from my mind the images of Jews I have betrayed screaming for mercy as I have screamed for mercy.

I drive to Tehran from Mashhad on my mission to find the fellow Jew Haji wants me to locate. An hour out of Mashhad, at Neyshabur, the home town of the great Iranian poet Omar Khayam, my mobile rings. It's Haji Samadi, hysterical with rage. He wants to know by what authority I have left Mashhad.

'But Haji, you told me to go to Tehran.'

'And I also told you that you must inform me whenever you step outside the boundaries of Mashhad!'

'But...'

'But nothing! You don't make a move of any sort without informing me!'

He permits me to continue my journey. But I am reminded that I am being watched all day and all night. I begin to feel that Haji is inside my head watching for thoughts that I may be punished for conceiving.

I rely on my Uncle Mansoor's connections to help me track down this Jew I am supposed to find. In Khorasan Square, so Mansoor told me when I was in Isfahan for Morvarid's funeral some years ago, his father-in-law, Esav Saparian, keeps a modest fabric shop. It's my intention to use Saparian's knowledge of the Jewish community of Tehran to put me into contact with my target, a certain Mansoor Gidanian.

After a night's rest at a hotel in Tehran, I find my way down to Khorasan Square, with my tape recorder concealed inside my jacket. As soon as I see the signboard of Saparian's shop I reach inside my jacket and activate the recorder as Haji instructed.

I know why he wants me to switch on the device before I meet with the target. It's to allow me no opportunity to give a verbal signal, to say 'Beware! I'm wired!'

I introduce myself to Saparian, making sure that I stand close enough for his voice to carry to the quietly revolving tape. He is an old man and his seamed face lights up with a smile as soon as he knows who I am. He embraces me with a warmth that sends a spasm of guilt through my chest.

'Dr Kooshyar Karimi,' he says. 'How kind of you to visit. We are proud of you, all of us are proud of you, not only a fine doctor but a writer, too.'

'Thank you for that, you are too kind, sir. You know, I was just passing and I thought I would say, hello.'

'I am honoured, most honoured.' The old man then lowers his voice. 'Oh, Dr Karimi, men like yourself with such skill, you should go to Israel. That is where you will be valued. Here, amongst these fanatics, what future for a talented man like yourself?'

I wince at the words Saparian is using. When the tape is played back to the *Tashkilat* people, they will smile and put a big black mark against Saparian's name and say, 'One fine day we will break his legs.'

I ask him if he knows anything about Mashhadi Jews who have resettled themselves in Tehran. He says that the Mashhadi Jews—or Khorasanis, as he calls them, since Mashhad is in the province of Khorasan—who have come to Tehran are snobbish, and try not to mix with Tehrani Jews. He says they have their own synagogue in Abbas Abad Street, and their own wedding hall in Takhtavoos Street. They consider themselves the aristocracy of Persian Jews. Then I ask Saparian if he has ever heard of a Khorasani Jew by the name of Mansoor Gidanian, said to be now living in Tehran. I tell him that I hope to get information from this Gidanian concerning the history of Persian Jews. Not only has Saparian heard of Gidanian, but he also has much to say about him.

As he chatters on I am acutely aware of how deeply he is incriminating himself and Gidanian. How Haji will relish hearing what this good old man has to say! I want to stand a little further back from Saparian in the hope of his voice not quite carrying to the recorder, but I know that Haji will be onto that in a flash and punish me for it. I stand listening to the old man, smiling at him even as I grieve for him, knowing that I cannot endure another session of torture. Saparian doesn't have Gidanian's telephone number, but he has the number of someone whom, he says, might be able to put me in contact with Gidanian. I accept the number with thanks and leave poor Saparian smiling in his shop, unaware that every word he spoke will be transcribed and handed over to people who detest him.

The contact I have is named Eli. When I call him he responds with a certain degree of suspicion, but agrees to see me at his shop. The suspicion in his voice is there in his face when I call on him. He's younger than Saparian, more alert. I explain my purpose—which is to say, my ostensible purpose—in wishing to see Gidanian. Eli won't give me Gidanian's number but he at least agrees to speak to Gidanian himself, and perhaps arrange a meeting. The meeting will be for the next day, if it can be negotiated. Back at my hotel, I transcribe the recording of the meeting with Eli, not missing a single syllable.

I return to Eli's shop the next day and he tells me that Gidanian has agreed to speak to me on the telephone. Eli gives me the number and watches as I dial on my mobile. The voice that responds is no-nonsense, just a little short of curt. I explain my purpose. Gidanian refers to my mother by name and asks me to confirm that she is indeed my mother. I'm surprised at the question, surprised that Gidanian knows of my mother. He says he will meet me the following day at 10 o'clock in the morning outside the Khorasani synagogue in Abbas Abad Street. He says that Eli will tell me how to get there. Eli draws me a map to the synagogue. There is not the least amount of trust in his face when he farewells me. I spend another fitful night in the hotel, pacing up and down and talking to myself, checking my reports against the tapes to make sure I have left nothing out.

I find my way to Abbas Abad Street a little earlier than the appointed hour. I hope to give myself time to look at the synagogue before Gidanian turns up, a little interval of peace between episodes of betrayal. It's a good thing I have the number of the building that houses the synagogue because there is no outward show of its purpose. The regime would not permit that. And it's a plain building, unexceptional in every way. Within, yes, it's a synagogue, it's the house of worship of my faith, but still very austere.

I find an old woman on a bench at the back of the synagogue, plainly distressed, wheezing, coughing. She's badly overweight, on the threshold of obesity, and to my professional eye, suffering from some cardiac complaint. I sit beside her and ask her if there is anything I can do for her. 'Oh,' she says, 'what can be done for me at my age!' But she shows me a prescription for heart medicine and says that she cannot find anyone here at the synagogue to fetch the medication from the pharmacy. I tell her I will get the medicine for her and bring it back to the synagogue a little later. She thanks me and attempts with what little strength she has to pat my hand. I think to myself, 'I wish to God this was my only task today, to be of some help to this old woman.' And then another thought slips into my consciousness, one I had not rehearsed, a surprise to me. It is this: 'I must get out of this country.'

It's right on 10 o'clock when I step onto the street again for my meeting with Gidanian. The tape recorder is ready to capture whatever he has to say. He could hang himself with a single

330

phrase, if he but knew it. And he's waiting for me, Gidanian, a man of about forty, with fair, freckled skin, very little hair left to him, but what there is of it, is a reddish colour. Not much Persian blood in him: it's all from Judea.

'Dr Kooshyar Karimi?'

We shake hands. He looks straight into my eyes, and not with warmth. We stand in the shade of the synagogue wall, Gidanian alert and candid, me feigning innocence.

'What is it you want?'

I tell him of my project, the book on the subject of Mashhadi Jews. I say that it is my hope that he will be able to help me.

'There's little I can contribute,' he says. 'The Mashhadi Jews have all left the city. Maybe one or two remain. But tell me this, Doctor. How long has your mother been working for the regime?'

'I beg your pardon?'

'I asked you how long your mother has been working for the regime.'

'I don't understand your meaning. My mother working for the government?'

Gidanian's piercing gaze is unsettling. Surely I am betraying myself with my anxious expression?

'Let me tell you something,' he says. 'I had a friend in Isfahan, where your mother was born. Yosefian was his name. Twelve shops he owned in the bazaar before the revolution. They were confiscated by the government after the revolution. All twelve. The revolutionary court said that he was an Israeli agent. But they had no proof. So he tried to get the shops back. He hired a lawyer and put together a case. Then he made a bad mistake. Such a pity, because his case was a good one and he might have prevailed. He went to see your mother when she was visiting Isfahan. He'd been told that your mother had some influence with the Revolutionary Court. You must have known that,

Doctor? You must have known of your mother's 'connections', surely?'

'I didn't know at all, I promise you.'

And this is true enough, but a man who is secretly recording a conversation has probably forfeited any claim to call himself 'honest'.

'So you say. So you say. Well, your mother didn't help Yosefian. Quite the opposite. She gave them all the information she could about him. Things he had told her in confidence. But you wouldn't know about that, of course.'

'No, I didn't know. I am sorry.'

As quiet and as focused as he is, Gidanian, I realise, is full of rage—of rage and disgust. He detests me.

'Do you know what happens to me when I go to Mashhad? Anytime my business takes me there? He asks, after taking a half step closer to me. 'I will tell you. Someone from the Revolutionary Guard finds me and takes me in for questioning. They push me about, insult me, then let me go. And the reason they let me go is that they have nothing to charge me with. Nothing. They listen to me day and night, every day of the year. They are listening now, listening and watching. It means nothing to me. I have never married because I have devoted my life to my people. I never will marry. One fine day they will kill me. Too bad.'

By this time we are walking side-by-side, strolling, a little this way, a little that way. I happen to notice that Eli from the bazaar is watching us from a window above the street. As soon as he sees that I've noticed him, he ducks out of sight.

'I have no information for you about Mashhadi Jews, Doctor. Nothing I would care to tell you. But I can give you some advice. You are still young, you are a successful writer, your popularity is growing steadily. Get out of Mashhad. Come to Tehran. Or better still, get out of this country. No Jew can prosper in Iran; not under this government. You will say that Khatami has made a difference. How wrong you would be to think that. Khatami is powerless. Go to the West, Doctor. This is the best advice I can give you.'

Haji would be expecting me to press Gidanian further, arrange a second meeting, ask him questions about other Jews. But I can see that any attempt at further engagement would be fruitless. He doesn't trust me in the least. He will tell me nothing. I shake Gidanian's hand and take my leave. I walk back in the direction of my hotel. It is only after a full ten minutes have passed that I turn off the recorder.

I lie on my bed in the hotel with the curtains drawn against the sun. The news of my mother's duplicity—or more accurately, the full extent of her duplicity—has left me feeling as if I could vomit. Over how many heads has she placed a noose? To keep hope alive in our hearts we are forever deceiving ourselves, forever finding excuses for ourselves, for others. When my mother became involved with Haji Heydar, choosing him over my father, I found a way of excusing her. I said, 'Her life has been one of endless strife, so she allows Haji to comfort her a little, put food on her table.' But it is now apparent that her relationship with Haji goes much further than mere expediency. He is a fundamentalist, a supporter of the regime. The fact that she finds it possible to cook for him, sleep with him, means something. I know that it means the money he pays her each month, essentially the fee one would pay a prostitute. But how profound are her feelings for her Jewish heritage when she becomes the whore of a man who hates Israel, hates Jews? My mother is herself a supporter of the regime. Or am I still deceiving myself? Perhaps there are hundreds of Jewish supporters of the regime! For all I know, *Tashkilat* could be running an entire network of Jewish agents!

As if this thought is not sickening enough, it suddenly occurs to me that Gidanian himself might be an agent of *Tashkilat*, like Sayar. I sit upright on the bed and stare about the hotel room in horror. The walls seem unstable, the floor is shifting. I no longer know anything reliable about anything. I am going mad. In Nabokov's story, 'Invitation to a Beheading', the condemned prisoner Cincinatus is lied to by everyone, even by his executioner, up to the very second when his head is severed by a blow of the axe. Is it possible that Azita works for *Tashkilat*? And when Newsha is older, will *Tashkilat* find a way to recruit her, find a way to put her to work, watching me? And my brother, Koorosh? My friends from university? And what of me? I tell myself that I am a slave, that I have no choice but to do the bidding of my masters, but maybe little by little I am turning into the Muslim I pretend to be. Where in my soul does the truth about me survive? Is there any truth left?

I light a cigarette and pace the floor. I say to myself, 'Kooshyar, don't permit yourself to go mad. Find something to hold onto.'

I suddenly recall the old woman in the synagogue, Tavoos. I said I'd fetch the medicine she needs from the pharmacy, and I'd forgotten. I pull on my shoes, throw on my jacket. Should I take the tape recorder? I leave it in the inside pocket, but with reluctance. It's not difficult to find a pharmacy that can fill the prescription, but whether or not Tavoos will still be waiting at the synagogue is doubtful. It's an hour and a half since I left her. But she is waiting, with all the patience of those who have spent their lives waiting for one thing or another. I sit beside her on the bench and allow her to thank me. I need her thanks, my soul needs it.

I haven't turned on the recorder, even though it's next to certain that one of Haji's men will be watching me, will have seen me return to the hotel, seen me leave it an hour later, seen me visit the pharmacy, seen me return to the synagogue. Haji is likely to say, 'When you talk to a Jew, you turn on the recorder, no exceptions.' But I can't. I hunger for a brief experience of being a normal human being showing normal concern for a distressed, dying old woman. In the paranoid state of mind I've been in since seeing Gidanian, I can if I let myself imagine this old woman, this Tavoos, to be in the employ of *Tashkilat*. In fact I have to fight against the impulse to treat her with suspicion. I think, 'If she works for Haji, there is no hope for me, no hope for Iran, no hope for the world.'

She tells me a tale of her son's disappearance some years ago. He was picked up by the national police for some reason or other, probably for being a Jew, nothing more, and beaten, tortured, then let go. He sent his wife and children to Israel, but he himself was unable to secure a passport. He tried to buy a fake passport, made all the arrangements, then went to Zahedan near the border with Pakistan to await delivery of the passport, and apart from one brief, terrified phone call to Tavoos, was never heard from again. Habib was his name. Tavoos still lives in hope of hearing from him, but I can see that it's a forlorn hope. My eyes fill with tears while I listen to the old woman, and I have wet cheeks when I leave her and walk back to the hotel. Perhaps this is what I can hold onto to fend off madness—the fact that I can still weep. It is something.

BAIT

In almost all cultures the concept of bait has been developed to a high level of effectiveness. The bait that fishermen employ is, of course, very well known. But in various places at various times, certainly in Iran and the lands surrounding us, living bait has been used to lure bears from their caves into the nets of waiting hunters, to tempt ibex down from mountain ledges, tigers from their cover of foliage. Sometimes the object is to catch the creature alive, sometimes the creature is shot dead as soon as it appears. I've become bait of a more sophisticated type, bait that attracts Jews and dissidents, and having attracted them, beguiles them, flatters them, leads them into the waiting nets or into range of the hunters' guns.

This image of myself as 'bait' takes hold in my imagination after my experience with my seductive fellow *Tashkilat* operative, Roxana. Using operatives like Roxana is something *Tashkilat* picked up from the East Germans, the Stasi, who kept whole harems of gorgeous young women and set them as bait for susceptible men from whom they hoped to learn something. 'Honey traps' these young women were called.

I am in a Tehran hotel room with her, a situation arranged by Haji Samadi. Roxana is candid about her employment.

She is happy to tell me that she works for *Tashkilat* just like me. 'They use me in any way they like,' she says. 'I have no choice.' Every word that comes out of her mouth is breathed with a caressing sensuality. Every movement of her body is designed to enhance her allure, to reveal more completely the swell of her hips, the thrust of her bosom. One could almost believe that if *Tashkilat* hadn't found a way to bring her into its harem, she could have made her living as a high class call girl. And we have high class call girls in Iran, we most certainly do. The regime's mullahs and pious men of faith are all capable of getting erections.

'You're a writer,' Roxana purrs. 'That's good. I like writing. I like reading. Shall I make myself more comfortable? Shall I... well, perhaps take a shower?'

And while Roxana is in the bathroom, I try to figure out what Haji hopes to gain by offering me this delectable bait. When I returned from Mashhad after the Gidanian affair, Haji was displeased.

'You didn't try hard enough,' he said. 'You should have made him trust you more. You should have taken it more slowly, much more slowly. You're hopeless. You know what, Doctor? I could get tired of you, very easily.'

Is it possible that he believes I learned something from Gidanian that I'm not sharing with him? What does he think transpired between us? Something communicated in sign language? Something that didn't register on the tape?

The flow of the shower is itself enticing. I imagine the water and suds running in streams down Roxana's flesh. And listen— she's singing. Singing in the shower. Who in the universe would blame me if I gave way to temptation and slipped into the bathroom, undressed, joined Roxana in the shower? Who in the universe? Well, Azita for one. She's likely to stick a knife right through my throat. And that might be the entire point, might it not? To get something on me that Haji can threaten to reveal to my wife? Isn't that the prime motive of using the honey trap? Not so much what the target might say to the woman in bed, but what the agency that employs the woman might say to others. 'We have these fascinating photographs, Mr X. I wonder if your wife would find them as fascinating as we do?' But why would Haji need more on me? He has enough to hang me fifty times over. Or perhaps he wants something to discredit me even further after he does hang me. Perhaps he wants to say, 'Oh, that Kooshyar Karimi, not only was he an abortionist, not only did he spy on his fellow Jews, he was an adulterer. Would you like to see the pictures?'

I'm paranoid, and it's getting worse. Haji sent me to spy on a gathering of anti-regime people after the Gidanian 'failure'. I wheedled my way into the group, pretending as ever that I am a devoted student of Persian Jewish culture and history. I was accepted, trusted. The leader of the group, a fellow by the name of Tahmasebi, had once been a supporter of the regime but like many, many such one-time supporters, he's become disillusioned. His group of broad-minded Muslims gathered to discuss political reform, not to plot sabotage, just a gathering of intellectuals who also take an interest in the Torah, since educated Muslims like Tahmasebi can find enjoyment in delving into texts commended by Muhammad in Islamic sacred literature. When Tahmasebi invited me to the meetings, I thanked him most sincerely.

'You are such a humble man,' I said. 'I have heard of your knowledge and I'm here to learn from you. People like you are assets to our society. I appreciate your trust and I will look forward to coming to your sessions.'

He had read my most recent book on the subject of Chinese and Persian myths and their interesting similarity. He had admired it. He admired me. He didn't know that a device in my pocket was recording everything he said. He didn't see that I was bait.

Roxana is calling to me from the bathroom. She has forgotten her robe. Will I bring it to her? Certainly I will. She stands in the doorway, inviting me to enjoy her nakedness. But I blush and turn away.

'What's wrong, shy boy? You can look if you like. Everything is permitted in this room.'

I don't look. And then I look. I'm too anxious. I've become obsessed with Haji's motive in leaving me here with this beautiful woman.

Roxana slips on her robe and strolls to the living room. She drapes herself along the sofa and pats a spot where I can sit. Even in my state of arousal and dread and paranoid fixation, I recognise the soap-opera quality of Roxana's performance. Every move she makes is alluring, yes, but it is also a cliché. Any minute now she's going to say, 'It's so hot in here! Why don't we slip out of our clothes?' And look at her, reclining on one elbow, the robe falling open over her breasts, an insouciant eyebrow raised. Side by side with the dread that the *Tashkilat* people induce in me, there's a type of contempt for the corniness of the scripts they write for themselves. I can imagine exactly what they would say when they pull a victim's first fingernail out. 'That wasn't very pleasant, was it? And guess what, nine more to go.' I suppose they can afford to be corny because in the end, they have the least corny thing in the world ready to inflict on you: enough pain to make you scream yourself hoarse.

Roxana asks me to tell her about myself.

'I'm m-married,' I stutter out. 'I live in Mashhad. One daughter. My heritage, you know, is Jewish.'

'Is that so?' says Roxana. 'Jewish? That's funny. *Tashkilat* already has a Jewish agent in Mashhad. A woman. Much older than me. Old enough to be your mother, in fact. I wonder why they want two Jews in Mashhad?'

339

And there it is. There's Haji's motive. I had already convinced myself after talking to Gidanian that my mother worked for *Tashkilat*. But he wants it confirmed without saying so in as many words. He wants any last spark of belief in the solidarity of Persian Jews in my heart to flicker and die. This is sadism in its pure form. I make an excuse, and leave the hotel room, leave Roxana as quickly as I can. Haji's message to me, spoken through Roxana is, 'Yes, your mother is a traitor to her people. Just as you are. So relax, do your job. It's all that's left on earth for you. Do your job, and do it well.'

We have spies because we are a species that keeps secrets; the only species that knows how to lie. All espionage corrupts— how can it not? We smile to cover deceit, and somewhere deep in our soul, something dies. Our great objective in life becomes not the discovery of some more profound truth about existence, but going undiscovered in our deceit. To walk out of a room having hoodwinked everyone in the room—that is a triumph. To have coaxed someone into saying, 'Well, damn the Islamic Republic, anyway!'—that is a triumph. To have pleased your handlers, that is a triumph. And all the while, you don't believe for a second in the importance, the virtue of what you are doing.

I am bait. And I am much more of a whore than Roxana. But the corruption that I hate most is the corruption of my reverence for scholarship. It once meant the world to me, the patient study of old texts, the joyful unearthing of new facts. Now I walk into a room in which eleven people have gathered to study the Torah, and I hear myself welcomed by Tahmasebi, my target. I hear myself praised for the books I have written; I see the eyes of those ready to give themselves to a couple of hours of scholarship and enquiry turn towards me with approval; and all the while the tape in my state-of-the-art recorder is whirring softly within the machine. What I love in life, what I honour, what I consider my only real accomplishments, become the aroma of the bait that encourages the prey to approach me.

Tahmasebi offers his guests tea and fruit. As he does so he mentions, for my benefit, the names of his guests and the profession of each: a professor of literature, a doctor, a computer engineer, a couple of students of psychology at the university, a journalist, another lecturer in literature now retired, three or four students of Persian literature. We sit in a circle sipping our tea and smiling and reaching towards the fruit platters to choose a slice of watermelon, a dried apricot, a ruby-red grape.

'So glad to have you in our little group,' says the professor of literature. 'Such a distinguished author as you—it makes me proud to be here.'

'Oh, Dr Karimi—how I honour the work you do,' says one of the psychology students. 'I apologise to you for the way this barbarous government treats your people, treats Jews.'

'Barbarous government' will please Haji.

Tahmasebi calls the meeting to order. 'Tonight I am pleased to be able to tell you that Dr Karimi will help me with my pronunciation of some of the Hebrew words I have difficulty with. Will you please put your hands together to thank him for being amongst us this evening? Good. And now let us look into the Book of Kings, the fifth book of the Torah, and in many ways, the most interesting...'

I have also made use of my scholarship to get myself in with the organisers and key figures of a conference on Assyrian culture and history held in Tehran. The regime sanctions the conference because the leading Assyrian scholar, Dr Wilson, who has come from the US to run the conference, has a grand scheme to establish a joint Assyrian and Kurdish homeland in Northern Iraq. The regime is in favour of anything likely to drive Saddam Hussein crazy, but at the same time they want me to infiltrate the meetings of the leaders of the conference and see what I can learn about possible Jewish influence in this 'homeland' idea. And I do it. I trade on my scholarship. I smile and smile and smile and draw attention to the work I've done on ancient Persian culture in exactly the way that Roxana draws attention to her bosom. It's no wonder Roxana makes me so nervous and jittery. Every time I see her, I'm looking at the female version of me.

But a new mantra becomes constant in the free periods of thought I have left to me now: Get out. Get out of Iran. Get out. In the barren hours of my journeys to Tehran, to other cities, always on the orders of Haji Samadi, I pursue schemes of escape that often approach pure fantasy in their unlikelihood. But even as I abandon one scheme, another suggests itself. My schemes are not restricted to my escape alone. I have to get Azita and Newsha out, too, and a new baby, waiting to be born.

I am giving *Tashkilat* substantial information. But Haji demands more. I think he believes that Jews have a natural talent for espionage, that they are born masters of duplicity. He was probably imagining that I would become his greatest creation, the Genius Jew who can float on the air like a mist and pluck the thoughts from the sleeping brains of enemies of the state. Now he thinks of me as pathetic. I don't try hard enough. I don't push hard enough. I don't smile for long enough. I don't go that extra yard.

That drumbeat: Get out. Get out. Get out.

Recent developments have made it more likely that I will get out of Iran and the world at one and the same time. Get out, that is, in a shroud. It is the year 1998 and fourteen Iranian writers have been murdered over the first few months—stabbed, shot, strangled. What all these writers have in common is opposition to the government—peaceful opposition. Journalists, editors, authors, politicians, exercising their rights under the constitution to criticise the government. And now the government is exercising its right, not mentioned at all in the constitution, to cut their throats.

And while this is happening—while throats are being cut in Tehran, Isfahan—the President of the Islamic Republic is delivering a speech to the United Nations General Assembly on 'The Dialogue of Civilizations'. The murders embarrass him, show his weakness. And indeed, when investigations into the murders are complete, it is revealed that they were carried out by a 'rogue' unit of the state security organisation. But it is what Haji Samadi has to say about the murders before the investigation that shocks me as much as the murders themselves. I am about to head off on yet another mission of infiltration and entrapment and have been given all the details when I pluck up my courage and request the right to ask a question.

'What question?' Haji asks, impatiently.

'Who is killing all these writers?'

Haji's eyes narrow. 'Who do you think?'

'I don't know.'

'Yes, you do. Who would do such a thing? Zionists.'

'Zionists?'

'To discredit the government. Zionists.'

He really believes what he's saying. I can see it in his eyes, that manic light. He really believes that Mossad has organised the murder of these fourteen writers, that Mossad has Zionist agents living in Iran.

'The Zionists,' says Haji, 'don't want Khatami to succeed. They don't want him to build friendly relations with the West.'

'Oh, I see.'

'Do you see, little Jew doctor? Do you? Maybe you have never seen these Zionists yourself. Maybe not. They are demons!'

By this time, I'm sorry I asked. I make my farewells and leave on my mission, but I'm left thinking this: every security organisation needs its Arch Villain, either an individual or a rival intelligence agency. In the Cold War, the CIA was the Arch Villain for the KGB, and vice versa. For MI5, and James Bond, SPECTRE was the Arch Villain. The Arch Villain fulfils the vital function of keeping the levels of paranoia extremely high. Intelligence agencies can't operate below a certain level of paranoid fixation. It's their life's blood. A demon is essential; Satan is essential. The fear the Arch Villain inspires becomes the licence for cruelty. People have to be burnt alive, have their faces torn from their skulls—a necessity if we are to be protected from Satan. Haji has to loathe the Zionists and Mossad with all his heart and soul and being or his motivation will wilt.

Like everyone else in Iran, I'm becoming accustomed to picking up the newspaper and reading that yet another reformist has been found dead with a gaping wound in his throat. There was a hiatus after those initial fourteen murders, but that interval is long past. Two bodies a week is the usual news. I struggle to fathom the system, and I dare not ask Haji any further questions. It must be pretty obvious by now, even to him, that this is not a great big Zionist plot. The thing is, the intelligence agencies in Iran do not coordinate their plans. The monsters carrying out the killing may belong to *Tashkilat*, or they may be part of the Revolutionary Guard's intelligence service; or they may even be a special unit deployed by Khamenei's people or by the Council of Guardians. So many people running around in Iran in this year of 1998 with unfettered licence to cut the throats of their fellow citizens! Even the repulsive teenagers of the government's Basij militia would probably have the right to kidnap reformists, torture and kill them.

For all I know, there may be competition between agencies to see who can murder the most reformists, journalists, academics. And as the number of reformists still alive declines, these homicidal lunatics are going to start looking for people like me, Jews, simply because we are Jews. I have some hope that Haji himself will protect me from being murdered, but I can't be sure of that. A frenzy has taken hold. No one is in overall command. Iran is like one of those Latin American countries in which death squads fan out across cities at night hungering for victims. I read that in Chile under Pinochet, the death squads resorted to picking up teenagers wearing sneakers to torture and kill on the basis of a ludicrous and lethal reasoning that young people who wear sneakers were more likely to have left-wing political views.

Leaving the home of yet another entirely innocent Jew after an hour of smiling at him, of flattering him, of accepting his hospitality and his kind words of endorsement for my writing, I sit slumped in my car yearning for release. I am hemmed in on all sides; I have no space on this earth that I can call my own. On one side stands the seemingly all-knowing and menacing presence of Haji Samadi whose last resort I have already tasted, whilst on the other side I have Azita's shrill insistence that I 'Do what they want'. Every time she says that, I know that the unspoken clause of her demand is, 'They are only Jews you betray, after all.' Oh dear God, I can't breathe.

The blood in my veins runs so sluggishly, as if it wants no further part in keeping me alive. I have it in my power to end my life. After all, I carry a gun these days, a pistol that Haji gave me and taught me how to shoot, perversely claiming that 'Zionist madmen' were after me, wanting to assassinate me. I think of ending my life a hundred times a day. But when I look at Newsha, my willingness to inject myself with something toxic from my medicine bag or settle the muzzle of my pistol against the roof of my mouth fades away. She knows nothing of this vile program of deceit and betrayal that I have been drawn into. I am the person she relies on for love and caresses and tender words, and ironically, safety. To her, I am a doctor who goes off to work each day to cure the sick. She is proud of me. I can't put myself into the earth and leave her mourning.

And so I rouse myself from this torpor of self-hatred and turn the ignition key and drive home. Even as I drive, it is likely that another reformist is being murdered somewhere. I barely have time to even contemplate my own part in this fevered carnival of throat-cutting going on all over Iran. I have to write up the report for Haji as soon as I get home. I have to transcribe the tape. I have to respond to calls from my patients. For even in all this mayhem of treachery and violence, I am implored by women to save their lives, save their reputations, save their sanity by ridding their womb of a foetus seeded there by coercion.

This latest report will tell the tale of Roxana's success in inveigling a tailor in the market, a person by the name of Bahrami, a converted Jew, into providing me with all sorts of information about his fellow converted Jews. Roxana's task is to help Bahrami enjoy my company more, trust me more, by virtue of my association with her. It's as if I am suggesting to him that if he wants to taste at greater leisure the bait that is Roxana, he'd better open up to me. So I've been watching Roxana flirt and tease and give glimpses of her shapely hips and her fabulous bosom to poor Bahrami, his temperature rising as he mentally undresses her. I have come into contact with Bahrami through his brother, another converted Jew (and I must tell you that Haji does not accept for a second that Jews ever really convert to Islam, just as many Jews themselves never really believe that any one-time gentile who claims to have converted to Judaism is a true Jew).

All my espionage is based on such links. One Jew leads me to another, and that Jew to another, and so on. My recorder captures everything. Behind me as I move from link to link, a trail of grief is blazed. Recently I was instructed to make friends with a fellow named Bijan, whom I came into contact with through my attendance at Tahmasebi's Torah study gatherings. I was then told to introduce Bijan to a venomous-looking thug by the name of Mohammad, saying that Mohammad was a great friend of mine. And I was told to make an excuse once the introduction had been effected and leave Mohammad alone with Bijan. ('I've just had a phone call from my wife. She says that my daughter is suffering an asthma attack. I've got to go!') Since then, nothing more has been heard of Bijan. And Tahmasebi? He was picked up, tortured, his discussion group dispersed. And at least one other member of the discussion group, a woman, was also taken into custody and tortured. In my report on Tahmasebi, I mentioned that both he and Bijan are passionate believers in the theory of the Jewish establishment of the Shi'a branch of Islam. It's an old theory, proposing that centuries ago, a particularly shrewd old Jew dreamed up the whole Shi'a rationale and foisted it on certain Islamic scholars. Nothing is more likely to bring on hysteria in Iranian fundamentalists than the idea of their faith having been dreamed up by a Jew.

I arrive home and turn off the engine of my car. But I can't move. I can't make myself open the door. After what I have done, who on earth, who in heaven will forgive me? My next mission is in Isfahan, my mother's birthplace. I pray God it's my last mission. May Adonai reach down with his strong hands, encircle my neck with his fingers and squeeze, squeeze, squeeze.

29

ZIONISTS

I n Isfahan once more. This city in which you will find some of the greatest monuments of world architecture, a city that at one time stood at the heart of Middle Eastern civilisation. It is also the city in which many of my relatives live. And it is those relatives, three of them, at least, who are my targets on this mission. I will be exploiting my good name amongst my relatives in order to locate the targets. My reputation has grown here in Isfahan over the years. An honoured doctor, a celebrated writer—yes, I am acceptable now. But these three relatives of mine I have never met them. They have been kept under surveillance by *Tashkilat* for more than a year, according to Haji. When he tells me of this particularly vile mission, I can see that little glitter of sadism in his eyes. He is thinking, I'm sure, 'We can make you do anything, can't we, little doctor? We can make you spy on your own family. We can make you show your little pink arse to people of your own faith. If we demanded it of you, you would be willing to put a noose around the neck of the Chief Rabbi of Israel.'

I call on my Aunt Nosrat as the first stage of the mission. It was Aunt Nosrat who told me of my mother's early life here in Isfahan, and of my heritage. Aunt Nosrat, in her sorrowing way greets me with tears and tea and cakes. I ask her about the three relatives. I ask where they conducted business, I write down the addresses. But I don't call on the three relatives. All three are said to be Zionists, fierce supporters of Israel. I don't necessarily accept this judgement of Haji Samadi's. Any Jew who has ever expressed even mild approval of the creation of the State of Israel is a raving Zionist to him. If I were to wander into the place of work (all are shopkeepers) of any of these relatives and coax them to talk about their political views, it would seem suspicious. Instead I contact a man whose name has been supplied to me by Haji Samadi, a certain Mr Nejat, another Jewish shopkeeper who is a friend of one of my relatives—the relative said to be the most fervent Zionist of the three. I turn on the tape recorder, walk into Nejat's shop and introduce myself. I am greeted in the Persian manner with embraces and a warm squeezing of my hand and excessive compliments on my work as a doctor and as a writer. This sort of flattery is common all over the Middle East, in Iran as much as anywhere, part of a culture of hospitality which is often employed to hide the true feelings of the host.

'A joy it is,' says Nejat, 'that you have come to my shop. A joy and an honour.'

He says it is 'a joy and an honour' without knowing exactly who I am, and when I fill him in, the 'joy and honour' is even greater. In Iran, members of social and political minorities take great comfort in the accomplishments of one of their number since it brings credit on all the members of that minority. Jews relish the achievements of fellow Jews, Kurds of fellow Kurds, Zoroastrians of fellow Zoroastrians. I am, of course, trading on my accomplishments. I can't think of a feature of my character and achievements that I have not exploited. If I were capable of standing on my head while drinking tea through my ears, I'd probably exploit that talent, too.

The result of all this charm I'm displaying is an invitation to Nejat's house that evening for dinner with his family. I accept, of course, and arrive at Nejat's house on the appointed minute of the appointed hour.

Nejat's wife is young and pretty. His two children are adorable. I don't actually tell Nejat that his wife is pretty. That's not acceptable in the Middle East amongst Jews or Muslims. But I do tell him and his wife that their children are a delight.

'Oh, thank you, Dr Karimi. Thank you, Doctor. You are too kind, too kind!'

All well and good, but it is after dinner when Nejat and I are alone drinking tea and smoking that my real purpose in coming to Isfahan is rewarded. Nejat speaks of my three relatives once I have mentioned them. All three, he says, to me and to my tape recorder, are passionate supporters of Israel.

'Would you call them Zionists?' I enquire.

'Zionists? Well, they encourage us Jews to send money to Israel, certainly. But it is only Shahram who is really a Zionist. Oh, he is a very fiery supporter of Israel. He hates the fundamentalists, hates them with all his heart and soul!'

An hour more of this, then it's, 'Thank you, thank you, a lovely meal, my compliments to your wife!'

I'm off back to the hotel to write my report, to transcribe from my machine. I sit on the side of the bed, the machine resting on a chair; I have my notepad on my lap. And I write, reaching constantly to pause the tape or to replay it. I hear Nejat saying, 'But it is only Shahram who is really a Zionist. Oh, he is a very fiery supporter of Israel. He hates the fundamentalists, hates them with all his heart and soul!' I think, 'I could delete that'. But Haji would know I'd deleted it. And I remember the experience of Sayar, who gave me information I didn't relay, and whom I next encountered with a burning cigarette in his hand searching for the painful spot on the flesh of my chest to apply the red tip.

I return to Mashhad, call Haji, and deliver my report and the tape. Haji is delighted. This is what he likes, Zionists incriminating themselves with their own words. He all but rubs his hands together with relish.

'You have done well,' he says. 'Yes, indeed. Good work.'

He departs and I am left with something of the sequence of emotions that Judas Iscariot must have experienced when he pointed out the figure of Jesus in the garden of Gethsemane: rationalisation, succeeded by self-disgust, succeeded by sorrow, succeeded by an urgent need to attach a rope to a rafter and choke to death.

But perhaps nothing will come of it all. This is what I whisper to myself. 'Haji knew about the political views of my Isfahani relatives long before I came along. They will watch them but do nothing. All that Zionist talk—it's just the bravado of young men. Haji knows that.'

Within two weeks, my hopes for a quiet end to the Isfahani mission are dashed. I pick up the newspaper one morning and read that thirteen Jews have been arrested in various Iranian cities, including Isfahan. The names of the thirteen Jews are printed on the page. My three Isfahani relatives are amongst them.

A horrible, curdling sickness seizes my gut. I stand up from the table at which I've been reading the newspaper and put my hands over my face.

I begin to moan.

Azita stares at me in alarm. Her pregnancy is far advanced and every time I look at her I despair for the life I've created for her and Newsha and the child in the womb.

'What's the matter with you?'

I push the newspaper across the table towards her. She reads the leading story of the 'Zionist traitors'.

'So what?' she says.

'So everything,' I say, and rush to the toilet to vomit.

It is revealed to me long after the arrests of the thirteen Iranian Jews that the government intended to negotiate a prisoner swap with Israel. The thirteen Iranian Jews for thirteen Hezbollah prisoners held by Israel. Hezbollah, a Shi'a organisation, is strongly supported by the Iranian regime and this prisoner swap will be popular all over the Muslim world, even amongst Sunnis. But before any deal can be negotiated, the Iranian Jews have to be tried, found guilty and sentenced. There's no doubt whatsoever that the Iranian Jews will be found guilty, of course. My report and my transcription of the tape will form part of the evidence against them.

It is at this time that I am called to Tehran to face the abuse and threats of Haji Samadi's colleague, the very man who will drive me to make the paranoid 3 a.m. call to Azita. I leave that meeting knowing with absolute certainty that I am to be executed. I believe that Haji Samadi was genuinely delighted with my Isfahan mission. But his more senior colleagues are getting sick and tired of me. They want me to devote my life to implicating Iranian Jews in espionage plots. They want me to show more initiative, find new ways to make myself trusted. They believe that Iranian Jews are involved in every sort and variety of anti-government activity. They believe that Iranian Jews are amassing weapons, burrowing deep beneath the foundations of the Iranian State, plotting to blow the regime sky high. It's utter nonsense, of course, but such is their paranoia that they believe it.

They want me to drag fifty Jews a month into the torture cells of *Tashkilat*. The fact is that I am unable to continue this betrayal of my own people, my very soul. They'd hoped, as I've mentioned before, that I would turn out to be a genius of a spy, and now their disappointment has reached the stage where they will get more satisfaction out of shooting or hanging me than out of letting me continue to spy for them. In reality, they will most probably put me on trial and, after enough torture, I will tell the court what they wish me to say—that I'm an Israeli spy. Haji knows that.

When I return to Mashhad from Tehran after my meeting with the Haji and his homicidal colleague, I tell Azita that I am as good as dead unless I flee. In her pregnant state, she can't begin to think of fleeing with me. She argues with me, demands that I give up such an insane idea. But I'm adamant. Azita follows me about the house as I pack imploring me to think of the unborn baby, to think of Newsha.

'The baby will be born without a father if I stay,' I shout over my shoulder, 'because its father will be dead. Azita, try to understand! They intend to kill me. Haji will call me and arrange a meeting and at that meeting, they will kill me.'

Azita is almost hysterical. She implores me to first consult Darvish Hossein.

'The Holy Man! Darvish Hossein! Please first speak with him!'

She's talking about a renowned cleric of the Sufi persuasion, a devout Muslim but not aligned with the regime—or not entirely. But I am in such a fever of preparation for my escape that I can't begin to think of wasting time with mystical hocus-pocus. I shriek at Azita, 'Are you completely out of your mind? It's Muslims who want to kill me and you're telling me to go and ask a Muslim in the mosque if I should run away? Use your brain!'

Now Azita is on her knees, clutching at me in her desperation.

'Please! You must do this! Speak first with that good man!'

To please my wife, I go to the mosque. But I'm in a high state of panic, almost frothing at the mouth with fear. In a quiet corner of the mosque, seated cross-legged on the floor, I find the holy man Darvish Hossein, a very ancient fellow, perfectly

qualified by the length and whiteness of his beard for the role he
has adopted in life. He sees me approaching and gestures for me
to sit. He's reading from a book, not the Koran, perhaps some
Sufi text of arcane wisdom.

So I sit, and as soon as I've done so, I feel the feverish panic
abate.

'Speak, if you will,' he says.

'Sir, I am in despair. I have come to a difficult moment in my
life and I don't know which way to turn.'

'Well, I have to admit, you look as troubled as you say you
are.'

I am about to explain my predicament in greater detail, but
the Sufi lifts his hand palm outwards, indicating, so I understand,
that I am to keep silent. He opens the book he is reading at what
seems a completely random page. Then he reads aloud these
words:

'*Haram dar pish, Harami dar pas, Choe rafti bordi, Cho
khofti mordi.*'

I listened transfixed. He speaks the words slowly, and only
the once. An adequate translation would be: 'Shrine, before
you. Killers, behind. You escape, you fly. You remain, you die.'

Once Darvish Hossein has spoken, he simply looks at me as
if the import of the words should be obvious, an almost matter-
of-fact look. I think, 'This is a blessing. Don't question him
further.' I bow slightly where I sit, then stand and bow again.
He says, '*Khodahafez*', which means 'In the hands of God'.

I take the words of the old Sufi back to Azita, and she accepts
the verdict of Darvish Hossein. It's absurd, and I know it, relying
on the old man to negotiate the way ahead when he knows
next to nothing about me. In a way, it's primitive, more related
to superstition than to modern thinking. Yet I must confess that
the old Sufi's words have calmed me down greatly. I know the
way ahead: run as fast as I can, and keep running.

THE PASSOVER

I run to Tehran. I run to the mountains. I find a village, I find an old farmhouse. And there I remain. Azita and Newsha are staying with Azita's mother. Azita's story is that I have gone to Bandar-e-Abbas to work in a hospital for a couple of months. Azita's mother knows the story is fishy, but Azita sticks to it, regardless.

In hiding, I am free. The joy of being liberated from treachery, liberated from conspiracies—my first experience of happiness in months. It is a relief and a happiness that I do not deserve, but I take it. I stand outside the farmhouse door with my eyes closed and my face raised to the sun. Tears of gratitude pick a path down my cheeks. I whisper prayers of thanks to a God who must be listening sceptically. And a great distance beneath my feet, in his immemorial home in Hell, Satan must be laughing quietly, saying to himself, 'Do you think I am finished with you, little doctor? Do you think in your escape from Mr Haji and the Bad Men you have escaped from me? Poor little fool. I have you for life.'

As I wait in my farmhouse this is what I don't know, but might have guessed: Haji Samadi in a fury goes to my father-in-law's house and screams at Azita:

'Where is he? Where is that Jew liar?'

He and his thugs have already ransacked my apartment, have already found my mobile in my safe. Haji takes Azita, nine months pregnant, into custody and keeps her for twelve hours. He bombards her with questions, waiting for a slip-up.

'Is he in Tehran? Tell me if you care about this baby inside you! Is he in Mashhad? Tell me if you care about this daughter of yours! Is he in Isfahan? Tell me if you care about your teeth and fingernails!'

'He divorced me. He is gone and I am glad of it,' Azita replies, as I have instructed her to reply.

And I do not know but hope with all my heart that Azita has gone to hospital and given birth to a new child, and that she is well.

One thing that I do know, because I have gone into the village and purchased a transistor radio, is that the thirteen 'Zionist spies' have been found guilty by the highest court in the land. The Supreme Leader has demanded the execution of the spies. Hearing that news destroys the relief I have experienced in my farmhouse. What I have done to assist the Iranian government returns with all its aching force, together with a renewed sense of the danger that I live with.

The country is in turmoil. It is not only the vicious campaign against Jews that is making news. The government is coming down brutally on student demonstrators, who have taken to the streets demanding reforms. The demands of the students are mild enough: a little more liberty in the subjects they are permitted to study, a little more liberty in what they are allowed to read, to listen to, to wear. The demonstrations are peaceful, the reprisals by the police, by the Basij militia, by the Revolutionary Guard are full of venom. Students are snatched from the streets— several thousands of them—and taken to secret locations for interrogation, meaning torture.

I can no longer stay where I am. A violent restlessness overtakes me. I stand and pace up and down, then sit for ten seconds before standing again. I must go back to Mashhad. It seems insane, but if I am to get out of Iran I must have a passport. And my only hope for a passport is to appeal to Ali Mazaheri—the man whose life was spared in my father's bus all those years ago—and who is now the Director of the Mashhad passport office. I have been getting about with a fake birth certificate hastily purchased in Gomrok, and under an assumed name, and that's been good enough to get me past ID checks on buses. But a passport is now imperative.

I say farewell to the strange respite of the farmhouse and walk into the village to catch the bus back to Tehran, and then a bus to Mashhad. I have entered the end game with *Tashkilat*, with Haji Samadi. I have come to realise that I have only average courage, and even that average complement has been eroded by years of dread. But if I don't take what courage I have left and act, I will die in the hell of a torture chamber. Haji Samadi will be studying closely every grimace of pain, revelling in every scream that can be wrung from me.

A passport is a document that serves the future. It takes you across the border you have not yet reached, and once you have crossed that border, it waits quietly for the next border you reach, wherever that might be. A passport, after all, is a document that permits you to have a future. When I hid Ali Mazeheri in my father's bus all those years ago, I had in effect given him a passport. In the years since I helped him cross the frontier to freedom, he has had ample opportunity to become quite a different man from the one I saved. He might have grown bitter as he grew older, he might have adopted more completely the ideology of the fundamentalist. He might have grown more resentful, meaner. He might have thought back to the boy who helped him cross the frontier and thought, 'So what?' In his life since I saw him that first time, a million episodes have transpired and any one of them could have destroyed his courage, spoiled his ability to feel gratitude. But when I finally make it to his office, terrified, feeling the barrel of a gun at the back of my neck, he remembers me.

'Tell me everything,' he says, showing me that he knows he has a debt to honour.

And it is for that reason—that a man may hold sacred a certain memory, year after year after year—that I am at this moment holding my newly-issued passport, travelling by bus from Mashhad back to Tehran, hoping to cross the frontier into Turkey.

In Mashhad, I send a written message by taxi to Azita, telling her to come to the Turkish border beyond Tabriz with Newsha and our new baby on a certain day, to bring all the money I'd left her with, and her passport. Sending the message is a horrible risk. Haji Samadi's hatred for me is so fierce that he may well be keeping my father-in-law's apartment under constant watch and checking every visitor. But it is not my scheme to escape from Iran without Azita and the two children. I want whatever life I may find to include my family. To have so harmed my immortal soul by betrayals of my fellow Jews— that is grotesque and vile. But to add to that the betrayal of my family? No, and thank God—thank God!—I have enough of my soul left to say no to that.

In the bus on the way to Tehran I am bathed in the scalding sweat of a fear, of liquid fire enclosing my every limb. Every glance from a stranger makes my heartbeat race. When we reach the bus station at Tehran, I show my fake birth certificate to the police, who check the identification papers of everyone heading on the bus to Tabriz. I feel as if I have violent red signs plastered all over me, screaming, 'Enemy of the State!' and 'Traitor to the Revolution!' I can scarcely believe it when I am permitted to buy a ticket to the Turkish border. I think, 'Can they not see my guilt?'

Then, in the bus station, a child's voice shrieks, '*Baba*!' I glance behind me and there, five metres away, stands Newsha wearing an ecstatic smile. Azita, with the new baby in her arms, quickly hushes Newsha. She knows that *Tashkilat* stooges will be watching and waiting to see if she or Newsha unwittingly identify me. Up until this point, I have not known if Azita has received my note, nor if the hundred things that would have had to go right for her to reach Tehran have indeed gone right. I can allow myself no more than a two second glance at my wife and daughter. Of the new baby, I can see nothing.

I have shaved my beard, cut my hair to avoid detection, and I'm wearing sunglasses. And I've wasted away during my two months of hiding. I know I look like a walking corpse. Even so, Newsha has recognised me. I would have given the wealth of a king to embrace her, my beloved child, but I turn my gaze away and steal into a remote corner, a sort of nook, and remain there for half an hour. Azita and the children will board a bus before me, surely, but that can't be helped.

Finally, I join the hordes of passengers around the ticket counters.

Over the next three hours, both at the bus station in Tehran and on the bus to Tabriz, my ID and passport are checked four times. I am so sick with fear that I would probably enjoy a brief period of relief if I were captured. Whatever death Haji Samadi has in store for me could not be worse than living with every nerve strained to the limit. But, dear God, I am so sick of dread.

At the border I wait, trembling, to join the queue to Iranian customs. I take one deep breath after another, hoping to locate somewhere in my core a last vestige of courage. Customs is the checkpoint at which I am most likely to be caught. My name will be on a list, but it is my desperate hope that Ali Mazaheri has made it possible for me to get through, that he has fashioned a doorway, an opening, through which I might wriggle. I think of my heroes in life, people who have risked everything to be free. I think especially of Moses, summoning his courage before he crosses the River Nile. I think of my great grandmother, Morvarid, and pray to God that she is watching in heaven, and that her influence will save me.

I join the line inching towards customs.

At the counter, a customs officer looks with unusual scrutiny at my passport. Then he looks closely at me. He studies my passport again.

'Dr Kooshyar Karimi?' he says.

'Yes. Yes I am…I am him. I mean he. Kooshyar Karimi.'

The customs officer raises an eyebrow. He is a young, handsome fellow, with a lush moustache. I think, 'He knows everything. I am dead.'

'Wait here,' he says and leaves me to enter an office behind the counter.

If I had the gun with me that I left behind in a hole in the ground, I would now use it to put a bullet through my agonised brain.

The handsome young customs officer and an older and more senior colleague come to the counter.

'This is your passport?' the senior officer asks.

'Yes, it is my passport.'

'So you claim to be Dr Kooshyar Karimi. Is that correct?'

'Yes, that is correct.'

'Really?'

'Yes, I am Kooshyar Karimi.'

'You've lost weight, doctor.'

'Pardon?'

'I said that you've lost weight. And you've also lost your beard and moustache.'

'I've been ill. Yes. Ill.'

'And so you shaved off your beard and moustache?'

'Pardon?'

'You shaved off your beard and moustache because you were ill. Strange.'

'That was a different reason.'

'For what different reason, if you don't mind me asking?'

'My wife…my wife…'

'Your wife, what?'

'My wife made me. She didn't like…she didn't like my beard.'

'I see. And you're travelling without your wife today?'

'No. Yes! Yes, I am travelling without my wife.'

'You seem a little confused, Doctor. Tell me this: why are you travelling to Turkey?'

'Holiday,' I manage to get out.

'A holiday. To help you recover from your illness, maybe?'

'Yes. Yes, to help me recover.'

The senior officer turns to the junior officer.

'That's fine,' he says, and he turns and departs.

Just like that. Was he teasing me? Does he know? Only God has the answer, but for me the relief eclipses everything. I almost piss myself with gratitude.

I am three metres from the end of my nightmare. Three metres will take me to Turkish customs, a stamp in my passport, and liberty. Three metres.

The Turkish customs officer has no great interest in me. He stamps my passport, hands it back.

'Welcome to Turkey.'

His words are repeated to everyone who arrives at his counter with a valid passport, generated in an automatic manner, but to me his three words have the beauty and richness of the world's most sublime music. 'Welcome to Turkey.' A blessing! A blessing! I smile for the first time in weeks.

'Thank you! Thank you!' I say, a little too loudly and with too big a smile.

The customs officer glances up and gives a brief smile. He thinks I'm a bit simple-minded.

'That's okay,' he says, and waves me along.

On the Turkish side of the customs hall, I hurry into a shop and do something that you cannot do in the Islamic Republic of Iran—not openly. I purchase a bottle of Johnny Walker Red Label. I have my ticket to Istanbul in my pocket. When the Istanbul bus arrives, I board cheerfully and as soon as we start our journey to Asia Minor I open the bottle and begin to sip. I make the whisky last, and with each hour that passes I am happier until finally, after three hours, I am delirious with joy. The man sitting next to me smiles sympathetically.

'Take it easy, brother. Plenty to drink in Istanbul.'

I watch the towns and the lights go by. I feel like singing. But instead of singing I sink into what must be a mild coma. I am still aware of the people around me in the bus, but more vivid to me are the images that swim up from the deepest vault of my mind. I see my mother stretched out on the bed in our squalid Tehran basement flat when I'm a small child. She is reading to me and to Koorosh from a book of Torah stories. I see her lips moving, I feel her hand caressing my head and my shoulders. I ask, 'Who is Moses, Maman? Who is he?' I see my adored pigeons descending from the blue heavens to alight on the roof of the toilet at the back of our Mashhad house. I hear the flurry of their wings, their cooing calls. Then I am asleep. The whisky is all but gone. I awake for a minute when the man next to me relieves me of the bottle in a helpful way and tightens the lid before slipping it into the seat pocket in front of me.

'You have a nap,' he whispers to me. 'It'll do you good.'

Of what I dream, I do not know. But I know I dream. I awake with someone shaking my shoulder. In the instant before I open my eyes, I am convinced that I have been captured by Haji Samadi. I know it is his face I will see next. I have it on the tip of my tongue to shriek, 'I am ready to die! I am ready to die!'

But it is Newsha's face I see when my eyes open. It is Newsha. The lustre of her eyes is so deep that I can imagine it lasting forever, bottomless.

'Newsha?' I manage to whisper.

'*Baba*! *Baba*, wake up!'

Azita is bending above Newsha. 'It is you, Kushi! Oh, thank God! Thank God, you are here!'

The bus has stopped at a roadside restaurant. All of the other passengers have taken the opportunity to sip some tea, eat some rice and bread. I have been left behind, drunk and unconscious. Azita and Newsha must have been in the bus in front. They've waited to see if I made it. From the depths of my being a volume of emotion rises and emerges as a flood of tears. I kiss Azita's cheek and draw Newsha to my chest, to my lips, and cover her face in kisses. I know I stink of whisky but Newsha makes no protest.

'Thank God! Thank God!' I gasp.

I am talking of my God, Adonai, but I am happy to share my gratitude with any other god who has played a part in this deliverance. Azita is in tears, too, clutching our newborn Niloofar to her chest.

'You look so ugly!' she says laughing.

I realize then, seeing the sparkle in her eyes that has been absent for so long, that even though Azita never held me as I trembled, never stayed awake with me through my anxious wonderings, she has suffered with me in every step of my painful journey. And we have both survived.

We three laugh and embrace again, and laugh again and weep. I have returned to the world. Even with my daughter's face against my shoulder, I know that I have sins to atone for. A cry of grief comes from me, something I cannot control. In the midst of this happiness, I can't forget how much I owe God, how deep the debt.

'*Baba*, what's wrong?' Newsha anxiously asks.

I shake my head and hug her so forcefully that she cries out again.

'*Baba, Baba*, what's wrong?'

What's wrong is that I want to begin to atone, but don't know how.

People are beginning to return to the bus. The man who was sitting beside me looks down at me, smiling.

'Family reunion,' he says. 'Take your time.'

I want my atonement to come in a rush. I want it to drown the wrong I have done. But at the same time I know how long it will take, how terribly, terribly long.

The land in which I now live is as remote as I could wish from the Islamic Republic of Iran, but much too far from the Iran I love—the Iran free of ideologues, free of tyrants. In this second land, my daughters Newsha and Niloofar have thrived. I think at this moment of Newsha, in particular. Her love is literature and, of all the poets and all the poems that have delighted her, first amongst them is Coleridge and his *Rime of the Ancient Mariner*.

We all know the story: a sailor aboard a masted ship commits a terrible wrong and only finds his way back to the family of man when he repents in his heart. As he lies on the deck of the derelict ship, amongst his crewmates, dead each one, he hears the voices of spirits, two of them. The first voice is full of wrath—it is doubtful that this spirit will ever forgive the mariner. The second is milder, more generous. It speaks to him in a softer voice, soft as honey-dew, 'The man hath penance done, And penance more will do.'

I am once again gazing upon the Star of David. But this time it is not scratched hastily upon a wall. It is hanging silently around my neck. It carries a new oath, an oath of atonement. But atonement has yet to come.

The End

GLOSSARY

Achaemenid Empire (550-330 BCE)
The first Persian Empire, founded
by **Cyrus the Great**. One of
the greatest empires in history,
stretching at its peak from the
Indus valley to Greece.

Allah u Akbar
An Arabic expression, usually
translated as 'God is Great'.
Muslims use the expression in
varied contexts: in formal prayer,
and to express approval, defiance
and resolute determination.

Assyrian
An ethnic group whose origins lie
in Ancient Mesopotamia. They
speak Eastern Aramaic, and have
traditionally lived all over what
is now Iraq, northeast Syria,
northwest Iran, and southeast
Turkey. They were the first group
to accept Christianity and still
predominately keep up the
practice of this faith.

Aushe Sarka
A Persian-Afghan vinegar-based
flat noodle soup. Similar in taste
to Chinese hot and sour soup.

Ayatollah
A title granted to **Shi'ite Muslim**
scholars who have demonstrated
expertise in Islamic Studies.

Individuals who have been granted
this title are regarded as religious
authorities and can then teach
according to their specialty, act as
a reference for religious questions,
and as a judge.

Baba
Literally translated, means
'Father'. **Baba jan** means 'dear
Father'.

Balfour Declaration
A letter (dated 2nd November
1917) from British Foreign
Secretary Arthur James Balfour
to the leader of the British Jewish
community, Lord Rothschild,
declaring his support for the
establishment of a Jewish state in
Palestine. This declaration was
later incorporated into the Peace
Treaty of Sèvres with Turkey and
the Mandate for Palestine.

Basij
A volunteer paramilitary group
established in Iran by **Ayatollah
Khomeini**. An individual member
is known as a **Basiji**. While the
Basij was technically open to
individuals aged between 18 and
45, during the Iran-Iraq War it
became a grass-roots intelligence
organisation made up of young

boys aged between 10 and 16, and old unemployed men. Youth volunteers were targeted through school visits and media campaigns exploiting the idea of martyrdom.

Chelow

Saffron-seasoned basmati or Persian rice that has been carefully soaked, parboiled, drained and then steamed. The Iranian national dish is Chelow Kebab: chelow served with meat kebabs.

Cyrus the Great

The first Emperor of the **Achaemenid Empire**. He founded Persia by uniting the two original Iranian tribes–the Medes and the Persians–and went on to conquer vast areas and populations throughout the region.

Dariush Eghbali

A famous Iranian pop singer born in 1951. He has also acted in many Iranian films.

Darius the Great

The third Emperor of the **Achaemenid Empire**, ruling from 522 to 486 BCE, when the Persian Empire was at its peak.

Dhimmi

Non-Muslim citizens of a Muslim state. While dhimmis were traditionally accorded protected status and allowed to retain their faith, they were subject to some different civil laws and taxed by the state in return for that protection.

Dolma (Dolmades)

Literally means 'stuffed thing'. The dish varies across cuisines. In the Jewish Quarter of Isfahan,

dolmas are made from minced beef or lamb meat mixed with rice and wrapped in grape leaves.

Farsi

The official language of Iran. Dari, one of two official languages in Afghanistan, is a dialect of Farsi.

Hafiz (1320-1390)

The most famous Persian lyric poet, known for his sensuous lyrics that elevate descriptions of erotic love to the realm of metaphysics. His influence and inspiration go far beyond Persia and the Middle East, and include writers such as Goethe, Ralph Waldo Emerson and Nietzsche. His works continue to be amongst the most popular in the Persian-speaking world.

Imam

A position of leadership in the Islamic community. In the Koran the title is used to refer to leaders and to the biblical Abraham. The Imam is often the leader of a mosque.

Iran hostage crisis

A diplomatic crisis that took place in Iran during the chaotic aftermath of the **Iranian Islamic Revolution**. Islamist students and militants seized control of the US Embassy in Tehran on 4th November 1979 and occupied it till 20th January 1981. Fifty-two Americans were held for 444 days. A failed rescue operation by the US military contributed to Democratic US President Jimmy Carter's defeat at the election to conservative Republican Ronald Reagan.

Iranian Islamic Revolution

Also known as the Iranian Revolution, or 1979 Revolution. These terms refer to the popular uprising, led by **Ayatollah Ruhollah Khomeini**, resulting in the overthrow of the Pahlavi dynasty and the establishment of an Islamic Republic in Iran.

Iran-Iraq War

A brutal 8-year war triggered by Saddam Hussein's army invading Iran in September 1980. It was the longest conventional war of the 20th century.

Khomeini's Revolution

Refers to the Iranian Revolution in 1979. **Ayatollah Ruhollah Khomeini** became **Supreme Leader** of Iran as a result of this revolution.

Khoresht

A Persian stew. There are many different types of Khoresht, including vegetarian varieties. Khoresht is typically made with liberal amounts of saffron and served with a white rice dish.

Kosherfied

Persian recipes cooked using Kosher ingredients. Kosher food is prepared in specific ways to meet Jewish dietary laws.

Kurds

A largely **Sunni Muslim** ethnic minority, with their own language and culture. They live in a region that straddles parts of Turkey, Iraq, Iran, Armenia and Syria, generally known as Kurdistan.

Madar

Literally translated, means 'Mother'. **Madar jan** means 'dear Mother'.

Matzos

A brittle, flat piece of unleavened bread traditionally eaten by Jews during Passover.

Mikveh

A ritual bath designed for the Jewish rite of purification. The mikveh is composed of stationary water, a percentage of which is derived from a natural source. Full immersion in a mikveh allows an individual to regain religious purity after ritually impure incidents have occurred.

MOIS

Acronym for the Iranian Ministry of Intelligence and Security

Mossad

The national intelligence agency of Israel. The Mossad is responsible for espionage, intelligence gathering, and covert political operations in foreign countries.

Pahlavi monarchy

Only two generations of Shahs in this family: the father Reza Shah Pahlavi who was deposed by the British during World War II, and his son, Mohammad Reza Shah Pahlavi who fled into exile during the Islamic Revolution in 1979.

Parthian Empire

The Parthian dynasty ruled from 247 BC to 224 AD. It was one of the most enduring empires of the ancient Middle East.

Peacock Throne

A term that was frequently used in Iran to refer to the Pahlavi monarchy.

Reza Shah Pahlavi

Reigned as the Shah of Iran from 1925 to 1941. When he took a neutral stance during World War II, Britain and the USSR invaded Iran and forced him to abdicate in favour of his son.

Roosari

A scarf worn by women in Iran to cover the head and neck.

Ruhollah Khomeini (1902-1989)

An Iranian religious and political leader who led the revolution that overthrew the Pahlavi monarchy and was an Ayatollah and the **Supreme Leader** of Iran from 1979 to 1989.

SAVAK

The much-feared Organisation of Intelligence and National Security (or secret police) in Iran during the Pahlavi regime.

Sayyid Mohammad Khatami

Served as the fifth president of Iran from 1997 to 2005. During his two terms, President Khatami was an advocate of freedom of expression, tolerance and civil society. However, during his presidency over 80 Iranian dissident intellectuals were murdered or disappeared.

Shamaqsood

An expensive kind of rosary made of precious green stones. Carrying a Shamaqsood rosary is a sign of aristocracy.

Shemira

The Jewish tradition of keeping watch over a dead body. To honour the deceased, the body is not left alone from the moment of death until it is buried.

Shi'ite Islam

A branch of Islam that regards Ali, the Prophet Muhammad's son-in-law, whom they consider divinely appointed, as the rightful successor to Muhammad, and the first Imam. Shi'a Islam is the second largest denomination of Islam after Sunni Islam. Followers of Shi'a Islam are called Shi'ites or Shi'as.

Socialist Realism

A style of art developed in the Soviet Union which glorified the political and social ideals of communism, venerating the role of the poor and painted in a naïve poster style.

Sunni Islam

A branch of Islam that accepts the first four caliphs (heads of state) as rightful successors to Muhammad. Sunni Islam is the largest denomination of Islam. Followers of Sunni Islam are called **Sunni Muslims, Sunnis** or **Sunnites**.

Supreme Leader

The highest ranking political and religious authority in the Islamic Republic of Iran. The Supreme Leader is responsible for general policies, is commander-in-chief of the armed forces, controls military intelligence, and has the sole power to declare war. He is also more powerful than the President.

Sura Three

The third division in the Koran. Sura Three is broken into four sections. It includes: an explanation of the nature of the Koran; Muhammad's discussion with the Christians from Najran; an explanation of the Muslim military defeat at the battle of Uhud; and a closing reflection and prayer.

Timur (1336-1405)

Also called Tamerlane, referred to as the son of a Mongolian chief from central Asia. Amassed huge multi-ethnic armies that conquered nations from central Asia right across the Middle East, founding the Timurid dynasty. His conquests were characterised by exceptional brutality and were feared far and wide. When Isfahan revolted against his punitive taxes, Timur ordered the complete massacre of the city.

Toman

A unit of Iran's official currency. One toman equals ten rials.

Tsimmes

A Jewish sweet stew that is often part of the Rosh Hashanah meal. It is typically made from carrots and dried fruits, and is often combined with other root vegetables that have been sweetened with honey or sugar.

Ya Allah

Means 'O God!' The term can be used to express frustration or relief.

Zoroastrianism

A monotheistic religion and the official religion of Persia from 600 BCE to 650 CE. It was founded by the Prophet Zoroaster in Ancient Iran 3,500 years ago. Followers of Zoroastrianism worship a supreme God, Ahura Mazda, who battles the evil destructive spirit, Angra Mainyu.